CARDINAL WOLSEY

CARDINAL WOLSEY
A Life in Renaissance Europe

Stella Fletcher

continuum

Continuum UK, The Tower Building, 11 York Road, London SE1 7NX
Continuum US, 80 Maiden Lane, Suite 704, New York, NY 10038

www.continuumbooks.com

First published 2009

British Library Cataloguing-in-Publication Data
A catalogue record for this book is available from the British Library.

ISBN 978 1 84725 245 1

Typeset by Pindar NZ, Auckland, New Zealand
Printed and bound by MPG Books Ltd, Cornwall, Great Britain

Contents

Illustrations   vii

Foreword   ix

Acknowledgements   xi

Introduction   1

1 Apprenticeship, *c.* 1471–1515   5

2 Grand Chancellor, 1515–20   37

3 Papal Pretensions, 1520–3   69

4 Heretics and Rebels, 1524–7   99

5 A Great Fall, 1527–9   127

6 Pastor Bonus, 1529–30   161

7 At the Sign of the Red Hat, 1530–2009   171

   Notes   195

   Bibliography   207

   Index of names   217

Illustrations

Between Pages 100 and 101

1   Magdalen College Tower

2   Henry VIII, Charles V and Leo X, and Wolsey

3   Parliament Roll of Arms

4   Henry VIII letter

5   Pope Clement VII

6   Herbert Beerbohm Tree as Wolsey

7   Christ Church portrait of Wolsey

For Dominic

Foreword

The Lord Chancellor occupies one of the most historic offices of State, with a lineage that can be traced back to the ninth century. Despite the many convulsions of our history it has survived centuries as a working, not titular, office – one which straddles this country's feudal past and democratic present.

Lord Chancellors throughout history have displayed the adaptability that has been the source of their longevity. The ancient trappings, rituals and robes of office belie a contemporary relevance today, as in every other age. Never more keenly has this been exemplified than in the person of that quintessential Lord Chancellor and thoroughly modern politician: Cardinal Wolsey.

Wolsey was modern in the sense that he was able to rise from nowhere, 'an upstart from the dung-cart' in the description of poet laureate John Skelton, to high office in both church and state. The master administrator, shrewd advisor and accomplished statesman, Wolsey wielded such power and influence that the French ambassador, du Bellay, remarked that 'in every honour the Sovereign and his Minister were equal'.

It is a description which would no doubt have greatly flattered Wolsey, who could be self-serving and would thoroughly enjoy the trappings of power, but he was, first and foremost, the king's servant. In common with politicians across the ages he had a canny knack of anticipating his master's wishes, even when they were as capricious as those of Henry VIII, and, in common with politicians from time immemorial, also knew when to keep his own counsel.

Wolsey provoked the king's displeasure at the failure to secure an annulment of his marriage to Catherine of Aragon. In so doing, Wolsey was the accidental father of the modern practice whereby laymen typically, rather than clergy, are appointed Lord Chancellor.

I write this foreword as the first Lord Chancellor for nearly 500 years to sit in the House of Commons. Such is the history and continuity of this ancient office that in some respects change can be measured in centuries. Very rarely, a figure comes along who makes this sort of transformation in a lifetime. Wolsey was one of them.

Cardinal Wolsey: A Life in Renaissance Europe is an impressive work of scholarship providing a fascinating portrait of the man in the ecclesiastical, cultural and political context of his time.

Rt Hon Jack Straw MP
Lord Chancellor and Secretary of State for Justice

Acknowledgements

This book concludes with an appeal to any surviving little Englanders or latter-day Whigs to cease over-indulging in the 'island story' and, instead, regard the life of Cardinal Wolsey as their gateway to the wider history of Renaissance Europe. Ironically, the cardinal has had the opposite effect on me. During the book's brief gestation I have much enjoyed exploring English locations associated with episodes in his life, and am grateful to my enthusiastic companions on the Wolsey trail. Much to my surprise, that trail led to Wolsey-centred conversations with Jack Straw and Archbishop John Sentamu, between whom at least some of the cardinal's governmental and ecclesiastical responsibilities are currently divided. The second of those encounters could not have occurred in a more appropriate venue: the hall of Christ Church, Oxford. In the course of the journey I have also received valuable information from John Blatchly, Claire Cross, Judith Curthoys (archivist, Christ Church College, Oxford), David Dawson (Landmark Trust), Sarah Foot, David Rundle and Julie Wright (Lincoln Cathedral Library), and I am delighted to have this opportunity to record my thanks to all of them.

Stella Fletcher

29 November 2008,
anniversary of the death of Thomas Wolsey

Introduction

When, in the late nineteenth century, the Oxford historian Edward Armstrong surveyed the history of Renaissance Italy with a view to creating a new under-graduate special subject, he identified the lifespan of Niccolò Machiavelli – 1469–1527 – as being ideal for his purpose.[1] Not only did the period from the death of Piero de' Medici to the sack of Rome present the opportunity to compare and contrast the Italian states on either side of the French invasion of 1494; it also offered a healthy range of primary source material, by Machiavelli and others, for Armstrong's students to dissect. A couple of academic genera-tions later, Armstrong's indirect successor J. R. Hale brought the content of the special subject course to a wider public with *Machiavelli and Renaissance Italy*.[2] The possibilities of such a dual-focused approach to history, switching between an individual figure in the foreground and the wider panorama of his or her lifetime, are as numerous as the men and women in the documentary record, but for the purposes of the present exercise I have chosen to focus on the life and the times of Thomas Wolsey. In one sense this offers little variation from the Machiavelli model, for Wolsey's lifespan – from some time in the early 1470s to 1530 – largely overlapped with that of the Florentine bureaucrat and political theorist. On the other hand, geography provided one of the clearest distinctions between them, for there was no geographical overlap between Machiavelli's personal knowledge of the states of Italy and Wolsey's sphere of influence, which straddled the English Channel and from which he strayed furthest when he ventured into Yorkshire during the final months of his life. Another key distinction was that the underemployed Florentine had plenty of time to reflect on the lives of great men and try to discern their motives, while Wolsey was a man of action rather than contemplation, a figure who sat at the political top table, who occasionally enjoyed quasi-monarchical authority, and who was therefore treated as something of an equal by the emperor-elect Charles V and the French king Francis I.

During the years immediately either side of 1520 Wolsey effectively redrew the diplomatic map of Europe, and thereby gave England a considerably more prominent role than she had hitherto enjoyed or than her relatively limited economic resources could realistically support. It was a stunning achievement and, as its architect discovered even before his dramatic fall from power in the later 1520s, one that could not be sustained for long. His virtuoso command of the interplay of forces at work between Habsburg power in Spain, Germany and the Low Countries, Valois France, the papacy and their various satellites, was what set Wolsey apart from other English statesmen of the fifteenth and sixteenth centuries. In domestic terms, Wolsey was one of the longest serving lord chancellors of England, matched in length of service by Lord Thurlow in the eighteenth century, and exceeded in that respect only by Ranulf in the twelfth century, Ralph de Neville and Robert Burnell in thirteenth, John Stafford in the fifteenth, the earl of Hardwicke in the eighteenth, and Lord Eldon in the nineteenth century.[3] No less remarkable than the length of Wolsey's tenure of the chancellorship was his deliberate employment of the courts of chancery and star chamber to break the legal logjams created by the common law courts, to ensure swift justice for poorer claimants, and to bring recalcitrant nobles to heel. In a parallel development, his dominance over the English Church was exercised by means of extraordinary legatine powers, as well as through holding the bishoprics of Lincoln, Bath and Wells, Durham and Winchester, and the archbishopric of York. Among these episcopal connections, that with York was the most enduring, though numerous archbishops, from Wilfrid in the eighth century to Cosmo Gordon Lang in the twentieth, have served for longer in the northern province and have devoted more of their time and energy to ministry there. The longevity of Archbishop Warham at Canterbury meant that Wolsey was denied the primacy of all England, but it also meant that he was the archbishop of York who exercised most influence over the entire English Church in any period, pre- or post-Reformation, and was the one who enjoyed the highest profile in secular government. In purely political terms, he was also the most significant of England's cardinals, largely because of the diplomatic niche he created for himself but also, ironically enough, because he steered well clear of Rome, from where he derived the cardinalitial title and where he could easily have exercised its unique powers of election and counsel. As chancellor, archbishop, cardinal and legate, Thomas Wolsey accumulated a remarkable degree of power and influence, yet he insisted that his exercise of it was not for any personal aggrandisement, but consistently in the service of his king.

In the light of the points made above, the present work keeps the figure of Thomas Wolsey in the foreground while providing an account of the political, ecclesiastical and cultural history of his time. Its most distinctive features are to be found at either end of the text. The first four decades of Wolsey's life, the years prior to his receipt of the coveted red hat, are generally passed over in some haste by his biographers. Although it is true that there is little biographical material with which to work, Wolsey was nevertheless a prelate moulded in the late fifteenth century, rather than one who appeared fully-formed in the sixteenth, and this is reflected in the attention given to the period before 1515, and to the statesmen and clerics who shaped much of Wolsey's career and who presumably influenced his thinking on matters political and ecclesiastical. After the fourteen years when he combined the chancellorship and the cardinalate came the single year of his political disgrace, but Wolsey's story did not end there, and the final chapter of this study is devoted to an exploration of his posthumous reputation, the uses and abuses to which he has been subjected by subsequent generations of historians and novelists, painters and sculptors, playwrights, filmmakers and actors. This is an even more striking departure from earlier studies of the cardinal.

1

Apprenticeship, c. 1471–1515

Thomas Wolsey's reputed birthplace on the corner of St Nicholas Street and Silent Street in Ipswich has been known to generations of his fellow citizens as the Wolsey Pharmacy. Until 2008 the site of his death in Leicester was overlooked by a large industrial building identified as the Wolsey Mill, a prominent reminder of how his name was appropriated by a well-known knitwear manufacturer. England's last pre-Reformation cardinal makes a somewhat unlikely talisman for the modern business community, but the attraction may lie in a combination of his father's reputation as a tradesman, the ease and lack of scruple with which he accumulated wealth, the reassuring solidity of his presumed physical appearance, and his creation of a brand image based on the red robes and broad-brimmed hat which marked him out as a prince of the Church. Wolsey's associations with the arts of healing and of knitting have been entirely posthumous, but the pope who raised him to the cardinalate, Leo X, quite literally came from a family of doctors – Medici – who invested the profits from their international banking interests in the manufacture of cloth. The wholesale merchants of Florence operated on a vastly different scale to that of the tradesmen of Ipswich, but Giovanni de' Medici and Thomas Wolsey were nevertheless united in being targets for the anti-commercial scorn of their nobly born contemporaries. It is by making connections of this nature, by setting Wolsey firmly in his European context, that the present work is intended to make a distinctive contribution to the study of a figure made all too familiar by English historical narratives.

Ipswich's location at the head of the Orwell estuary facilitated a range of international commercial connections, not least the export of locally produced woollen cloth on locally built ships. For Wolsey's biographer the significance of that location is that it provided him with an early appreciation of England's commercial interaction with communities and states from Scandinavia to Iberia. It was to the diplomatic and military counterparts of that interaction that Wolsey devoted much of his subsequent career. Thomas' father, Robert, was connected with another Ipswich industry dependent on proximity to water, tanning, for he dealt in various aspects of the meat trade, from grazing to butchery. These were, indeed, relatively humble occupations, but scholars have long appreciated that both Thomas' parents issued from among east Suffolk's more prominent families.[1] Ipswich as Robert Wolsey, his wife Joan Daundy and their four children knew it in the later fifteenth century can now be appreciated only in terms of architectural fragments, most substantially St Margaret's church, which stood outside the town walls, near the house of Augustinian canons dedicated to the Holy Trinity and popularly known as Christchurch. Augustinian abbeys and priories were the most numerous of England's religious houses and Ipswich had two of them, the other being that of St Peter and St Paul, which was dissolved in the 1520s in order to fund Wolsey's college in the town. Additionally, this busy port lacked only Austin friars to make up the full complement of mendicant orders, for Ipswich was also home to communities of Franciscans, Dominicans and Carmelites. Like religious houses throughout England, those in fifteenth-century Ipswich were past their numerical prime, a fact confirmed by the emergence of secular clerks as grammar masters employed to educate the sons of burgesses. In 1477 the corporation of Ipswich chose John Besett to fill that role, a choice confirmed by James Goldwell, the bibliophile bishop of Norwich. Besett and his successor, John Squyer, were presumably the men to whom it fell to educate the precocious talent that was Thomas Wolsey, who may well have been a pupil at the grammar school in 1483, when Squyer secured its first permanent home, in St Edmund Pountney Lane (now Foundation Street). According to the will of the school's benefactor on that occasion, Richard Felaw, the master and pupils were to sing a Mass of Our Lady at six o'clock every morning in the neighbouring Dominican church.[2] This observance presumably set the pattern for Wolsey's later life, for his first biographer, George Cavendish, assures us that he said his office assiduously and generally heard two Masses each day.[3]

At least two traditions have developed regarding the presumed date of Thomas Wolsey's birth: Mandell Creighton's assertion of March 1471 appears to be reflected in Sybil Jack's recent choice of 1470–71, as distinct from the preference of A. F. Pollard, Jasper Ridley and Peter Gwyn, all of whom opted for late 1472 or early 1473.[4] In 1519 the Venetian ambassador Sebastiano Giustinian reckoned him to be about forty-six years of age.[5] Others have suggested a date as late as 1475, so that Wolsey's age at death may have been anything between fifty-five and sixty. Beyond inferring that Wolsey was aged fifty-nine in 1530 because

he washed the feet of fifty-nine poor men on Maundy Thursday, Cavendish
sheds little light on this matter, but does state that Wolsey became known as
the boy-bachelor when he obtained his BA at fifteen, an age at which other
boys of his social background were more likely to begin their undergraduate
studies.[6] Robert Wolsey died in early October 1496, bequeathing ten marks for
the singing of Masses for himself and his friends, a task to be performed by
Thomas, providing he was ordained priest within the following twelve months.
In the event, Thomas' priestly ordination took place at St Peter's, Marlborough,
on 10 March 1498, at the hands of Augustine Church, titular bishop of Lydda
and suffragan of John Blyth, bishop of Salisbury, and if there is no reason to
imagine that this occurred much beyond his attainment of the canonical age
of twenty-four, it lends credence to the Pollard tradition, rather than that of
Creighton. Robert's widow remarried and lived until 1509.

It has been assumed that Thomas advanced the careers of his two younger
brothers to the extent that a 'Mr Wulsey' became a gentleman of Henry VIII's
privy chamber, a position which presented the potential for wielding political
influence and accumulating substantial wealth, but neither of them prospered
to any remarkable degree. The contrast with Venetian clerical dynasticism must
have been particularly glaring to Giustinian, who explained in 1519 that the
cardinal had two brothers, one a clerk with an untitled benefice, while the other
'pushed his fortune'.[7] More shadowy still is Thomas's sister. If the young cleric
known as Thomas Wynter really was, as claimed in the 1520s, the cardinal's
nephew, and not his illegitimate son, then he could have been the offspring
of that sister, but this entirely uncontroversial scenario has generated little
interest.[8]

There is no means of knowing whether Wolsey regarded any of his kinsmen
with genuine affection, and one is tempted to conclude that his university
inspired greater and more abiding enthusiasm. His studies at Oxford began
either during the brief reign of Richard III (1483–5) or at the very beginning
of Henry VII's, our lack of precise information on this point conveniently reflecting wider confusion in the political sphere. Oxford experienced the change
of regime through the persons of its chancellors. Lionel Woodville, bishop of
Salisbury, did not long survive the death of his brother-in-law, Edward IV,
in April 1483, for he supported the duke of Buckingham's rebellion against
Richard in the autumn of that year and accordingly lost the chancellorship. His
successor was William Dudley, bishop of Durham, but he died little more than a
month after his election. The university's choice then fell upon John Russell, the

learned bishop of Lincoln, who lost the chancellorship of England after the bat-tle of Bosworth but retained sufficient royal favour to remain a valuable patron to the university, as was confirmed by the building projects for which he raised the necessary funding. After Russell died at the end of 1494, the next chancellor was Archbishop John Morton of Canterbury, who had already proved himself as a builder of palaces, including the prominent brick gatehouse at Lambeth, and continued Russell's rebuilding of the university church and repair of the canon law school. Even setting aside this form of cultural patronage, Morton provided an obvious role model for Wolsey, for he combined the status of a non-curial cardinal with the office of lord chancellor (keeper of the great seal) and the reputation of being one of the architects of the Tudor regime.

A more immediate source of inspiration for the young Wolsey was the vener-able William Waynflete, bishop of Winchester since 1447 and lord chancellor between 1456 and 1460. Waynflete was Henry VI's choice as provost of the king's new college at Eton and was responsible for forging the connection between that foundation and King's College, Cambridge, a connection modelled on William of Wykeham's foundation of Winchester College and New College, Oxford. At the height of his fortunes, Waynflete followed the example of both Wykeham and King Henry by founding his own Oxford college, dedicated to St Mary Magdalen. During the lean years of Yorkist rule from 1460, the Lancastrian Waynflete threw his energy into educational patronage, but nevertheless had to wait until 1467 to begin the physical construction of Magdalen College, a process which continued throughout the remaining years of the fifteenth century. In 1484 Waynflete authorized the building of a grammar school in his native town, Wainfleet in Lincolnshire, from which boys would proceed to Magdalen. Wolsey was a youthful member of the college when the aged bishop died in 1486, but he nevertheless lived within walls that stood as testimony to Waynflete's devotion to the university and his determination that the college should survive the caprices of princes. When Wolsey founded his colleges in Oxford and Ipswich in the 1520s, Magdalen and Wainfleet were still the most recent model of such linked educational institutions. By that stage Wolsey was also lord chancellor, though he had to wait until 1529 to become Waynflete's indirect successor as bishop of Winchester.

Magdalen's early history also contained a warning to ambitious clerical statesmen, for it was surely no coincidence that the college's construction did not commence until after the disgrace of the university's then chancellor George Neville who, prefiguring Wolsey, combined the chancellorship of England with the archbishopric of York. Along with his brother, the 'kingmaking' earl of Warwick, Archbishop Neville lost Edward IV's favour in 1467 and, with it, the great seal. After the Nevilles' failed restoration of Henry VI as a puppet monarch in 1470–71, Edward twice had his former chancellor arrested for treason, confining him in the Pale of Calais between 1472 and 1474. Neville was therefore very much a non-resident primate but, much to Edward's annoyance, he could not be deprived of his archbishopric, though he could be prevented from travelling there and from developing it as a power base. In a curious parallel to the last phase of Wolsey's life, George Neville did finally head northwards in 1476, but died in the east Midlands without setting eyes on his cathedral church. Edward IV's role in Neville's fall was very much a model for his grandson Henry VIII's treatment of Wolsey, not least in the seizure of the estates and goods of his archiepiscopal victim.

Aristocrats such as George Neville did not pass their university careers in the obscurity enjoyed by other students. Thomas Wolsey's Oxford career began in complete obscurity, and quite literally comes to light by degrees. Speculation remains about what caused Wolsey to be sent to Magdalen. The connection between Ipswich School and Pembroke College, Cambridge, had yet to be established, and it is not known whether the Ipswich schoolmaster John Squyer was a graduate of Oxford or Cambridge. Wolsey's length of residence at Magdalen cannot be determined for certain, but it was longer than his boyhood in Ipswich, which itself can have lasted no more than eleven years. He was admitted to the college fellowship by 1497, by which time he had proceeded to his MA.[9] His fellowship provided the title to which he was ordained the following year, for he did not begin to acquire benefices until 1499. If he wished to continue in an academic career he had two basic options, to study for a doctorate in law or one in theology. The legal option had been taken by virtually every English cleric who reached episcopal rank in the fifteenth century. Wolsey did not take it, suggesting that he was not regarded as a clerical high-flyer. Academic theology was enjoying something of a revival during Wolsey's time at Oxford and it seems that his interests lay more in that direction. His early years at Magdalen overlapped with those of William Grocyn, who was reader in divinity between 1483 and 1488. After three years in Italy pursuing his study of Greek, Grocyn presumably returned to Oxford until c. 1500, during which time his friend John Colet began lecturing there on St Paul's epistles, and the king's mother, Lady Margaret Beaufort, countess of Richmond and Derby, founded readerships in divinity in both universities. These were intellectually exciting times, but there is no indication that Wolsey was enthused by Colet's appeal for a return to the purity of primitive Christianity, or aspired to join the circle of scholars which so impressed Erasmus when he first arrived in England in 1499. Indeed, so unclear was Wolsey's way forward that, between 1498 and 1500, he served his college in two capacities simultaneously, each of which nevertheless proved to be valuable in equipping him for a non-academic career. On the one hand, he was Magdalen's junior bursar in 1498–9 and senior bursar in 1499–1500, providing him with practical administrative and financial experience, whether or not he was guilty of any alleged financial impropriety with regard to the construction of the college's elegant tower. On the other, he became master of Magdalen School.

Public schoolmastering or private tutoring provided an income for many a young scholar in this period, but for Wolsey its greatest advantage lay in offering him a route out of Oxford and into the favour of a useful patron. Cavendish relates that the marquis of Dorset had three sons at Magdalen School and invited their master to join the family for a Christmas season, presumably that of 1499–1500.[10] The marquis, Thomas Grey, was the elder son of Elizabeth Woodville's first marriage and prospered conspicuously after his mother became Edward IV's queen in 1464. She sought to advance Thomas's interests by arranging a marriage with the duke of Exeter's only daughter, but the girl died without issue, and a match was contracted with Cicely Bonville, heiress to extensive estates in the south-west of England. The Greys were a Leicestershire family, and Thomas's power in the Midlands was enhanced by his acquisition of a substantial portion of the estates of Edward's brother George, duke of Clarence, whose disgrace and execution in 1478 were subsequently attributed to the hostility of Queen Elizabeth. Edward's death in 1483 left the Woodville faction desperately trying to hold on to the person of the young Edward V but falling prey to their vengeful enemies, led by the boy king's uncle Richard, duke of Gloucester. Dorset's role in the usurpation crisis is well known from Mancini's near-contemporary account and from the insular literary tradition that ultimately reached the stage in Shakespeare's *Tragedy of King Richard III*, but his later career attracts comparatively little interest.[11] From 1486 he enjoyed the distinction of being half-brother to the new queen, Elizabeth of York, but did not enjoy the trust of King Henry VII. He nevertheless remained seriously wealthy and threw his energies into building Bradgate Hall, to the north of Leicester, where Wolsey enjoyed the Christmas festivities and evidently created a positive impression, for he was chosen by the marquis to fill a vacant living a few months later.[12] The first marquis died in 1501 and was succeeded by his son, also Thomas, whose reputation for jousting duly made him a popular figure at the court of Henry VIII.

In terms of identifying a potentially useful patron, Wolsey did remarkably well at this first attempt. In 1500 the English nobility boasted only one marquis, above whom there ranked just one non-princely duke, that of Buckingham, for the Yorkist claimant, Edward's IV's nephew Edmund de la Pole, lacked the means to maintain his ducal title and was forced to downgrade it to the earldom of Suffolk in 1493, while Thomas Howard did not immediately succeed to his father's dukedom of Norfolk because they had been staunch partisans of King Richard. Thomas Howard was not restored to his earldom of Surrey until 1489 and did not gain his father's ducal title until 1514, after his decisive victory over the Scots at Flodden convincingly proved his loyalty to the Tudor dynasty. The Howards had been instrumental in putting down the rebellion against Richard III by Henry Stafford, duke of Buckingham, in the autumn of 1483, a rebellion in which the marquis of Dorset had also participated. Henry was succeeded by his young son Edward, who became the third Stafford duke of Buckingham and who, by the beginning of the sixteenth century, cut a dashing figure at court. Henry VII certainly needed to keep Buckingham close, not merely because of his kinsmen's history of rebellion against the crown, but also because his descent from two of Edward III's sons made him the most convincing threat to the Tudor monarch and his young children, especially after the executions in November 1499 of the pretender Perkin Warbeck and Clarence's son, the uncomfortably legitimate Edward, earl of Warwick.

The living to which the marquis appointed Wolsey was the Somerset rectory of Limington, in the diocese of Bath and Wells.[13] He was admitted to the benefice on 10 October 1500 and held it until some time before July 1509. In one of his most memorable vignettes, Cavendish tells of Wolsey incurring the displeasure of the Somerset worthy Sir Amias Paulet, who had the young rector placed in the stocks for an unspecified misdemeanour. With the cardinal as his sole source for this episode, Cavendish relates that the former rector got the better of his persecutor in due course by not permitting him to leave London 'for the space of five or six years, or more' and that Paulet, who was treasurer of the Middle Temple, sought to appease Wolsey by decorating the gatehouse of that institution with 'cardinals' hats and arms, badges and cognisaunces of the cardinal, with divers other devices'.[14] It is impossible to be sure how much the anecdote itself became embellished in its telling by Wolsey and in its retelling by his devoted servant. In reality, Wolsey had more pressing commitments far from deepest Somerset, for he was dean of divinity at Magdalen in 1500–1, and went straight from there to serve as chaplain to Archbishop Henry Deane. It was in the context of his move from Oxford that he received a dispensation to hold two incompatible benefices – that is, both with cure of souls – and became vicar of Lydd, precariously located amid the marshes of the Dungeness peninsula.

Patronage was the lifeblood of this society and a humbly born young cleric, who had already feasted with his social superiors, could not afford to waste time in acquiring a new patron after the marquis's death. How he came to be chaplain – effectively private secretary and gatekeeper – to the primate of all England remains a mystery, not least because Cavendish is conspicuously silent about the relationship. Archbishop Deane was an Oxford man who retained great affection for his university, so the connection may have been forged in that context, but of that there can be no certainty. Socially, intellectually, architectur- ally and even ceremonially, Deane was the perfect role model for Wolsey, for his birth was obscure, his talent for administration widely recognized, his rise to ecclesiastical eminence secured by a combination of personal ability and royal favour, his enthusiasm for building manifested at the archiepiscopal manor of Otford, and his taste for extravagance amply illustrated by the detailed instruc- tions he left for the transporting of his corpse from Lambeth to Canterbury. The most obvious distinction between the archbishop and his chaplain was that Deane was an Augustinian canon of Llanthony, Gloucester, and Wolsey a secular priest, but it was precisely because of his reputation as a monastic administrator that Deane was invited to join Henry VII's council and sent in 1494 to serve as chancellor of Ireland. He remained there throughout the following year and succeeded Sir Edward Poynings as deputy governor in 1496. Meanwhile, the king confirmed his appreciation of Deane's abilities by ensuring his steady rise through the Anglo-Welsh ecclesiastical hierarchy: he became bishop of Bangor in 1494, succeeded John Blyth at Salisbury in the winter of 1499–1500, and was Henry's second choice for Canterbury after Thomas Langton of Winchester followed Cardinal Morton to the grave without being able to take possession of the primatial see. Deane succeeded Morton as lord chancellor on the cardinal's death in October 1500, and was translated to Canterbury the following spring, thereby providing his chaplain with an opportunity to watch his execution of simultaneous primacy in Church and State.

It was a primacy notable above all else for the successful conclusion of long negotiations with the Spanish monarchs over the marriage of their youngest daughter, Catalina (hereafter Katherine), with Henry's fifteen-year-old elder son, Arthur. Archbishop Deane performed the marriage ceremony in St Paul's Cathedral on 14 November 1501 with a show of pomp and display appropriate to England's return to European dynastic politics, the like of which had not been seen since Margaret of York wed Charles the Bold of Burgundy in 1468. Flush with this triumph, Deane led the English delegation which concluded the Anglo-Scottish 'perpetual peace' of January 1502, though the thirteen-year-old Princess Margaret did not travel northwards to meet her somewhat more mature husband, King James IV, until the following year, after Archbishop Deane's death on 15 February 1503. For a period of less than two years, there-fore, Thomas Wolsey effectively received an apprenticeship in statecraft by living in Deane's household and serving as his chaplain. He could observe the archbishop's handling of matters secular and ecclesiastical and was close to one of the major players in the marital saga that ultimately led to his own downfall. It is too easy to dismiss Wolsey as a self-made man who worshipped his own maker. There were no self-made men in a society composed of interlocking patronage networks. Wolsey was the client and, arguably, the protégé of a gifted but now largely forgotten prelate.

While Wolsey was receiving this valuable education in statecraft, the Florentine civil servant Niccolò Machiavelli was observing its practice in rela-tions between and within the Italian states. Between 1499 and 1503 he watched admiringly as Alexander VI's son Cesare Borgia dispatched his opponents with brutal efficiency and then observed the fickleness of Fortuna when that pope died in August 1503, leaving Cesare to the mercy of his numerous enemies. Fortune's wheel turned with less dramatic consequences when Archbishop Deane died, but Wolsey was once more left in need of a patron. This time, Cavendish assures us that his master became acquainted with the 'very grave and ancient' royal councillor Sir Richard Nanfan, who had been part of the English mission which negotiated the Anglo-Spanish marriage under the terms of the treaty of Medina del Campo (1489).[15] Diplomatic missions had featured highly in the careers of numerous fifteenth-century English clerics destined to hold high office, Archbishops Kemp and Morton providing cases in point, but this route was presumably denied to Wolsey because he had not chosen to specialize in law. In 1503 Nanfan was appointed to the lieutenancy of Calais in the absence of Giles, Lord Daubenay, and took Wolsey there as his chaplain. Calais and its Pale bordered both the kingdom of France and the counties of Artois and Flanders, which had been ruled by the Valois dukes of Burgundy in the fifteenth century but fell into Habsburg hands when Charles the Bold's daughter Marie died in 1482. All parts of the Burgundian inheritance which fell within the Holy Roman Empire and outside the kingdom of France were ruled thereafter by her widower, Maximilian, but when he succeeded his father as emperor in 1493, the Low Countries were reallocated to Maximilian and Marie's son, who is known in English as Archduke Philip. In 1506 the archduke and his wife, Juana, made their way from the Low Countries, via England, to Castile, where Juana had succeeded her mother as 'queen proprietress' in 1504, and where her husband was acknowledged as Felipe I. A footnote to their English visit was the Habsburg surrender of the Yorkist claimant Edmund de la Pole into Henry's hands. Edmund remained imprisoned in the Tower of London until his execution in 1513, by which time his younger brother Richard was courting and being courted by the European powers as an alternative to the Tudor monarch. Meanwhile, Louis XII of France felt justifiably threatened by the presence of Habsburg territory across virtually all his kingdom's land borders. Personal experience of Calais and its political geography – suffocatingly close to both French and Habsburg territory – loomed large in Wolsey's subsequent thinking about international relations, especially his apparent conception of England's role in balancing the two greater powers in that region.

Wolsey remained in Nanfan's service until the knight died in 1507 and he acted as executor of the will, but his appointment to the Suffolk rectory of Redgrave between June 1506 and March 1507 suggests that he was already looking to re-establish himself in England. According to Cavendish, it was Nanfan who secured Wolsey his next position, as chaplain to King Henry, but two more pieces were still required to complete the patronage puzzle. Among the king's councillors Wolsey identified Richard Fox, bishop of Winchester, and Sir Thomas Lovell as the men most likely to be of use to his career.[16] Lovell was an East Anglian lawyer, whose attractions for Wolsey included his likely association with the marquis of Dorset in the 1483 revolt against Richard III, his service to Henry VII in a sequence of senior financial offices, and even his visits to Calais to collect Henry's French pension. Fox's attractions were even more numerous. It is impossible to confirm the later assertion that he had been among the earliest members of Magdalen College though, as bishop of Winchester from 1500 to 1528, he was certainly its visitor. Having served Henry during the invasion of 1485, he remained among the king's closest and most trusted councillors, including as keeper of the privy seal from 1487. His diplomatic experience was extensive and included several missions to France between 1487 and 1492, the last of which culminated in the treaty of Étaples and ensured that pretenders to the English throne would cease to enjoy French support. Turning to England's essentially commercial relations with the Low Countries, Fox negotiated the treaty known as the *Intercursus magnus* in 1496, and attended meetings between Henry and Archduke Philip at Calais in 1501 and Windsor in 1506. He was directly involved in marriage negotiations for all of the king's children. Those for Princess Margaret were, for Fox, the culmination of fifteen years of talks punctuated by episodes of cross-border warfare. Negotiating the Spanish match for Prince Arthur and renegotiating it for the somewhat reluctant Prince Henry occupied him intermittently for two decades. For Princess Mary, Fox and his colleagues aimed even higher: in 1507 they negotiated a match with Philip and Juana's eldest son, Charles of Ghent (the future emperor Charles V), who had already succeeded his father as ruler of the Low Countries and offered a potential alternative to his allegedly mentally unstable mother in Castile.[17] All the while, Fox filled a succession of episcopal vacancies – Exeter in 1487, Bath and Wells in 1492, Durham in 1494, Winchester in 1501 – but was again overlooked for Canterbury and the chancellorship in 1503, both of which went to the bishop of London, William Warham.

Cavendish's account of Wolsey's rise to eminence and power acquires greater detail and conviction when he tells of how Fox and Lovell spied a means for the ambitious chaplain to distinguish himself in the eyes of his king. An emissary to the emperor was required and Wolsey was dispatched. After leaving the king's presence at Richmond Palace around noon on a certain day, he reached London in four hours, Gravesend by barge in a further three, and Dover after a night ride. A fair wind took him to Calais in three hours, and post horses to Maximilian in Flanders. Retracing his route with equal celerity he was back at Richmond within eighty hours of his departure. When the king saw him, he asked the chaplain why he had not yet set out on his mission and was suitably impressed to be furnished with proof that it had already been completed.[18] Cavendish reveals nothing of the content of this presumably sensitive mission, for the manner of its execution was what caused Wolsey to recount the episode over twenty years later, but when Pollard examined this striking anecdote, he found it to be 'inaccurate in various details'.[19]

It is from the chaplain's own correspondence with the king that we learn of two diplomatic missions undertaken by Wolsey in 1508: to James IV in Edinburgh in late March and early April, and in October to Charles's regent in the Low Countries. The regent was his aunt the emperor's daughter Margaret, a woman who had been betrothed to Charles VIII of France, widowed after brief marriages to Don Juan of Aragon and Castile and Duke Philibert II of Savoy, and who was now being sought in marriage by the somewhat older King Henry, himself a widower since 1503. Wolsey failed to persuade her of his master's charms, though she was happy enough to confirm the existing Habsburg-Tudor alliance and the betrothal of her nephew to Princess Mary. However, towards the end of 1508 this mission was nothing more than a diplomatic sideshow, compared to which the main attraction was the league signed at Cambrai on 10 December between Maximilian, Louis XII, Ferdinand of Aragon and Pope Julius II.[20] Henry VII was needed neither for the signatories' ostensible purpose, a crusade against the Ottomans, nor for their real objective, a military campaign against the republic of Venice to take back various territories incorporated into the Venetian state during the previous century. That objective was achieved on the battlefield of Agnadello, near Crema, the following 14 May. Even if a snub was not intended by the various signatories, the league of Cambrai was precisely the sort of pan-European initiative from which Wolsey was determined that England should not be excluded in future.

Between the Scottish and Netherlandish missions, Wolsey obtained his first cathedral canonry, at Hereford, where his appointment was surely explained by a personal relationship with the bishop. This was Richard Mayhew, whose career prefigured Wolsey's in that he had been an episcopal chaplain, to William Smith of Lincoln, and later chaplain and almoner to Henry VII, but the most telling connection was that he had been president of Magdalen throughout Wolsey's entire Oxford career. Wolsey's next preferment, to the deanery of Lincoln in February 1509, gave him capitular responsibilities to dovetail with those of Bishop Smith in the diocese. The canons were evidently a disorderly bunch, but Smith's responsibilities as lord president of the council of the Marches of Wales, and Wolsey's at court, suggest that neither was able to exert much control over their subordinates. Smith was a protégé of Lady Margaret Beaufort, who secured his appointments to the bishoprics of Coventry and Lichfield in 1492 and Lincoln in 1496, and remained close to her throughout Henry VII's reign. In the realm of education, their foundation of Oxbridge colleges reads like something of a dialogue between the universities: Lady Margaret founded Christ's at Cambridge in 1505, Smith responded by co-founding Brasenose at Oxford in 1509, and Lady Margaret effectively clinched the argument with St John's in 1511. After Smith's death in 1514, Oxford's cause was championed in style by his friend Richard Fox, founder of Corpus Christi College in 1517.

More immediately, an era ended with the death of Henry VII on 21 April 1509 and that of his mother a little over two months later, on 29 June, that is eighteen days after the new king's marriage with his brother's twenty-three-year-old widow, five days after their joint coronation, and just one day after his eighteenth birthday. Continuity characterized the first phase of Henry VIII's reign, for many of his father's most experienced and trusted servants continued in high office: Archbishop Warham as lord chancellor, Thomas Howard, earl of Surrey, as lord treasurer, and Richard Fox as keeper of the privy seal. Thomas Ruthall, bishop of Durham, remained secretary of state, an office he had held since 1500. Wolsey's sometime patron Sir Thomas Lovell provided another element of continuity in the king's council. The prompt arrests of Henry VII's least popular ministers, the 'new men' Sir Richard Empson and Edmund Dudley, confirmed the character of the council as both noble and clerical. The character of the court, on the other hand, changed dramatically, to match the exuberance of the young monarch, whose personal servants and close associates were young, hearty and devoted to the noble diversions of hunting and tournaments. Meanwhile, the new queen became pregnant straightaway and was launched on her career of maternal misfortune: her first child miscarried in January 1510 and the second lived for less than two months early in 1511. The most appropriate company for the ambitious dean of Lincoln was among the greybeards of the council, but it appears to have been in this period that Wolsey, who was by now in his mid thirties, participated in the rejuvenated spirit of the court by indulging in a liaison with a woman known to posterity as Mistress Larke, for the boy taken to be their son, Thomas Wynter, was born around 1510 and his sister, Dorothy (who went by the surname Clansey), perhaps a couple of years later. The temptation to regard this sort of behaviour as somehow characteristic of Renaissance prelates should be resisted, for it emerged at the papal court only when popes granted cardinals' hats to men of greater nobility than learning, and when some of their social inferiors chose to ape aristocratic mores. In the context of the early sixteenth-century English Church, the part of the noble-but-worldly prelate was taken by James Stanley, bishop of Ely, who acknowledged three illegitimate children by his housekeeper, leaving Wolsey to follow in his wake as the ambitious parvenu. The connection did not end there. At Stanley's death in 1515 his Lancashire rectory of Winwick was re-allocated to Thomas Larke, Wolsey's chaplain and the brother of Jane or Joan, the cardinal's sometime mistress. That put Larke in contact with the many-branched Legh family, some of whose family memorials can still be seen at St Oswald's, Winwick. Around 1519 Jane Larke married George Legh of Adlington in Cheshire, complete with a dowry provided by Wolsey, and went on to have four more children, the youngest of whom was named Thomas.

Wolsey's liaison may have been facilitated by his acquisition of the disgraced Empson's London house at Bridewell, which stood at the confluence of the Fleet and the Thames, but it certainly provided no immediate bar to his promotion in either Church or State.[21] Indeed, Peter Gwyn argues that he did not have to wait until November 1509, as previously assumed, to be appointed as Henry's almoner, but rather entered into this office in September, immediately after the death of the previous holder.[22] This appointment appears to have been engineered by Fox and brought with it membership of the king's council, where the bishop felt in need of allies.[23] In another passage based on no more than the cardinal's own recollections, Cavendish captures the flavour of this period and explains that the secret of Wolsey's success lay in his appreciation of the young king's need to channel his energies into action and pleasure, ingratiating himself by relieving Henry of the more burdensome aspects of kingship: 'Thus the almoner ruled all them that before ruled him; such things did his policy and wit bring to pass. Who was now in high favour, but Master Almoner? Who had all the suit, but Master Almoner? And who ruled all under the king, but Master Almoner?'[24] In reality Wolsey's ascent still proceeded steadily and was very far from complete, especially as Henry declared the venerable Fox to be the councillor he most trusted and commentators were keen to chart rivalry between Fox and the lugubrious Warham, complete with speculation that Winchester, rather than Canterbury, would be graced with a cardinal's hat. Meanwhile, Wolsey became registrar of the Order of the Garter in April 1510 and supplicated for the degrees of BTh and DTh from his university.

The opening months of 1511 saw Wolsey made a canon of St George's Chapel, Windsor, as well as rector of Great Torrington in Devon, the former providing the more accurate reflection of his ambitions at court and in the council chamber. Henry was now thought ready to display his prowess as a military leader and the opportunity for this emerged in the post-Cambrai realignment of the European powers. The league's victory at Agnadello had created a power vacuum in areas where Venetian patricians had previously governed on behalf of their state. Louis XII and his armies rapidly filled that vacuum, adding much of the Venetian *terraferma* to their existing occupation of the duchy of Milan. Julius II therefore initiated an anti-French strategy that meshed diplomatic and military initiatives. It was in the course of this conflict, in the region around

Bologna and Ferrara, that the pope demonstrated his resolve to oust the French from Italy by heading north to supervise the campaign in person.

If a pope could go to war, then a king could convene a general council of the Church. Conciliarists had argued since the papal schism of the fourteenth century that such councils had the authority to overrule and even depose popes. The taxable wealth of the Gallic Church meant that kings of France tended to be well versed in this argument, but only Louis went as far as to summon an anti-papal council, which a small number of dissident cardinals declared would meet in the Florentine subject city of Pisa from 1 September 1511.[25] When this damp squib of a council finally opened on the feast of All Saints, it did little more than decide to adjourn to the relative safety of Milan. Maximilian soon dissociated himself from the project, and Ferdinand of Aragon was opposed to it from the start. Julius responded to the French challenge by summoning a perfectly valid general council to meet at the Lateran in Rome at Easter 1512, while at the same time creating an anti-French Holy League to isolate Louis diplomatically and drive the French out of northern Italy by military means. Maximilian, Ferdinand and Venice spied potential territorial advantages in this, the emperor because he was overlord of Milan, the king of Aragon because he had long-standing disputes with France along their Pyrenean border, and Venice because it was the quickest opportunity to reassert control over her lost *terraferma* possessions. Henry followed his father-in-law's lead, not least because it offered an opportunity to put into practice the grand design which had inspired the Anglo-Spanish marriage in the first place, the exertion of concerted pressure on France. There was, however, a difference of opinion among Henry's councillors over how best to deal with this opportunity, a division which has created misleading assumptions about the existence of peace and war factions, with Fox and Wolsey allegedly heading the former and the earl of Surrey the latter. The differences between them were more subtle than that. Scotland remained one of France's few reliable allies. Surrey used his prior experience of Anglo-Scottish affairs and his continuing involvement in countering Scottish piracy at sea to argue in favour of a traditional cross-border attack. Wolsey clearly regarded this as an unnecessary and costly distraction. Writing from Windsor on 30 September, he informed Fox that Surrey might easily be excluded from influence with the king and that the earl's younger son, Edward Howard, continued to press the cause of an expensive Scottish campaign. Concluding that 'your presence shall be very necessary to repress this appetite', Wolsey confirmed his own allegiance to Fox.[26] Such distinctions were for private consumption. To the outside world, the king's councillors presented a more united front, so that it was Surrey who led the negotiations which culminated in the signing of the treaty of Westminster on 17 November, a treaty which committed England to an anti-French policy in concert with the Spanish kingdoms. Four days earlier Henry had formally adhered to the Holy League.

One means of presenting a united front and a clear sense of purpose was the production of printed propaganda. The French-born printer Richard Pynson had worked for Bishop Fox and Archbishop Morton before receiving his first commission from Henry VII in 1504, but it was not until 1512 that he became the exclusive printer of government publications, a number of which were propaganda pieces designed to persuade the reading public of the merits of the Holy League and its war against King Louis. The timing of this development and the emphasis on foreign policy suggests that it was Wolsey's initiative and that the king's almoner fully appreciated the political potential of the printed word.

The campaigning season opened early in 1512 and witnessed a sequence of victories in northern Italy for the young French commander Gaston de Foix. These culminated in the battle of Ravenna on Easter Sunday (11 April), but the spirit of the French forces was broken by the death of their talismanic leader. Although the Holy League was defeated at Ravenna and the papal legate, Cardinal Giovanni de' Medici, captured and briefly held in Milan, Julius remained resolutely determined to drive the French from Italy, a resolution largely encouraged by the intervention of 18,000 troops from the Swiss Confederation, but also by assurances from Ferdinand and Henry that they were keen to attack the French from a different direction. The pope's determination was rewarded when the French, including their schismatic council, evacuated Milan before the end of June, allowing Massimiliano Sforza to claim the ducal title which his family had enjoyed since 1450, but which Louis had challenged since 1499. The French retreat from his native Liguria gave Julius the keenest pleasure of all. Meanwhile, the Fifth Lateran Council opened on 3 May, though Louis did not finally concede defeat on the ecclesiastical front until the following year. The withdrawal of French forces from the peninsula provided Julius with the opportunity to send a Spanish army to subdue France's long-term Tuscan ally, Florence. The government headed by Piero Soderini promptly fell and the remaining members of the Medici family, led by Cardinal Giovanni, returned to their native city after nearly eighteen years in exile.[27]

The French cause in Italy was therefore roundly defeated when Wolsey's sometime pupil, the second marquis of Dorset, put his former schoolmaster's policy into practice by leading an English force from Southampton to Fuentarrabía with a view to launching a combined Anglo-Spanish invasion of Gascony and reviving England's claim to the region. The expedition was designed to introduce Henry of England as a serious player on the European stage, a young, vigorous man of action who provided a contrast with his older fellow monarchs. It also offered the prospect of greater glory than would a perfectly conventional strike against the Scots. The reality of the expedition was utterly inglorious. There was no coordinated campaign against the French because Ferdinand had more immediate designs on Spanish Navarre, which he occupied in the name of his new wife Germaine de Foix, while the English had orders only for a campaign against the French. Between June and October the inactive English soldiers were sitting targets for infectious diseases in the sweltering summer heat, and mutinied when they could endure the situation no longer. The diplomat William Knight accompanied Dorset and the English troops and reported home that Wolsey was being singled out by those who sought to apportion blame for this ill-conceived and catastrophically executed policy.

It was doubtless a chastening experience for Wolsey, but the only thing he resigned towards the end of 1512 was the administration of the deanery of Hereford, from which he nevertheless retained a pension, of £45 per annum for the next three years and £40 a year thereafter. Thus, from February 1513 he was non-resident dean of just two cathedrals, Lincoln and York. By the end of that year he had gained footholds in three other chapters, as precentor of St Paul's, London, and as a canon of Bath and Wells and of St David's. All of these were vacated when he became a bishop, but the acquisition of such geographically diverse interests creates the impression that Wolsey used those personal connections, however nominal, to fashion something of a power base spread across various regions of the country. Indeed, far from forcing Wolsey into retreat at home or abroad, the humiliation generated by the 1512 expedition only succeeded in galvanizing him into further action. It gave him a clearer idea about the scale of organization needed for successful English intervention in the affairs of larger, wealthier states, as well as the degree of wariness required when dealing with princes as unscrupulous as Ferdinand of Aragon. An interventionist foreign policy could not be one-dimensional, as the Spanish fiasco proved, but had to operate on many fronts simultaneously. That necessitated a level of diplomatic sophistication founded on the employment of permanent ambassadors sending regular dispatches to their home governments, a practice which began among the Italian states in the fifteenth century and soon became standard among the extra-Italian states as well.

Rome was the diplomatic hub of Renaissance Europe, and never more so than in the last days of an aged or ailing pope, during the *sede vacante* following a papal death, or when princes and prelates jockeyed for position in the opening phase of a new pontificate. The grizzled warrior Julius II died on 21 February 1513 and the conclave to elect his successor opened on 4 March. The Sacred College of Cardinals had become more geographically diverse during the pontificate of the Spanish pope Alexander VI (1492–1503), but Julius reversed this trend, so that it was again predominantly Italian by the time of his death. A survey of the college's membership at that point introduces us to Christendom's most exclusive club, a club to which Wolsey shortly gained admission.

The most senior of the twenty-five electors was Raffaele Sansoni-Riario, the only cardinal to survive from the pontificate of his uncle, Sixtus IV (pope 1471–84). Innocent VIII (pope 1484–92) had created eight cardinals, of whom only Giovanni de' Medici remained. Ten of the electors had been created by Pope Alexander: the Aragonese-Neapolitans Luigi d'Aragona, Jaime Serra and Francisco de Remolins, Alessandro Farnese and Adriano Castellesi from the Papal States, the Venetian patricians Domenico Grimani and Marco Corner and their Genoese counterpart Niccolò Fieschi, the Florentine Francesco Soderini, brother of the exiled Piero, and Tamás Bakócz, primate of Hungary.[28] The remaining thirteen were the creations of Julius II and included his *nipoti* Marco Vigerio della Rovere, Leonardo Grosso della Rovere and Sisto Gara della Rovere, vice-chancellor of the Church. Julius's other Italians were Carlo Domenico del Carretto, Sigismondo Gonzaga from the ruling family of Mantua, Antonio Maria Ciocchi del Monte, Pietro Accolti, Achille Grassi, the Genoese Bandinello Sauli and the Sienese Alfonso Petrucci. Only three of the electors were non-Italians promoted by Julius: the Breton Robert Guibé, the Englishman Christopher Bainbridge and the Swiss Matthäus Schiner, the last of whom had facilitated the late pope's employment of Swiss mercenaries. Half a dozen cardinals were eligible to vote but did not do so: Ippolito d'Este was the brother of Duke Alfonso d'Este of Ferrara, a papal subject but a French ally, and sympathized with the schismatic Pisan council; Philippe de Luxembourg, Amanieu d'Albret and François Guillaume de Castelnau displayed varying degrees of patriotic opposition to Julius but not to the extent of being excommunicated by him; Francisco Jiménez de Cisneros, primate of Spain, loomed large in Castilian government; elsewhere, Matthäus Lang was preoccupied as Maximilian's chancellor. A further four cardinals had been excommunicated by Julius for their part in the Council of Pisa-Milan and consequently did not participate in the conclave. Of these Francesco di Sanseverino came from a family of *condottieri*, was more inclined to action than contemplation, and vengefully sought to depose the pope after Julius subjected him to a period of incarceration. The Castilian Bernardino López de Carvajal was a man of a radically different stamp, devoted to the cult of the Holy Cross, under which his fellow countrymen had triumphed against the Moors of Granada in 1492. He had since taken their crusading fervour into north Africa, and hoped to conquer Jerusalem by means of the considerably longer route opened up by Columbus. Carvajal was a long-term critic of clerical abuses and advocate of a reforming general council. He longed for the election of an angelic pope, so was bitterly disappointed by the reality of Julius II. Guillaume Briçonnet had been among the architects of Charles VIII's Neapolitan campaign in 1494 and owed his hat to Alexander VI's need to placate the invading power. The fourth of the excommunicates, René de Prie, had accompanied Louis XII on campaign in northern Italy.

There had been two previous conclaves since the French invasions of Naples in 1494 and Milan in 1499 initiated the conflicts now known as the Italian Wars, both of them in 1503. In the first of these the cardinals elected Francesco Todeschini-Piccolomini – Pius III – because he was neither French nor Spanish, nor close to either of those powers, his principal connections being with his native Siena and with the German lands. When the rigours of the papal office killed Pius after a pontificate of just twenty-six days, the same set of electors took a different tack and chose Giuliano della Rovere – Julius II – as an Italian patriot who made it his mission to drive all the 'barbarians' from Italy. The conclave of 1513 proved to be the last, before the twentieth century, in which none of the larger European powers tried to engineer the result. Again the cardinals chose an Italian pontiff, the thirty-seven-year-old Giovanni de' Medici, who took the name Leo X and resolved to live up to his family name by healing the wounds of the Church, which he did by pardoning the rebel cardinals. King Louis rejoiced at the election of a Florentine and again turned his attention to Milan, where Massimiliano Sforza's rule was weak. However, another French invasion was abandoned when Sforza's Swiss mercenaries got the better of a French army at Novara on 6 June.

As in 1512, therefore, the French had already suffered a significant reversal in Italy when the English launched their invasion of Picardy in the middle of the campaigning season. Wolsey's dominance among Henry's councillors was underlined by the fact that he coordinated national preparations for the campaign, while his former mentor Fox had a subordinate role, albeit one appropriate for the bishop of Winchester, organizing provisions for the Portsmouth-based fleet. Both clerics accompanied Henry when the invasion got under way at the end of June, Wolsey commanding a contingent of two hundred men. In total an estimated 30,000 men crossed the Channel. The English possession of Calais made Picardy particularly vulnerable to attack, to which the building of a fortress at Thérouanne was the principal defensive response. The English set about besieging it, while the defenders included Richard de la Pole, whose Yorkist claim to the English throne was consistently supported by Louis and who declared himself to be duke of Suffolk following the execution of his brother Edmund in May. While the fortress was besieged, Henry himself ventured further south with another force and came upon an ill-prepared French army in open country at Guingatte (now Enguinegatte) on 16 August. The speed with which the French fled caused this encounter to become known as the Battle of the Spurs, after which Thérouanne soon surrendered. By this stage Henry had been joined by Maximilian, and their joint forces then headed eastwards to the city of Tournai, a French possession surrounded by Habsburg territory. That too surrendered at the end of September, though not without controversy as both Henry and Maximilian staked claims to it. With that the military campaign concluded, but the Anglo-imperial diplomacy continued, for Henry was eager to cement the relationship through the marriage of his sister Mary and her betrothed, the emperor's eldest grandson, Charles. It was agreed that the marriage would take place before the following 15 May. As events transpired, the most enduring consequences of the 1513 expedition concerned Wolsey personally, for Henry sought his appointment to the lucrative bishopric of Tournai, but encountered stiffer opposition from Louis's alternative candidate than he had from the French king's army.

Between the fall of Thérouanne and that of Tournai there occurred a military encounter of genuine significance when, on 9 September, the inferior forces of the septuagenarian earl of Surrey met James IV's invading army at Flodden in Northumberland. This battle was as bloody and hard-fought as Henry's victories were easy and inglorious. Up to 10,000 Scots, including James himself, were killed in a matter of hours, leaving those who survived with a seventeen-month-old king and a regency government, initially headed by the pro-English queen dowager. However, when she married Archibald Douglas, earl of Angus, in August 1514 she broke the terms of her late husband's will and lost the regency, which was assumed by the French nobleman of Scottish descent John Stewart, duke of Albany. James V could not assert himself until the late 1520s, leaving the northern kingdom in a state of anarchy throughout his lengthy minority.

In February 1514 Surrey's heroism was rewarded by his long-delayed succession to the dukedom of Norfolk. On the same occasion the king's favourite Charles Brandon became duke of Suffolk, without any exceptional feats of arms to his credit. Wolsey also experienced a dramatic inflation of titles in 1514, for he began the year as a dean and ended it as archbishop of York, having been bishop of Lincoln for seven months in the meantime. There had been no English episcopal vacancies since that at Durham in 1509, when Thomas Ruthall became Henry VII's last addition to the bench. The first vacancy of Henry VIII's reign did not occur until William Smith died at his Huntingdonshire manor of Buckden on 2 January 1514. As the Tournai episode indicated, Wolsey was clearly next in line for a bishopric, wherever a vacancy happened to occur. On 6 February he was papally provided to the Lincoln vacancy and consecrated at Lambeth on 26 March, a chronology that reveals the labyrinthine bureaucratic processes of the Roman Curia being completed more swiftly than the later formalities in England. This can be attributed to the intervention of Silvestro Gigli, who was the king's agent in Rome and with whom it seems that Wolsey had developed a good working relationship.

Wolsey himself never made the journey to Rome, but Anglo-Roman connections proved to be so crucial in his career as a cardinal and papal legate that it is worth tracing the history of that particular diplomatic axis throughout his earlier life, thereby setting Gigli's contribution to it in context. As a resident of Ipswich Wolsey's first diocesan bishop was James Goldwell of Norwich, who acted as Edward IV's orator or proctor in Rome in 1468, 1469 and 1471–2 and received the bishopric upon completion of his third Roman mission. Indeed, ensuring the papal provision of the king's candidates to vacant English, Welsh and Irish bishoprics, together with a small number of abbacies, was crucial to the orator's role. Each candidate required cardinalitial sponsorship, so the orator cultivated curial cardinals to fulfil that duty. The most assiduous of the late fifteenth-century English 'Rome-runners' was John Sherwood, a protégé of Archbishop George Neville and Richard III's successful choice for the bishopric of Durham in 1484, though the king failed in his bid to secure him a cardinal's hat. Sherwood was a great bibliophile and it was through succeeding him at Durham that Richard Fox acquired the library of Italian books which he subsequently bequeathed to Corpus Christi College, Oxford.

Although Sherwood served Henry VII after 1485, the new king deliberately cultivated a number of interrelated Anglo-Roman connections, including the dispatch of a large, high-profile embassy in 1487, in the hope of securing his tenuous hold on the English throne. Giovanni Gigli of Lucca, who had been collector of Peter's pence in the kingdom since 1476, served as Henry's orator in Rome from 1490 onwards and opened up a new chapter in Anglo-papal relations in 1492 by ensuring that Francesco Todeschini-Piccolomini, the future Pius III, became the first cardinal protector of England.[29] Indeed, Todeschini-Piccolomini made history as the first officially recognized cardinal protector of any nation. In 1497 Gigli became the first of three Italians to be chosen by Henry VII for English bishoprics. When he died the following year, his kinsman and former secretary Silvestro Gigli succeeded him as bishop of Worcester and as the king's orator in Rome. On the other side of the Anglo-papal coin, the future cardinal Adriano Castellesi held the lucrative English collectorship of Peter's pence from the point at which Giovanni Gigli returned to Rome in 1490, but later went to Rome himself, creating some confusion about which of them was Henry's principal representative. Castellesi appeared to be in the ascendant when he became bishop of Hereford in 1502, a cardinal in 1503, and bishop of Bath and Wells in 1504, but it was Gigli who proved to be the more reliable royal servant, renewing his English contacts during his diplomatic mission to the kingdom in 1505.

By the time of Henry VIII's accession in 1509 the papal favourite Francesco Alidosi was cardinal protector of England and Castellesi had fled from Rome to Venice for reasons that are still not understood, but a fresh approach to Anglo-papal relations began in September that year when Christopher Bainbridge, the recently appointed archbishop of York, was sent to Rome to reinforce England's anti-French position in the wake of the battle of Agnadello.[30] Pope Julius's appreciation of this English support was duly expressed in his gift of a cardinal's hat for Bainbridge in March 1511. The new English cardinal was not only far too grand to be Henry's confidential agent in Rome, let alone that of the king's almoner; he was immediately preoccupied with a legation in the war zone of northern Italy, thereby creating a vacancy at the Curia. This was filled by Silvestro Gigli, who arrived back in Rome in October 1512 and acted as the king's representative at the Lateran Council and in all the usual capacities of a curial proctor. Bainbridge's brash attempts to assert himself as the principal link between Henry and Julius were consistently thwarted by Gigli's more subtle mode of operating, presumably on behalf of both the king and the almoner. In 1513, as we have seen, Bainbridge became the first English cardinal since 1370 to vote in a conclave. He was certainly not *papabile* and Gigli signalled his masters' preferred outcome by persuading Castellesi to vote for Giovanni de' Medici. In other words, in a conclave with an unusually large 'English' component, the bishop of Worcester persuaded the bishop of Bath and Wells not to vote for the archbishop of York. By February 1514 Gigli was operating with supreme confidence and ensured that none other than Pope Leo's cousin and right-hand man, Giulio de' Medici, became the next cardinal protector of England.[31] This was the context in which he facilitated Wolsey's appointment to the vacancy at Lincoln. Bainbridge and Castellesi were both well aware that Gigli was acting as Wolsey's agent, but responded in radically different ways, Bainbridge informing Henry that Gigli was intriguing with the French and Castellesi trying to trump his rival by making a bid for a cardinal's hat for the new bishop of Lincoln.

From February 1514, therefore, Wolsey was the most junior of the nineteen English and Welsh bishops, seven of whom had been in their current sees for more than a decade. Indeed, this was an episcopal generation character-ized by longevity: John Fisher was bishop of Rochester for thirty-one years, William Warham archbishop of Canterbury for twenty-nine years, Robert Sherborn bishop of Chichester and Richard Fox bishop of Winchester each for twenty-eight years, Geoffrey Blyth bishop of Coventry and Lichfield for twenty-seven years, Thomas Skeffington bishop of Bangor for twenty-five years, and Edmund Audley bishop of Salisbury for twenty-two years. In addition to Fox of Winchester, Ruthall of Durham and Mayhew of Hereford, Wolsey may have found the bishop of Exeter, Hugh Oldham, among the more sympathetic older members of the episcopal bench. Oldham had been another protégé of William Smith and, consequently, of Lady Margaret Beaufort, and shared their commitment to educational patronage, which he expressed through the establishment of Manchester Grammar School in 1515 and in generous benefactions to Corpus Christi College, Oxford. Richard Fitzjames, bishop of London, would have been a familiar figure from Wolsey's Oxford days, for he had been a long-serving warden of Merton College, from 1483 to 1507. Among the younger bishops, the dedicated pastor John Fisher claimed that Fox had been responsible for his appointment to Rochester in 1504, an assertion that reinforces the impression of a deaf, emaciated but wily *fox* talent-spotting the brightest stars in the English ecclesiastical firmament and moulding the bench to his own exacting standards. A little light is shed on the relationship between Fisher and Wolsey by the fact that Fisher offered to resign as vice-chancellor of Cambridge in 1514 so that Wolsey, the coming man, might take his place. Only after Wolsey declined the honour was Fisher re-elected for life. Fox's friendship and patronage was no absolute guarantee of Wolsey finding allies among his fellow bishops, for Richard Nix, bishop of Norwich, was sufficiently close to Fox to have been his vicar-general at Bath and Wells, and subsequently at Durham, but he had a difficult relationship with the much younger Wolsey.

In terms of social origins, these bishops ranged from untraceable obscurity in the case of Edward Vaughan of St David's to unequivocally noble in those of Audley, the son of James Tuchet, fifth baron Audley, and James Stanley, the son of Thomas Stanley, first earl of Derby. Stanley's ecclesiastical career was advanced through the intervention of his stepmother, Margaret Beaufort, whose Cambridge colleges were founded during his episcopate at Ely. Wolsey's social inferiority may appear glaring when set in such company, but the most decisive advantage enjoyed by a number of his fellow prelates was their kinship with an earlier generation of bishops. Geoffrey Blyth was the nephew of Archbishop Thomas Rotherham of York. Rotherham's indirect successor in the northern province, Bainbridge, was the nephew of Thomas Langton, the bishop of Winchester who died before his translation to Canterbury could take effect. The mother of Richard Nix was a Stillington, making him a kinsman of Robert Stillington, the bishop of Bath and Wells who preached in favour of Richard of Gloucester in 1483 and died in 1491. No less typical of the period was the practice of installing religious in poorer, peripheral sees, as illustrated by the case of John Penny, the Augustinian abbot of Leicester who was bishop of Bangor from 1505 and translated to Carlisle in 1508.

Those members of religious orders who had higher degrees were more likely to be theologians than canon lawyers, but there was no hard and fast distinction in this matter and the secular priests Audley, Blyth and Fitzjames received doctorates in theology. By far the most distinguished theologian in this group was John Fisher, Margaret Beaufort's spiritual director and the first holder of her Cambridge chair in theology. Warham, Stanley and Vaughan held doctorates in canon law and were more obviously clerical careerists. Nix and Bainbridge followed in the footsteps of fifteenth-century English prelates such as William Grey and Robert Flemming, who became bishop of Ely and dean of Lincoln respectively, by completing their education in Italy. Both Nix and Bainbridge were initially attracted to Ferrara, although the great Ferrarese educator Guarino da Verona had died in 1460, and then proceeded to Bologna, the second city and the premier university of the Papal States, where Nix was admitted as a doctor of civil and canon law in 1483 and Bainbridge as DCL in 1492. Each man could therefore boast a flawless *curriculum vitae*. By way of comparison, Wolsey's record was certainly flawed, for his academic profile was not exceptional and his lack of useful clerical kinsmen necessitated career deviations such as the time-consuming detour to Calais.

Wolsey's distinguished predecessors at Lincoln – Thomas Rotherham, John Russell and William Smith – had enhanced the episcopal dwellings dotted throughout their sprawling diocese, as may still be seen at Buckden, with its Tattershall-style tower, or at Lyddington's charming Bede House. However, the latest successor of St Hugh was not in post long enough to appreciate these attractions, let alone enhance them further, for Cardinal Bainbridge died in Rome on 14 July, thereby creating the archiepiscopal vacancy at York to which Wolsey was duly provided. One of Bainbridge's servants confessed under torture to having poisoned the cardinal on instruction from Gigli, but a combination of diplomatic immunity and persuasion from England secured the orator's formal absolution by Leo towards the end of the year. Meanwhile, Wolsey received the temporalities of the see of York as soon as 5 August, in anticipation of Rome approving his translation, which did not occur until 15 September. Together with the patriarchate of Aquileia and the archbishoprics of Auch, Canterbury, Cologne, Mainz, Rouen, Salzburg, Trier and Winchester, York was one of the ten wealthiest sees in Catholic Christendom. As a metropolitan Archbishop Wolsey also received a pallium, the distinctive strip of woollen cloth which had come to signify the particularly close connection between the pope and archbishops throughout Western Christendom. On this occasion the act of investiture was entrusted to the bishops of Winchester and Norwich. As archbishop of York, Wolsey was entitled to have a metropolitical cross carried before him, but diplomatic convention dictated that this practice be confined to his province and not apply when he happened to be in the province of Canterbury. Wolsey had no obvious intention of visiting his province, but every intention of asserting his new status, much to the annoyance of Archbishop Warham.

Of less symbolic and considerably more practical significance was Wolsey's acquisition of York Place, the archbishop's London residence, the site of which can no longer be traced with ease in the area of Whitehall Court and Whitehall Place. The archbishops had a second London house at Brigge (Bridge) Court, Battersea, which Wolsey used as an operational centre for his building projects at York Place and Hampton Court, but the archiepiscopal palaces and manors in the distant northern province were of no immediate use to him and consequently fell into some disrepair. In southern England bishops' manors radiated outwards from London so that, for example, the bishop of Winchester could travel in stages from his palace in Southwark to his cathedral city by way of his estates at Esher in Surrey and Farnham in Hampshire, and the archbishop of Canterbury could make his way from Lambeth to Canterbury by stopping at Croydon, Otford, Knole, Maidstone and Charing. Late fifteenth- and early sixteenth-century bishops routinely maintained and augmented such buildings, a number of which were of a similar architectural style, ranged around a series of courtyards in a manner reminiscent of Oxbridge colleges, with emphasis given to monumental entrance gateways. The surviving remains vary in size from Archbishop Bourchier's sprawling palace at Knole, to more picturesque fragments at Otford and Esher. The last of these stands on the bank of the river Mole three miles from its confluence with the Thames. Opposite the entrance to the Mole stands Hampton Court Palace. From the twelfth century the manor of Hampton had been associated with the Knights Hospitaller but was leased by them to a number of laymen in the late fifteenth century. In 1494 John Kendall, prior of the English Hospitallers, signed an eighty-year lease with Giles Daubeney. Daubeney was one of Henry VII's most trusted councillors, for whom a country house seven miles upriver from the royal palace at Richmond was a particularly useful acquisition. The moated house which Daubeney then created at Hampton stood on the site of the present Clock Court and has been likened to Oxburgh Hall in Norfolk, but only the great kitchen and some adjacent rooms survive from before Wolsey's dramatic rebuilding. Daubeney's heir evidently experienced financial difficulties and disposed of the property as soon as he came of age. Kendall's successor, Thomas Docwra, had no difficulty in finding another leaseholder, for he and Wolsey were both councillors and, moreover, shared an interest in diplomacy. Consequently, in January 1515, just four months after he became archbishop of York, Wolsey signed a ninety-nine-year lease on Hampton Court, with a view to creating a palace fit for entertaining kings.[32]

One cultural distinction that can be made between Wolsey and some of his fellow bishops is that he did not share their personal involvement in literary matters: he was more of a patron than a practitioner of scholarly activities. To put it somewhat crudely, Wolsey's connections to northern Europe's most renowned humanist scholar, Erasmus, were generally by means of intermediaries such as John Fisher, William Warham and William Blount, Lord Mountjoy. Fisher was responsible for inviting the Dutchman to lecture at Cambridge, which he did between 1511 and 1514, but it was Warham's generosity that secured the dedications of a sequence of Erasmian publications, from two plays by Euripides in 1506–7 through to the New Testament of 1516. Mountjoy had been Erasmus' first English patron and became governor of English-occupied Tournai from January 1515. There he liaised with Wolsey's vicar-general, Richard Sampson, in the hope of securing a prebend for the illustrious scholar, but this scheme proved to be over-optimistic. The disappointment was not sufficient to place Wolsey among the victims of Erasmus' barbed wit, but he did fall victim to the pen of another foreign humanist who initially found a congenial home in England.

The Urbinese Polidoro Virgili – anglicized as Polydore Vergil – was sent to England in 1502 as sub-collector of Peter's pence, deputizing for Adriano Castellesi. It was not necessary for foreign scholars to 'go native' in order to acquire Henry VII's favour and, with it, benefices such as Vergil's archdeaconry of Wells, but only Vergil became so immersed in his adopted culture as to write a history of England, which he began in 1508 at the king's request.[33] When Cardinal Castellesi fled from Julius II's Rome, Vergil lost his curial patron. Consequently he also lost the sub-collectorship, but did not relinquish it to Pietro Griffo without a fight and claimed it back on Griffo's departure in 1512. Leo X's election offered Castellesi an opportunity to revive his fortunes in Rome, but it also happened to coincide with the flourishing of Wolsey's cardinalitial ambitions. In 1514, therefore, Vergil was sent to Rome to discuss with Castellesi the possibility of a red hat for the bishop of Lincoln. As we have seen, Castellesi was not Wolsey's most intimate contact in Rome and Vergil now became seriously embroiled in the rivalry between Castellesi and Gigli. By the time Vergil returned to England in 1515, the king was seeking to oust Castellesi from the collectorship and replace him with Gigli's fellow Lucchese Andrea della Rena, who is better known by his literary name of Andreas Ammonius. Like Vergil, Ammonius was a natural associate of Erasmus' erudite English friends, including Thomas More, Thomas Linacre and John Colet. Unlike Vergil, he never found himself in scholarly rivalry with Erasmus but, rather, enjoyed the great man's friendship as well as the literary privileges of being secretary to Lord

Mountjoy. From 1511 Ammonius served as Henry VIII's Latin secretary but also sought the collectorship, so therefore had both the capacity and the self-interest to see that Vergil's correspondence with Castellesi was intercepted.[34] This was found to contain criticism of Wolsey, in consequence of which Vergil was imprisoned in the Tower of London in April 1515 and Ammonius obtained the coveted collectorship.

A period of confusion followed, in which Vergil's supporters, from the pope downwards, petitioned for his release. Although it seems likely that it was Wolsey who effected this at the end of December, Vergil nevertheless identified the cardinal as the source of his woes and gained revenge in the same manner as Platina, the fifteenth-century papal historian, had done after being imprisoned by Paul II, by creating in the *Anglica Historia* so compelling an image of Wolsey's arrogance and ambition that it was long accepted as gospel:

> English affairs thus daily prospered, and in this prosperity Thomas Wolsey gloried exceedingly, as though he alone were responsible for the great good fortune, in that his authority was now supreme with the king. But he was also more hated, not only on account of his arrogance and his low reputation for integrity, but also on account of his recent origins.[35]

Ammonius was finally assured of the collectorship in June 1517, but he proved to be as short-lived as his victory, for he died of the sweating sickness just two months later.

As 1514 opened with the death of Bishop Smith, so in the secular sphere it did so with a death that led to a chain of events even less predictable than the king of England's almoner becoming a *grand prelat*. Louis XII's wife Anne of Brittany died at Blois on 9 January, her numerous pregnancies leaving the king with only two daughters, fourteen-year-old Claude and four-year-old Renée. It had already been decided that Claude would marry the king's heir presumptive, François, count of Angoulême, an arrangement reminiscent of Louis's own first marriage, to Jeanne de France, daughter of Louis XI. The grieving monarch declared that he would not remarry and his court was still in mourning for the much-loved queen when Claude and François were married on 14 May, the very day before what the English thought of as the deadline for their princess to marry Charles of Ghent. There was no enthusiasm for that match among Charles's advisers and no guarantee that the notoriously unreliable Maximilian would honour his word. Consequently, on 2 May, William Knight sent an unequivocal message from the Low Countries, advising Wolsey that English interests would be better served by making peace with France. As the emptiness of Maximilian's promise became apparent, it was no wonder that Bainbridge reported from Rome that Gigli was negotiating with the French. A *volte-face* was indeed taking place in English foreign policy, one that has been attributed to Gigli's master, Wolsey, though Bishop Fox and the duke of Norfolk were also at the heart of making and implementing policy. The first public sign of this came on 30 July, when Princess Mary formally renounced her betrothal to Charles, but this was merely a preliminary to the signing of an Anglo-French peace at St-Germain-en-Laye on 7 August. The crux of the deal was that Henry would cease to pursue the traditional English claim to the French throne, in exchange for an appropriate financial pay-off and the cession of Tournai. In exchange Louis, the gouty widower, would receive the beautiful eighteen-year-old Tudor princess as his bride. With regard to Scotland, Louis promised to rein in the duke of Albany and prevent him leaving France to threaten the regency of the pro-English dowager queen. It had been rumoured that the Yorkist claimant Richard de la Pole was due to accompany Albany, and the English negotiators insisted that Louis surrender him. That request was refused and de la Pole was encouraged to seek sanctuary in the duchy of Lorraine. In the relatively small print, the French withdrew the claim of their canonically underage candidate for the bishopric of Tournai and recognized Wolsey as its holder. Following proxy marriages at Richmond and Paris, Mary travelled to France with an impressive retinue led by Norfolk and was formally wedded at Abbeville on 9 October to the man known as *le père du peuple* and who, at fifty-two, was certainly old enough to be *her* father. Festivities of one kind or another continued for the remainder of the year and proved too demanding for Louis, who died on 1 January 1515, leaving the twenty-one-year-old count of Angoulême as King Francis I, Mary as queen of France in name only, and a gaping hole at the heart of the Anglo-French alliance.[36]

The mission sent to ensure that Francis observed his treaty obligations was headed by the duke of Suffolk and included the Hospitaller Thomas Docwra, the experienced diplomat Sir Richard Wingfield and another clerical protégé of Bishop Fox, Nicholas West. Suffolk and West both emerged from this bout of diplomatic activity with obvious benefits, the former as Queen Mary's second husband and the latter as bishop of Ely, for the only English episcopal death in 1515 was that of James Stanley on 22 March. Thus the Anglo-French alliance was renewed on 5 April, but Francis was only interested in it as a means of neutralizing his northern neighbours ahead of a summer campaign against

Massimiliano Sforza. The young king inspired his armies as his ageing predecessor had ceased to do and his descent into Italy was viewed with particular alarm by Pope Leo, the self-appointed custodian of what was left of Italian independence. What Mandell Creighton describes as Leo's 'ingenious policy of being secretly allied with everyone' was certainly subtle, but not subtle enough to prevent the secular princes continuing to treat the peninsula as a battlefield.[37] Leo had previously held out against appeals from Henry and Gigli for Wolsey to be made a cardinal, but on 10 September he capitulated in the hope that the English might again intervene and deflect French attention from Milan. It was a vain hope: later in the same week the French broke Sforza's Swiss infantry in battle at Marignano. Milan and Genoa both reverted to French control before the end of the year. Meanwhile, Margaret Tudor's marriage to the earl of Angus had played into French hands and Francis had no hesitation in sending the duke of Albany to head the anti-English majority among the Scottish nobility.

Leo X's determination to keep the papacy as neutral as possible in its relations with the non-Italian powers had been reflected in his choice of four new cardinals on 23 September 1513. The first three were his fellow Florentines: Lorenzo Pucci, Giulio de' Medici and the notable *litterato* Bernardo Dovizi. The fourth, Innocenzo Cibo, was Leo's nephew but named after his non-Medicean paternal grandfather, Pope Innocent VIII. The promotion of papal kinsmen to the cardinalate was perfectly standard practice and, like bishops forwarding the careers of their clerical nephews, would have excited greater contemporary comment if it had not taken place. While the creation of new cardinals was in the exclusive gift of the pope, the other standard means by which the overall composition of the Sacred College was determined – death – was generally outside the pontiff's control. Nevertheless, the deaths of Robert Guibé in 1513, followed by those of Christopher Bainbridge, Carlo Domenico del Carretto and Guillaume Briçonnet in 1514, combined with the promotion of Pucci, Medici, Dovizi and Cibo to create a more Italianate college – but also a more politically neutral one. Non-Italians would have to be admitted in due course, but preferably at times of the pope's choosing and not under threat from the secular powers. Leo's desperation can be measured not only by the fact that he broke his earlier resolve and conceded to Henry's requests for a hat, but that Wolsey was the only cardinal created in September 1515. There was, however, nothing significant about Wolsey's designation as cardinal-priest of S. Cecilia, one of the most venerable churches in the Trastevere district of Rome: it had merely become vacant at the death of Cardinal del Carretto. However, it had been allocated to an Englishman on one previous occasion and, in a patriotic touch which would presumably have appealed to Wolsey, the arms of England can still be seen there on the tomb of the Benedictine Adam Easton, who died in 1398.

In the course of the fifteenth century the increasing assertiveness of secular states *vis-à-vis* the papacy had been measured in the burgeoning number of red hats bestowed for service to princes, rather than as marks of exceptional piety, erudition or devotion to the Holy See. The proportion of non-curial cardinals was therefore inclined to increase, as the record of the English cardinals attested: Henry Beaufort (created 1426), John Kemp (1439), Thomas Bourchier (1467) and John Morton (1493) all resided in their native land. The collective example of these four prelates suggests that archbishops of Canterbury were increasingly likely to be chosen for the hat: Beaufort was bishop of Winchester when he received it, Kemp was archbishop of York but subsequently translated to Canterbury, Bourchier and Morton were both already primates of *all* England when they were admitted to the Sacred College. In terms of residence and title, therefore, Christopher Bainbridge bucked the trend, but he did avoid the problems of precedence created by Martin V and Eugenius IV when they bestowed hats on Beaufort and Kemp rather than on Archbishop Chichele of Canterbury. Among these English cases, only Morton was a serving lord chancellor at the time of his promotion, but Georg Hessler and Matthäus Lang were imperial chancellors when promoted in 1477 and 1511 respectively.

With which other Renaissance cardinals might Wolsey usefully be compared? In view of the fact that he was likened to a tyrant by a chaplain of Archbishop Warham, one might venture to compare him to Pierre de Foix, who was viceroy of Navarre around 1480, or Paolo Fregoso, who was doge of Genoa on three separate occasions in the fifteenth century. Both of these cardinals ended up as exiles in Rome, but the principal distinction between them and Wolsey was that they were born into the ruling elite of states less powerful than England and effectively inherited their secular responsibilities. Pedro González de Mendoza offers a better model of a cardinal who chose to eschew Rome and exercise considerable power in his homeland. Mendoza became known as the 'third king of Spain' during the reigns of Ferdinand and Isabella, but he was too socially exalted to be regarded as a 'first minister' and, instead, personified an alliance between the crown and the high nobility of Castile. By elimination, therefore, we are left with Cardinal Georges I d'Amboise, Louis XI's almoner, Charles VIII's choice as archbishop of Rouen, and Louis XII's first minister, as

the most reasonable model for the omnicompetent Wolsey. In matters of state
Cardinal d'Amboise oversaw French diplomacy and accompanied the king
on campaign in Italy. On the ecclesiastical front he was repeatedly named as
legate to France and entered the two conclaves of 1503 as the French candidate.
Indeed, so perfect a model was he that he even succeeded where Wolsey most
conspicuously failed, in securing the papal annulment of Louis's first marriage.
It was only after the cardinal's death that the king began to suffer the foreign
policy reversals which we have already charted.

Without the competitive presence of any other cardinals on English soil,
Wolsey effectively initiated a new cult, that of the red hat, which he alone was
entitled to wear. The hat itself arrived in London on 15 November 1514 and lay
on the high altar of Westminster Abbey for three days, after which a Mass was
celebrated the like of which Cavendish could not imagine, 'unless it had been
at the coronation of a mighty prince or king'.[38] John Colet, dean of St Paul's,
preached on humility, reminding his audience that whoever exalts himself
will be humbled and whoever humbles himself will be exalted. Colet died in
1519, so did not live to see the humbling of Wolsey a full decade later. As if the
symbolism of the hat were not enough, from that day onwards Archbishop
Warham ceased to have his primatial cross carried before him, even in his own
province, because the cardinal's presence meant that he was constantly outranked. Wolsey, on the other hand, came to be preceded by two silver crosses,
one for his archbishopric, the other for his legacy.[39]

Approximately two-thirds of Thomas Wolsey's life has been covered by
this chapter, yet the man himself remains an enigma, his character more or
less a blank, his life and career pieced together by reference to those of his
contemporaries, and his contributions to royal policy shrouded in the collective
responsibility of conciliar government. It is to the amply documented final third
of his life that we now turn.

2

Grand Chancellor, 1515–20

As building accounts from 1515–16 confirm, the newly created cardinal wasted no time in beginning the transformation of Hampton Court from moated manor house to palatial residence.[1] By inviting Henry and Katherine to visit his new estate shortly after its acquisition he also confirmed its intended purpose as a conveniently located riverside retreat for the king and his court. Giles Daubeney's house had faced southwards, towards the Thames, but the master plan for Wolsey's palace involved infilling part of the moat in order to build an extensive range of lodgings around a large rectangular courtyard, the present Base Court, thereby turning its orientation by 90° and creating what remains the principal entrance, the Great Gatehouse, on the western side of the complex. This means of dramatically extending an existing property was modelled on precedents at the archiepiscopal residences of Otford and Knole, but the arrangement of double- and single-roomed lodgings for guests, accessed by enclosed corridors around three sides of the courtyard, was based on the design of the archbishop of Canterbury's palace at Croydon. The Great Gatehouse was also a natural evolution from its counterparts at Esher and Lambeth, which had been built respectively for William Waynflete in 1475–80 and Cardinal Morton in 1490.[2] Where Wolsey's palace departed from those precedents, but possibly followed that of Edward IV's Eltham Palace, was in the construction of an extensively glazed long gallery, projecting out to the south-east of Daubeney's house and evidently designed to make the most of views over gardens to both north and south. The addition of such galleries became a common feature of Wolsey's houses in both town and country. Among contemporary building projects, the duke of Buckingham's reconstruction of Thornbury Castle in Gloucestershire also featured considerable quantities of glazing, but the vertical emphasis of the oriel windows and stacked lodgings reflected that building's essentially military character. Hampton Court, by contrast, was horizontally palatial, with defensive features limited to the new moat and imposing gatehouse. In terms of design and materials, the diapered brickwork and limestone dressings of Wolsey's Base Court reflected much that had become typical of domestic and collegiate buildings in southern England, but the exterior of the long gallery departed from tradition by incorporating decorative elements in the latest 'antique' style. Wolsey made a point of employing the best craftsmen, led by the king's master mason John Lebons. His glaziers came from Flanders, as did the tapestries and paintings with which the interiors of his various houses and chapels were decorated.[3] By 1520 he had amassed an astonishing large collection of 600 tapestries, so many that Giustinian was able to assure his fellow Venetian patricians that they were changed weekly.[4]

Building work and the acquisition of *objets d'art* proceeded with such rapidity that the cardinal was soon able to reside at Hampton Court on a regular basis, including at Christmas 1517, and to entertain the king and queen in their respective lodgings. Progress was facilitated by the establishment of an office of works at Brigge House in Battersea, from where the construction at both Hampton Court and York Place was simultaneously coordinated. The central London house inherited by Wolsey from his archiepiscopal predecessors was essentially that created for the ambitious George Neville in the mid fifteenth century, a tight complex of buildings constrained by proximity to the unembanked river and to other properties. While work at Hampton Court could proceed even when the cardinal was in residence, Wolsey's initial refashioning of York Place in 1516 necessitated his removal to Bishop Ruthall's Durham Place, one of the episcopal inns located between the river and the Strand.[5]

York Place was perfectly located for access to the palace of Westminster, where Wolsey sat in the courts of chancery and star chamber over a period of fourteen years, but not so close as to deny him the opportunity to make a theatrical performance out of his daily term-time progresses, clad in brilliant scarlet, with the great seal of England, his broad-brimmed *galero*, two silver crosses, twin 'antique'-style silver pillars, and a great mace carried in procession before him.[6] By way of contrast, his predecessor as lord chancellor, Archbishop Warham, had been obliged to make his way from Lambeth to Westminster by barge, a more discreet form of transport well suited to his less ostentatious manner. Warham resigned the great seal on 22 December 1515, just five weeks after the arrival of Wolsey's hat, and the cardinal took the oath of office two days later, making him the king's principal minister and England's senior judge, despite having no formal education in the law. Wolsey's contemporary detractors, among them the aggrieved Polydore Vergil, had no qualms about casting Warham as an innocent victim of Wolsey's seemingly boundless ambition, but more recent historians

have been at pains to counter this by citing Warham's relatively advanced
years and Thomas More's assertion that the primate was eager to retreat from
the rigours of secular government and devote himself to his spiritual duties.[7]
Warham was a quiet, cerebral cleric in his mid sixties and did not have the
capacity either to tame or to flatter the ebullient twenty-four-year-old monarch.
Wolsey could do both. Thus it is likely that Warham was reasonably content to
concentrate on the administration of his diocese, the reform of its clergy and the
chancellorship of Oxford, which he retained from 1506 through to his death in
1532. Warham's sheer longevity also frustrated any ambition Wolsey may have
harboured for the Canterbury archbishopric.

Yet more light can be shed on this ministerial transition by reflecting on
Warham's defence of ecclesiastical liberties in the face of a renewed assault by
the secular authorities. At issue was an act passed by the parliament of 1512
which denied 'benefit of clergy' to clerks in minor orders and insisted that any
such men charged with serious offences be tried in the secular courts rather
than the ecclesiastical ones. Naturally enough, this had been opposed by senior
clerics sitting in the Lords and meeting in convocation, the clerical assembly
which met at the same time as each parliament. Thus it was determined that
the act would apply for an initial period of three years, expiring in 1515. In
the meantime relations between Church and State were tested by the case of
the wealthy London merchant tailor Richard Hunne, who had been sued by a
priest in an ecclesiastical court for non-payment of a mortuary fee, was excommunicated, and then brought his own action against the priest in the court
of king's bench, accusing him of slander, supplementing this with a charge
of *praemunire* against those involved in the original case, the implication of
which was that the archbishop's court lacked the jurisdiction to try him. The
ecclesiastical authorities responded by investigating Hunne's beliefs and arrest-
ing him for heresy, which would have been unremarkable except that, in early
December 1514, he was found hanging in his cell within forty-eight hours of
appearing before the bishop of London, Richard Fitzjames, and much heated
debate ensued over whether he had committed suicide or been murdered by the
bishop's officers. The Hunne case has arguably received more scholarly attention
than it deserves. For our purposes, we may note that it polarized clerical
opinion between those, such as the Franciscan Henry Standish, who sided with
the king as a nearer and more potent authority than the pope, and those clerics
who defended their rights and privileges in the manner of latter-day Beckets.
In November 1515 the king presided over a conference at Baynard's Castle,

at which these matters were debated. Richard Fox took issue with Standish, and Warham cited his predecessor's martyrdom for the sake of ecclesiastical liberties. Presumably with his own twelfth-century predecessor and namesake in mind, Henry brought proceedings to a definitive conclusion:

> By the ordinance and sufferance of God, we are king of England, and kings of England in time past have never had any superior but God only. Wherefore know you well that we will maintain the right of our Crown and of our temporal jurisdiction as well in this point as in all others, in as ample a wise as any of our progenitors have done before us.[8]

This confrontation, above all else, must have convinced Warham that he could no longer continue to serve in the secular government.

The fourteenth-century statutes of *praemunire* – the illegal importing of an alien jurisdiction – had been passed by English parliaments during the period of the Avignon papacy, when French popes were protected by England's French enemies. England was among numerous states to take advantage of papal weakness at that time. A common theme was that secular powers insisted on their candidates being appointed to bishoprics and other major benefices, with the papal Curia doing no more than formally approving their choices. As the Hunne case and the debate about benefit of clergy illustrate, the English statutes stated that legal cases which could be heard in the king's courts should not be diverted to papal courts outside England or even, by implication, to ecclesiastical courts within the realm. *Praemunire* was therefore a sword of Damocles hanging over all pre-Reformation English clerics, not least Wolsey. How did he respond to this particular crisis in the long history of conflict between the jurisdictions of his spiritual and temporal masters? The cardinal of York had spoken first at the Baynard's Castle conference. Contriving to kneel before his king while metaphorically sitting on the fence, he declared that:

> to his knowledge none of the clergy had ever meant to do anything in derogation of the king's prerogative, and for his own part he owed his whole advancement solely to our lord the king; wherefore he said he would assent to nothing that would tend to annul or derogate from his royal authority for all the world. Nevertheless, to all the clergy this matter of conventing of clerks before the temporal judges seems contrary to the laws of God and the liberties of the Holy Church, the which he himself and all the prelates of Holy church are bound by their oath to maintain according to their power.[9]

By way of conclusion, he sought to defuse the tension and play for time by proposing that the matter be referred to Rome. In the event, a similar result was achieved by parliament not renewing the act regarding criminous clerks, and by Wolsey persuading the pope to issue a bull which created a technicality effectively eliminating the category of clerk with which the act had been concerned. Sabres were rattled again in 1519 when a similar conference was held to discuss the right of sanctuary claimed by criminals, and the various abuses to which this practice was prone. Sanctuaries were potential centres of social disorder, so it was natural that the crown sought to impose tighter restrictions on them. By that stage Wolsey's status had been enhanced in both Church and State, for he was papal legate as well as lord chancellor, but there seems to be little doubt that he was acting on the crown's behalf when he attempted to regulate practices in the sanctuary at Westminster Abbey. However, Abbot John Islip would accept no alteration of the abbey's royal charter and the sanctuary survived until the wholesale reformation all the kingdom's sanctuaries in 1540.

The most prominent example of public disorder during the early years of Wolsey's chancellorship was the 'evil May day' riot against foreign merchants in 1517, when London apprentices and others indulged in an outburst of xenophobia that was efficiently put down by the duke of Norfolk. It was followed by a carefully choreographed ceremony in Westminster Hall, in which Wolsey the chancellor made a suitable oration on the theme of keeping the peace, and Wolsey the prelate was among those who begged the king's mercy for the people who had been arrested. By 1520 Wolsey's impact on law and order was such that Nicholas West, bishop of Ely, could assure him that

> the honourable renown and great fame of your Grace in administration of indifferent justice and keeping this noble realm in such good order, tranquillity and peace as never was seen within memory of man, specially in punishing misdoers and exalting noble and virtuous men, so spreadeth over all to your great honour, glory and merit.[10]

The physical distance between the Inns of Court and the royal courts at Westminster was somewhat greater than that of Wolsey's daily mule ride from York Place. Arguably greater still was the distance between the common law and the equity jurisdiction sought by plaintiffs who resorted to the king's courts because the common law courts had somehow failed to deal with their cases. Sir John Fyneux, who served as chief justice of king's bench for three decades from 1495, led attempts to reform the procedures of the common law courts, but these bore relatively little fruit in Wolsey's time. Since the fourteenth century Wolsey's predecessors as lord chancellor had heard petitions sent to the king in council, petitions dealing with debts, wills and inheritance, marriage settlements and related matters. He could not impose damages, which were the preserve of the common law, but more imaginative sanctions were open to him. Thus the court of chancery grew increasingly popular with claimants throughout the fifteenth century and was supplemented from 1483 by the court of requests, which was designed to deal with smaller claims made by poorer people, many of whom were women. From 1519 the court of requests came under the authority of the keeper of the privy seal but, before then, its judges were answerable to the king's almoner and the dean of the chapel royal, which explains how Wolsey, with five years' experience as almoner, could adapt so readily to his legal responsibilities as chancellor. Those responsibilities extended well beyond Westminster and brought him into contact with the legal structures of every county, for then, as now, the lord chancellor had authority over the appointment and conduct of justices of the peace. Thus he was able to cultivate the gentry in all parts of the kingdom and build up a network of clients such as all men of consequence enjoyed in that period.

Cavendish's account of Wolsey's typical day during the legal term relates that the cardinal sat in chancery 'till eleven of the clock, hearing suitors, and determining of divers matters'. It concludes: 'And from thence, he would divers times go into the star chamber, as occasion did serve; where he spared neither high nor low, but judged every estate according to their merits and deserts.'[11] Like the court of requests, that of star chamber dated from the late fifteenth century, when it was created to 'punish divers misdemeanours', particularly public disorder and riot. Although Wolsey always sat with numerous other judges, his leadership was largely responsible for making it a popular choice among claimants, who emphasized the riotous elements of property disputes and other civil cases.[12] Cavendish reminisced about the later 1520s after the passage of three decades, but the poet John Skelton captured the essence of the chancellor in action in 1522, at the height of his power, presenting him as a foul-tempered, overwhelming character who behaved as though he were the monarch himself, not least by asserting royal authority over the nobility:

> In the Chancery where he sits
> But such as he admits
> None so hardy to speak
> He sayeth, 'Thou huddy-peke!
> Thy learnyng is too lewd
> Thy tongue is not well thewed
> To seek before our grace.'
> And openly in that place
> He rages and he raves
> And calls them cankered knaves.

Thus royally he doth deal
Under the king's broad seal;
And in the Checker he them checks
In the Star Chamber he nods and becks
And beareth him there so stout
That no man dare rout;
Duke, earl, baron, nor lord
But to his sentence must accord.
Whether he be knight or squire
All men must follow his desire.[13]

By way of contrast, another contemporary, the Venetian ambassador Sebastiano Giustinian, was singularly impressed by the master at work and anticipated Cavendish when he reported in 1519 that the chancellor favoured the poor, whose suits he heard and dealt with swiftly, and made the lawyers waive their fees in such cases.[14] Wolsey's reputation as a champion of the poor was consequently matched by the antagonism of the common lawyers towards both the chancellor and his courts, but his enthusiasm for star chamber also provided a means whereby Wolsey acquired powerful enemies.

In a speech delivered in star chamber on 2 May 1516 the chancellor set out the crown's need for a judicially responsible noble elite, which would abide by the law as well as execute it in the king's name. It was a bridling from which the nobility had been free since Henry VII's death and the more irresponsible elements did not take kindly to being lectured by a man they regarded as their social inferior. To illustrate the point, Henry Algernon Percy, the fifth earl of Northumberland, then appeared to answer for his violent actions. Over the next few days the chancellor's attention turned to the long-term problem of livery and maintenance. Lord Hastings and his kinsman Sir Richard Sacheverell had been seen visiting the fugitive Queen Margaret of Scotland at Baynard's Castle, accompanied by liveried retainers. Hastings was also party to a long-running struggle for dominance in Leicestershire, and soon the investigation spread to include his regional rival and Wolsey's former pupil, the marquis of Dorset. Dorset was one of the king's councillors, but he was not above the 'law of star chamber'. Nor was another councillor, George Neville, Lord Bergavenny, who was also caught up in the investigation. All four were charged with 'retaining ... riot, rout, unlawful assembly and trespass'.[15]

The following year it was the turn of another knight, Sir William Bulmer, to receive punishment in star chamber, this time in a session at which the king presided and in which he took a personal interest. Bulmer was a member of the royal household but was found guilty of wearing the duke of Buckingham's livery in the king's presence. Even if the royal line of succession been secured by the birth of one or more healthy princes, Buckingham was still the closest adult claimant to the crown: both Bulmer and the duke had to be shown that Henry was very firmly the master of his realm. The Bulmer case confirmed the duke of Buckingham's conviction that Wolsey was an enemy of the entire nobility, who should unite in his destruction, though we cannot be certain quite how the chronology of the case relates to an undated letter which the king wrote with his own hand and sent to Wolsey one April, telling him to 'make good watch on' the dukes of Suffolk and Buckingham, the earls of Northumberland, Derby and Wiltshire, 'and on others which you think suspect'. The closer to the crown, the less they could be trusted: Suffolk was the king's brother-in-law Charles Brandon and the earl of Wiltshire was Buckingham's brother Henry Stafford.[16]

King and cardinal had good reason to be pleased with the thoroughness and efficiency of star chamber procedures. On the other hand, excessive thoroughness was a theme running through many of the charges levelled against the cardinal. As we have already observed in the arguably apocryphal dealings between Wolsey and Sir Amias Paulet, the cardinal's detractors were able to make a memorable argument for vindictive behaviour on his part. The same character trait was alleged by Sir Robert Sheffield in the course of his dealings with Wolsey. Sheffield was MP for the city of London and had acted as the Commons' speaker in the 1512 parliament. He was also aristocratically connected, his wife being the sister of Thomas Stanley, second earl of Derby. In the years immediately before his death in the Tower of London in 1518, Sheffield's fortunes descended into a spiral of hefty fines, imprisonment and allegations that Wolsey had unjustly accused him of complicity in a murder, an accusation prompted by the overtly anticlerical opinions voiced by Sheffield in the parliament of 1515. Although Sheffield withdrew the allegation and admitted he had lied to the king's council, he certainly knew where Wolsey was vulnerable to attack and how to make a reasonably convincing assault on his reputation.[17]

Wolsey's zeal for the legal rights of the less wealthy and, by implication, the source of much festering animosity towards him on the part of the social elite was in large measure associated with his strict implementation of the anti-enclosure acts of 1489 and 1514–15. England had grown rich on the export of wool and many landowners, especially in the Midlands, sought to maximize their income by enclosing land for the pasturing of sheep. Not only did tenants lose their traditional rights to graze animals on common land, but many also lost their houses as 'the sheep ate the men'. The more extensive a nobleman's estates, the more land he had to enclose, and the duke of Buckingham possessed more extensive estates in England and Wales than any other nobleman. Excluded from political power by reason of his claim to the throne, Buckingham devoted much energy to the management of his estates and was an enthusiastic encloser. In 1517 Wolsey championed the anti-enclosure cause by launching a systematic, nationwide investigation into the amount of land that had been enclosed, and thereupon ensured that the legislation was observed. Hundreds of prosecutions were initiated, a substantial proportion of them resulting in guilty verdicts. Bishop Fox managed to persuade Wolsey that he and his diocesan officials were innocent of the charges laid against them, but other landlords, clerical and lay, felt the full force of the chancellor's zeal. By 1528 John Longland, the bishop of Lincoln, could assure Wolsey that 'There was never thing done in England more for the commonweal than to redress these enormous decays of towns and making enclosures.'[18]

Star chamber and the court of requests channelled and emphasized the legal role of the king's council, and more than a dozen councillors could sit in judgement in them at any one time. The councillor with whom Wolsey collaborated most closely on legal matters was the master of the rolls, who presided in the court of chancery in the chancellor's absence. Five clerics occupied this office during the period of Wolsey's chancellorship. The first of these was John Yonge, a protégé of Archbishop Warham who completed his education in Italy and attracted Wolsey's attention through his conduct of diplomatic missions, both before and after his appointment as master of the rolls in 1508. Yonge is easily overlooked as a key associate of Wolsey, but his significance can be measured by the fact that he became a canon of York while Wolsey was dean, succeeded Wolsey as prebendary of Bugthorpe in the same chapter, and was appointed his suffragan and titular bishop of Negroponte when Wolsey became archbishop of York in 1514. Yonge's record made him an ideal candidate for an English bishopric, but he died of the sweating sickness in April 1516, only four months after Wolsey took possession of the great seal. His successor, the polymath Cuthbert Tunstal, was another northerner, another Italian educated lawyer, another of Warham's protégés, and succeeded Wolsey as prebendary of Stow Longa in the diocese of Lincoln, but he was also a member of the Colet-Grocyn-Linacre-More circle of humanists whose company had not attracted Wolsey at Oxford and became one of Erasmus' closest English friends. Although Tunstal occupied the mastership of the rolls until 1522, when he succeeded Richard Fitzjames as bishop of London, it was in diplomatic service that he arguably achieved greater distinction during that period. A similar pattern is found in the careers of Tunstal's three immediate successors, for John Clerk, Thomas Hannibal and John Taylor were all prominent diplomats during their terms as master of the rolls. Of these three Clerk was easily the closest to and most trusted by Wolsey.

English government in the early Tudor period was conducted in the king's name by means of documents sealed with the great seal, the privy seal or the signet. The keepers of the privy seal during Wolsey's years as chancellor were Richard Fox, Thomas Ruthall, Sir Henry Marney and Cuthbert Tunstal. When Fox resigned the keepership in 1516 and retired to his Winchester diocese it looked like a clear parallel to Warham's resignation of the great seal a few months earlier, though there is no reason to believe that either of them was forced out of office by Wolsey, as it suited Polydore Vergil to maintain. Although Warham's personal relations with Wolsey happened to be lukewarm, Fox had long been and remained on friendly terms with the chancellor, and poured what energy remained in his fragile frame into diocesan administration, the foundation of his Oxford college, and the rebuilding of his cathedral. Fox's career was shadowed by that of Thomas Ruthall, who served as keeper of the privy seal from 1516 until his death in 1523, but likewise came to that office with experience as secretary of state. The secretary combined a number of crucial roles, acting as the king's personal secretary, keeping the signet, managing the council's agenda and coordinating diplomatic activity. Ruthall served for sixteen years in that office, thereby gaining more direct experience of international relations than Wolsey and causing Sebastiano Giustinian to identify him as the cardinal's *alter ego* in diplomatic affairs. It was surely no coincidence that Wolsey's most striking interventions in the international arena were made before Ruthall's death in 1523. The next secretary of state was a man of a very different stamp. Richard Pace – secretary from 1516 to 1526 – was one of Renaissance England's most notable men of letters, whose character and career were shaped by a humanist education at Padua, Bologna and Ferrara, by the friendship of Tunstal and other English scholars in Italy, by service as Bainbridge's secretary and conclavist, and by a deft transfer to Wolsey's patronage after Bainbridge's untimely death. He would have thrived among the scholarly secretaries employed by Leo X, but was unsuited to the rigours of the diplomatic missions on which he was sent by his 'invincible king' and 'the wise cardinal of York'. During his absences the secretarial duties were undertaken by Richard Sampson in 1521–2 and then by Thomas More who, in turn, required understudies when he sat in parliament or was sent on missions abroad. Pace was officially succeeded in 1526 by William Knight, another Oxford man who completed his legal education in Italy, and in 1528 by the exceptionally able Cantabrigian Stephen Gardiner, who came to the king's service via that of the cardinal.

These were some of the individual councillors with whom Wolsey dealt on a daily basis, scholarly clerics rather than noble warriors. Conciliar government continued, but it did so at Westminster during the legal terms, rather than at the king's court all year round, with policy very firmly under Wolsey's control.[19] As long as he made some effort to cultivate the noble councillors and steered them towards sitting as judges in star chamber, and as long as England's fortunes prospered internationally, many of them were prepared to acquiesce in this arrangement, but it was a tide waiting to turn.

The office of lord treasurer was largely honorific and was held throughout Wolsey's governmental career by just two men, the second and third Howard dukes of Norfolk. The most distinguished of the under-treasurers in this period was Thomas More, who held this lucrative office between 1521 and 1525. The crown's senior financial officers belonged to the royal household and formed an arm of central government over which Wolsey exercised no formal control, though he insisted on the proper keeping of accounts and, in the person of Sir Thomas Lovell, had a staunch ally with extensive experience of royal finances, at least until Lovell's death in 1524. Extraordinary expenditure to meet foreign policy commitments necessitated the raising of extraordinary income – subsidies – for which parliamentary approval was required. Only once did parliament meet during the fourteen years of Wolsey's chancellorship, in 1523, and the longest period between Henry's parliaments, from December 1515 to April 1523, coincided with the height of the cardinal's dominance over all aspects of policy.

The nature of Wolsey's working relationship with the king has generated no little comment, for this was not a clear-cut case of an all-powerful minister making up for the deficiencies of the hereditary system. From Henry's better known grandparents came the imposing physical presence of Edward IV and the subtle intellect of Margaret Beaufort, which combined to create a

Renaissance man and a Renaissance monarch, but the king's reluctance to apply his undoubted gifts to the quotidian reality of government may have constituted a reaction against his father's devotion to its minutiae. When occasion demanded, Henry was perfectly capable of putting business before the pleasures of hunting with his boon companions, but his quixotic nature only increased the challenges encountered by those who served him. According to J. J. Scarisbrick, the cardinal's

> quick, strong hands grasped everything because Henry seemed unable, or unwilling, to make the smallest decision himself . . . . Wolsey must be servant yet master, creature yet impressario; he must abase himself and yet dominate, playing a part which only a man of superlative energy, self-confidence and loyalty could have achieved.[20]

More recently, Peter Gwyn has stressed that Henry was no figurehead in the early years of his reign and never ceased to be actively engaged in the business of government.[21] Either way, the political chemistry worked extraordinarily well.

Nevertheless, Wolsey was only ever a royal servant and could potentially lose the king's favour at any point. Measures had to be taken to minimize that risk. One such measure was the attempt in 1519 to remove the so-called 'minions' from Henry's privy chamber and their replace them with gentlemen favourable to the cardinal. Within a matter of months the 'minions' were back in the king's company and the scheme had been foiled.

As far as the practicalities of government allowed, Wolsey followed Fox's advice and stayed close to Henry, to facilitate business as well as to prevent potential rivals from influencing the monarch. They tended to meet weekly when the king was in or around London. Richmond and Windsor were accessible from Hampton Court. York Place was convenient for Blackfriars and not altogether inconvenient for Greenwich Palace, for Cavendish relates that the cardinal travelled there by barge each Sunday, breaking his journey in order to assert royal authority by processing through the city of London, 'with his crosses, his pillars, his hat, and the great seal' carried before him.[22] It was at Greenwich that Henry had been born in 1491 and baptized by Fox in the adjacent church of the Observant Franciscans. It was also at Greenwich, on 18 February 1516, that Queen Katherine gave birth to a daughter, Mary, who was baptized in the Franciscans' church two days later. Two of the princess's godmothers were the last surviving members of the house of York, Edward IV's sister Katherine, countess of Devon, and Margaret Pole, countess of Salisbury, daughter of George, duke of Clarence. The countess of Salisbury had been a member of Queen Katherine's household since 1501 and became Mary's governess in 1519. The appearance of the two widowed countesses was more than spiritually significant, for the house of Tudor consisted of nothing more than Henry, his elder sister Margaret, countess of Angus, younger sister Mary, duchess of Suffolk, and the baby princess, who might have proved to be as short-lived as her siblings and, even if she did survive, would be obliged to marry a foreign prince. The prospect of a succession crisis loomed large throughout the decade, and it was a crisis from which the duke of Buckingham convinced himself he would emerge as king. His hopes were encouraged by the prophecies of the Somerset Carthusian Nicholas Hopkins, but the seer became uncomfortably reticent after Mary's birth. The princess's third godmother was Agnes, duchess of Norfolk, and the sole godfather was Wolsey. Non-curial cardinals made suitably princely godfathers for royal offspring, but more remarkable was the fact that Henry also chose Wolsey to be godfather to his illegitimate son Henry Fitzroy, who was born to the king's young mistress Elizabeth Blount in 1519, the year after the last of Katherine's unsuccessful pregnancies. Wolsey's supervision of the boy's upbringing confirms that Henry regarded Fitzroy as a potential heir.

That supervision was a task to which the cardinal came with relevant experience, for the education of his son Thomas Wynter provided something of a trial run. It was natural enough that Wolsey should entrust Wynter's tuition to a recent Magdalen graduate, Maurice Birchinshaw, but the fact that Birchinshaw was also second master at Colet's recently founded St Paul's School and assistant to another Magdalen man, the Italian-educated grammarian William Lily, confirms that Wolsey was abreast of the latest developments in English education. His appreciation was not exclusively insular, for 1517 saw the foundation of the Collegium Trilingue at Louvain, which was dedicated to implementing the ideals of Erasmian humanism by teaching the three scriptural languages, Latin, Greek and Hebrew. It was to Louvain that Birchinshaw accompanied his less than promising pupil the following year, young Wynter matriculating there on 30 August 1518. Neither in years nor aptitude was the boy suitable for Oxford's latest collegiate foundation, for Bishop Fox's Corpus Christi College opened in 1517 and was dedicated to the training of priests by means of strict moral discipline and the highest standards of scriptural and patristic study. It was a beacon of Christian humanism, with particular emphasis on the teaching of Greek. After Brasenose in 1509, Corpus was only the second new college in

Oxford since Waynflete's foundation of Magdalen, and Fox ensured that its first president and many of its original fellows were Magdalen men. Wolsey's employment of Birchinshaw was thus a small reflection of current trends in educational practice and patronage, while there fermented in his brain ambitious plans for the foundation of an Oxford college to dwarf those of Waynflete and Fox.

More immediately, in 1518, Fox's statutes for Corpus inspired those of Thomas Linacre's College of Physicians. By means of this institution Linacre and a small number of his fellow Italian-educated physicians sought to ensure the highest standards of professional practice in the London area and to do so by working in conjunction with the civic authorities. The need for such coordination was underlined in 1517–18 by an epidemic of the sweating sickness, an exceptionally severe disease that killed its victims within a matter of hours and was consequently feared even more than plague. The king fled from London, but Wolsey remained and suffered four life-threatening attacks of 'the sweat' in June 1517. Linacre's cultivation of the cardinal included the dedication of his edition of Galen, printed in Paris in 1517. The cultivation worked, for it was Wolsey's patronage that ensured the success of Linacre's petition to the king.

Apart from the strong tradition of fifteenth- and early sixteenth-century English bishops as educational benefactors, Wolsey also had before him the contemporary example of Cardinal Cisneros, who had founded an entire university at Alcalá de Henares, where some of Europe's leading scholars were employed between 1514 and 1517 to create the Complutensian polyglot Bible. Austere and devoid of personal ambition, Cisneros stood out among the non-curial cardinals of that era, many of whom served their kings better than they served God, even if Wolsey was alone in admitting as much. The dynastic confusion which followed the death of Queen Isabella in 1504 left Cisneros as *de facto* ruler of Castile while the widowed King Ferdinand give priority to a more traditionally Aragonese policy of rivalry with France, both in Italy and along the Pyrenean frontier. Castile's boy king remained in the Low Countries in the care of his Erasmian tutors. Ferdinand proved to be no more fortunate than his English son-in-law in the matter of fathering legitimate male heirs, for his nineteen-year-old son Juan predeceased him in 1497, and a second marriage, to Germaine de Foix, produced a boy who did not live long. Although the history of the smaller Italian states provided examples of illegitimate sons succeeding their fathers, the larger European states did not resort to such expedients, making Henry VIII's ambitions for Henry Fitzroy a sign of sheer desperation.

Ferdinand's insistence on his underage illegitimate son being made archbishop of Zaragoza was more typical of elite practice. When Ferdinand died in January 1516, less than fourteen months after Louis XII, it completed the royal cast list for the next three decades of inter-state relations in western Europe: Henry VIII in England, Francis I in France, and Charles I in Aragon, Sicily, Naples, Castile, the Low Countries and Franche Comté.

Thanks to a sequence of papal concessions, Ferdinand and Isabella bequeathed their grandson a remarkable degree of control over the Church in Iberia and the New World, not least in terms of appointments to bishoprics. Thus the king of England could but envy his wife's nephew. Nor could he feel any less jealous of his Gallic counterpart. While English prelates disputed the relative jurisdictions of king and pope with reference to benefit of clergy and Archbishop Warham resigned the great seal in the cause of ecclesiastical liberties, the king of France was busy negotiating a comprehensive deal with the papacy, covering joint action in a crusade against the Ottomans, papal permission for Francis to levy a *decime* on the French clergy and, most significantly, royal nomination to hundreds of major benefices. This was the concordat of Bologna, the deal struck by Francis and Pope Leo between 11 and 15 December 1515 in the wake of the Franco-Venetian military victory at Marignano.[23] The Bolognese summit was not a meeting of equals: Leo arrived in the city three days before Francis, who could afford to play on a combination of his recent military success and generations of Medicean allegiance to the French crown. Pushing his luck, Francis even revived the Angevin claim to the kingdom of Naples and suggested that Leo invest him with the Regno when Ferdinand died. While the *parlement* of Paris feared that the concordat might represent a diluted version of the Gallicanism which had triumphed in Franco-papal relations since the pragmatic sanction of Bourges (1438), Leo was sufficiently satisfied to commission a frescoed version of the Bolognese meeting in the Vatican's Sala del Incendio, where Raphael gave Pope Leo III the features of his namesake and Francis appeared as Charlemagne receiving his imperial coronation by the pope in 800. In a bid to mollify Henry, Wolsey's agent Silvestro Gigli secured papal approval for the English king to be known as 'Christianae fidei defensor', but Henry's 'most Christian' counterpart scotched that and it was not revived until after the publication of Henry's anti-Lutheran *Assertio septem sacramentorum* in 1521. There was a similar tussle when Leo made his cousin Giulio de' Medici cardinal protector of France in 1516 and Francis responded by arguing that this was incompatible with Giulio's existing protectorship of England and tried to force his resignation. On that occasion, Leo did not live up to Wolsey's taunt that he was merely the French king's chaplain. Giulio retained both protectorships and even gained that over Ireland in 1517.

Henry's response to the battle of Marignano and the French reconquest of Milan in 1515 was to revive the policy of 1513 and threaten an English invasion of northern France. His councillors balked at the expenditure and Wolsey sought a cheaper, if less spectacular, alternative by creating an anti-French alliance with Maximilian, who was still engaged in military action against Francis's Venetian allies, and those Swiss cantons which were threatened by the proximity of the French in Milan. His ally in this scheme was the staunchly anti-French Swiss cardinal Matthäus Schiner, whose objective was to restore to power in Milan what little was left of the Sforza dynasty. Richard Pace was sent to hire Swiss mercenaries in October 1515, a thankless task to which he devoted two years of his life. In the course of the mission he nearly lost that life to French poison, two periods of imprisonment and various fevers, all the while dealing with vexations from his own side in the person of Sir Robert Wingfield, Henry's ambassador to the imperial court. Pace's old friend Cuthbert Tunstal fared better with his diplomatic mission to the Low Countries, where he concluded that Henry should not put any faith in Maximilian as a reliable ally and made a close study of Charles and his principal ministers, Guillaume de Croy, seigneur de Chièvres, and Jean le Sauvage. After Ferdinand's death, their priority was to convey the teenage king to Iberia, where the fragile unification of Aragon and Castile was in danger of breaking and there was considerable resentment at the prospect of both being ruled by an absentee monarch. For this mission they required French cooperation and acquired it by making a range of concessions in the treaty of Noyon, signed on 13 August 1516. Under the terms of this treaty, Charles acknowledged French possession of Milan, an imperial fief, and bowed to the Angevin cause by agreeing to pay a hefty annual tribute of 100,000 *écus* to France for his own possession of Naples, a papal fief. He also broke off his proposed marriage with Louis XII's dynastically devalued daughter Renée in favour of one with Francis's twelve-month-old daughter Louise. According to Mandell Creighton's magisterial analysis of the treaty, had Charles 'been older and wiser he would have seen that it was safer to accept the gold of Henry VIII, from whose future projects he had nothing to fear, rather than try and secure a precarious peace for the Netherlands by an alliance with France.'[24] Wolsey was not unduly worried by this turn of events because he recognized that Noyon was designed to achieve short-term objectives and that Francis would soon come to regret tying himself to so unreliable an ally as Maximilian. The cardinal was playing a long game, waiting for Francis to realize his mistake. In the meantime, the English cause appeared to be weakened by further bouts of diplomacy. In October the English promised to fund Maximilian's bid to defend Verona against Venetian determination to regain what had been the strategic heart of her *terraferma* state. On 29 November the 'perpetual peace' of Fribourg effectively neutralized the Swiss threat to the French in Milan. Five days later, Maximilian's lack of loyalty to England was confirmed in the treaty of Brussels, by which he gave up Verona in exchange for monetary compensation from France and Venice. The English response to Maximilian's duplicity was to send William Knight to the Low Countries at the end of December with orders to break this daunting Habsburg-Valois alliance, but he was soon aware of the futility of the mission and asked to be recalled early in 1517.

Two members of the English and Welsh hierarchy died in 1516: Wolsey's sometime patron Richard Mayhew of Hereford and Miles Salley (Sawley) of Llandaff. Their successors came from radically different origins. The new bishop of Hereford was Charles Booth, a kinsman of three members of the fifteenth-century episcopate whose career had prospered under the patronage of his fellow Lancastrian William Smith and who was therefore squarely in the tradition of those bishops ultimately associated with Margaret Beaufort. Booth's appointment to Hereford was logical in that he had long been among Smith's colleagues on the council of the Marches. That put him in the circle of Prince Arthur and made him a consistent supporter of the widowed and remarried Katherine. The new bishop of Llandaff was appointed early in 1517 and was considerably closer to the queen, for he was her Spanish chaplain Jorge de Ateca.

Two English episcopal deaths in a single year was a relatively high figure for the period of Wolsey's prominence, but the deaths of his fellow cardinals occurred at a consistently steady rate: two in 1516, three in 1517. Among these were two of Pope Julius's kinsmen, Marco Vigerio della Rovere and Sisto Gara della Rovere, the second of whom was replaced as vice-chancellor of the Church by Pope Leo's kinsman Giulio de' Medici. What made 1517 remarkable in papal history was not the deaths of cardinals, but Leo's creation of an unprecedented thirty-one new cardinals on a single day, a figure unbeaten until 1946. The annual rate of cardinalitial deaths therefore increased in subsequent years, but this was also in large measure the College which determined the papal elections of 1521–22 and 1523, those in which Wolsey was a contender. This extraordinary turn of events had its roots in long-standing antagonism between the Tuscan republics and rather less deep-rooted hostility between certain Tuscan families, but it nevertheless came to have consequences for Wolsey's relations with Rome. Despite Florence's continuing republican status, Leo was its *de facto* ruler. Siena was also technically a republic but had been effectively ruled by members of the Petrucci family since 1487. Siena represented a threat to Leo, located as it was between Florence and the Papal States, so he sought to make it more amenable by expelling its first citizen, Borghese Petrucci, in 1516 and replacing him with Raffaele Petrucci, bishop of Grosseto. Borghese's brother, Cardinal Alfonso Petrucci, objected to this interference and, in April 1517, it emerged that Petrucci and four other cardinals had apparently been involved in a plot to poison the pope and replace him with Cardinal Raffaele Sansoni-Riario. How much substance lay behind the confessions made under torture by Petrucci's servant remains difficult to assess. Cardinals Petrucci and Bandinello Sauli were arrested on 19 May, and were soon joined in Castel S. Angelo by Sansoni-Riario. Francesco Soderini, whose brother Piero had been the *gonfaloniere di giustizia* during the recent period of Medicean exile from Florence, and Adriano Castellesi were rooted out as the fourth and fifth alleged conspirators, but they fled to Naples and Venice respectively. All five were stripped of their titles and benefices.

On 1 July, therefore, Leo sought to diminish the authority of individual cardinals by creating those thirty-one new ecclesiastical princes, a substantial minority of whom were his fellow Florentines. Another was the Milanese-born lawyer Lorenzo Campeggi, who entered the clerical state after his wife's death in 1509 and became bishop of Feltre just three years later. The generals of three religious orders – Tommaso de Vio, Egidio da Viterbo, and Cristoforo Numai – helped to make up the numbers. The Iberian powers were cultivated by the promotions of Afonso, son of King Manuel of Portugal, and Adriaan Florenszoon Dedel of Utrecht, who governed Castile for the still-absent Charles. Louis II de Bourbon de Vendôme, the twenty-four-year-old bishop of Laon, represented the interests of his king. Three days after this mass creation Petrucci was found strangled in his cell. Sansoni-Riario and Sauli were released upon payment of substantial fines, though Sauli died as early as the following March. Leo's handling of this episode was much criticized by the secular powers, as it bore the signs of a vendetta.[25]

Wolsey took the opportunity to pursue a vendetta of his own, for Castellesi's flight from Rome effectively settled the long-running dispute over the English collectorship of Peter's pence. In August 1517 Wolsey's loyal Roman agent Silvestro Gigli was appointed to that vacancy. Castellesi still retained his English bishopric of Bath and Wells, and hoped to use it as a bargaining tool with Henry and Wolsey, but this was a desperate throw and they were not interested in granting him a pension in exchange for its resignation. It was not until almost twelve months later that Leo deprived Castellesi of both the bishopric and the cardinalate, but Wolsey was eager to clinch victory and Gigli secured his master's papal provision to Bath and Wells on 30 July 1518. In accordance with a practice which was perfectly familiar in parts of continental Europe – Albrecht of Brandenburg, archbishop of both Magdeburg and Mainz, and a cardinal from 1518, provides a case in point – but which was then unparalleled in England, Wolsey held Bath and Wells *in commendam* with York, administering the see during what was effectively an elongated interregnum and taking the revenues from it, but without having cure of souls. In practical terms this arrangement made little difference because bishops were routinely absent on royal service, and depended heavily on their vicars-general to undertake administrative responsibilities and on suffragan bishops with Irish sees or titles *in partibus infidelium* for spiritual ones.[26]

1517 was a year of crisis for a number of the more significant prelatical players in our story. The pope's illness and its far-reaching consequences coincided with the cardinal of York's bouts of the sweating sickness, which in turn seem to have provided the inspiration for his pilgrimage to Walsingham in September, presumably in fulfilment of a vow made at the height of his illness. As a rule the cardinal's devotions were a private matter and did not intrude so conspicuously into time which could otherwise be devoted to business. Neither for Leo nor for Wolsey was 1517 a year of crisis because an Augustinian friar and university teacher in distant Saxony objected to the sale of indulgences, the income from which was intended to repay Albrecht of Brandenburg's debts and to fund the rebuilding of St Peter's basilica in Rome. What did matter to them were events even further from Rome or London, for the Ottoman sultan Selim had been inspired by reading a life of Alexander the Great and set about attempting to become nothing less than master of the world. His domains were rapidly expanded by the conquest of Syria in 1516 and that of the Mamluk sultanate early in the following year. As the new ruler of Egypt, Selim became overlord of Cyprus and therefore the recipient of tribute from Venice, which had ruled the island since 1489. It was in this context that the republic renewed its existing treaty with the Porte in September 1517. Venice, in turn, remained allied to France because the latter's possession of Milan made it an effective counterweight to Maximilian's ambitions in northern Italy. Crusading suddenly loomed large in the pope's priorities for Christendom, as well as in the empty words expressed on behalf of secular princes. It featured in a treaty of mutual defence signed on 11 March 1517 by Francis, Maximilian and Charles, a treaty that was unlikely to come into force as it was highly improbable that any state would risk taking on all three of them at once. The fact that their agreement was signed at Cambrai should have been a none-too-subtle indication of their real intent, to dismember Venice's fast-reviving state in northern Italy, though the really subtle player was Francis who, far from seeking to humble Venice, actually renewed his league with the republic seven months later.

Diplomatic business in England was hardly interrupted by the cardinal's illness and East Anglian expedition. By the summer of 1517 it was apparent that Charles would require English support, not least financial, in order to make his much-delayed journey to Spain. To that end a defensive alliance between Henry and his wife's illustrious but needy nephew was agreed on 5 July. In September Charles finally left the Low Countries to claim his Iberian inheritance. All things considered, Wolsey's diplomacy was maturing nicely. Charles had been neatly duped, for he did not realize that Anglo-French negotiations for the restoration of Tournai to Francis, in defiance of his own claim, had been in progress since March. The garrison ate up funds and, in stark contrast to Calais, was of no obvious use to the English. Tournai was therefore the gateway to a new chapter in Anglo-French relations. The two kingdoms had gone as far as they could in being enemies, leaving Wolsey convinced that the time had come to explore the possibility of an alternative relationship. Fortune – or the French king's prayers to St Martin of Tours – favoured the cardinal when Queen Claude gave birth to a son, named François, on 28 February 1518. Her first-born, Louise, died in 1517, which meant that Louise's younger sister Charlotte became both the intended consort as well as the namesake of the Spanish king. That left England without corresponding plans. As Princess Mary was England's only dynastic bargaining chip, Wolsey had great need of a suitable prince with whom to match her. The dauphin's birth could not have occurred at a more convenient moment.

Meanwhile in Rome, a plan was coming to fruition. Leo sought to bind all the Christian powers in a five-year truce, during which period they would devote their energies not to fighting each other, but to a crusade, the prime objective of which would be the recovery of Constantinople for Christendom. There was no time to delay, for the speed of Selim's conquests in the near east suggested that he might be emboldened to head westwards in the imminent campaigning season. The truce was proclaimed in a bull dated 6 March and published eight days later in S. Maria sopra Minerva, on which occasion the papal secretary Jacopo Sadoleto spoke effusively about Maximilian's crusading plans and detailed messages of support from the kings of France, Spain, Portugal, Hungary, Poland, Denmark and Scotland.[27] The Venetian doge Leonardo Loredan was conspicuously absent from this list. In time-honoured fashion, the pope appointed legates to preach the new crusade to the powers of Christendom. To the French legation he reappointed his long-term confidant Bernardo Dovizi, who was known to contemporaries as a playwright, is known to posterity as one of the speakers in Castiglione's *Libro del cortegiano*, and was one of Leo's first four choices for the hat. If Dovizi's courtly sophistication made him a suitable choice for France, then Egidio da Viterbo's record of textual scholarship, service to his order, and experience of similar diplomatic missions made him particularly eligible for the Spanish legation. Alessandro Farnese was Leo's initial choice for the German legation, but illness forced him to be replaced by another of the recently promoted religious, the Dominican Tommaso de Vio (known as Cajetan on account of his birthplace, Gaeta), who happened to be his generation's leading commentator on Thomas Aquinas. It is fruitless to speculate on the difference to the course of the Protestant Reformation that might have been made by Farnese going to Germany, but there is no denying that Martin Luther's theological differences with Rome evolved out of traditional disputes between his fellow Augustinian friars and their Dominican rivals. In the much-told Reformation story that traditional dispute has acquired a personal dimension in the pitting of Luther against Cajetan at the diet of Augsburg in October 1518, so much so that the legate's crusading mission has often been overlooked. For our Wolsey-centred account of the period, the most relevant aspect of the German legation was the even more easily overlooked imperial demand that the legate not be permitted to enter Germany unless Maximilian's chancellor, Cardinal Lang, could share his legatine status. Wolsey took Lang as his model and not without good cause: the imperial chancellor was the son of an Augsburg merchant and the father of three illegitimate children; he proceeded from episcopal service to that of the emperor, for whom he acted as councillor and diplomat before attaining the chancellorship in 1508.

When Sixtus IV sent legates to preach a crusade in the early 1470s, their destinations were the Italian states, Iberia, central Europe, and a combination of France, Burgundy and England. That Leo's legates were sent to France, Spain, Germany and England reveals much about the changing fortunes of the secular powers over a couple of generations, most particularly the enhanced status of England, now considered sufficiently wealthy and influential to merit her own legate. This was the lawyer Lorenzo Campeggi. Taking their cue from Maximilian and Lang, Henry and Wolsey sought to turn this situation to their advantage. Typically, Henry took the less subtle approach, conveniently ignoring more than four centuries of Anglo-papal relations with his claim that 'it was not the manner of this realm to admit *legatos a latere*'.[28] This assertion had not been tested in 1472, because the legate Bessarion found Louis XI to be so uncooperative that he did not travel as far as England, but the fifteenth-century popes Pius II and Innocent VIII had successfully dispatched legates to the kingdom. Ably assisted by Gigli in Rome, Wolsey held up proceedings by demanding that he be granted equal status with Campeggi. The problem with this was that Campeggi was a legate *a latere*, literally sent 'from the side' of the pope, yet Wolsey had never been to Rome and had never even met the pope. Moreover, such a legate was invested with specific quasi-papal powers to deal with particular problems in the provinces to which he was sent and such powers were fundamentally incompatible with active service to a secular monarch. Archbishops Kemp and Morton had both been cardinals when they served as chancellor to Henry VI and Henry VII respectively, but neither of them sought to complicate matters further by seeking the powers of a legate *a latere*. Earlier in the fifteenth century Henry Beaufort had been chancellor of England, Martin V's legate *a latere* to the kingdom and a cardinal, but not necessarily all at once. His precise status was a matter of great contention. *Legati nati*, native legates such as Warham in his capacity as archbishop of Canterbury or Wolsey as archbishop of York, were a different matter because they did not act as diplomatic agents for the papacy, a role which fell between legations to lower-status nuncios, such Francesco Chiericati of Vicenza in the 1510s. *Legati nati* represented the papacy in a judicial capacity only. One of the features distinguishing a *legatus a latere* from a *legatus natus* was that the former was sent on an *ad hoc* basis, in response to particular circumstances, and lacked the permanence of the latter.

On 17 May 1518 Leo acceded to Wolsey's demands: the second time he had bowed to sustained pressure from the Englishman and granted something which should have been freely-bestowed. Campeggi was kept waiting at Boulogne for six weeks while news of the papal concession reached London.

He arrived in the city on 29 July, made Wolsey's acquaintance and travelled with him to meet the king at Greenwich, where they formally announced the crusade on 3 August.

The new English legate had not the slightest intention of committing his nation's resources to any crusading scheme, but was instead determined to hijack the pope's plan for a 'universal' peace. Thus, in Scarisbrick's words, 'through 1518 he played a skilful game, appearing to follow when he was in fact leading, to co-operate when he was in fact twisting the papal design to his own prepared pattern'.[29] Wolsey's priority was an Anglo-French treaty, but he found no harm in containing that project within a universal peace of his own devising. Prelates formed a crucial channel of communication between the two kingdoms: Nicholas West of Ely was among the English agents sent to cultivate relations with France from the autumn of 1517 onwards, and Wolsey engaged in correspondence with Étienne Poncher, bishop of Paris, from April 1518. By August Poncher was in London, operating incognito and laying the groundwork for the formal French embassy which arrived there towards the end of September. Magnificence and display were established features of diplomatic practice, but Wolsey now employed them on a scale which had certainly never been seen before in England. The stakes were high, for he had a number of audiences to satisfy at once: the French delegation, who would not wish to commit their dauphin to marriage with a pauper; the ambassadors of the other powers, who were needed for the universal peace and could not be alienated by the Anglo-French *rapprochement*; and the sceptical English nobility, led by the duke of Buckingham, who had been kept in the dark about Wolsey's initiative and for whom hostility towards the French was a default position. The English cardinal was master of gorgeous ceremonies, sacred and secular, including a dinner 'the like of which was never given by Cleopatra or Caligula, the whole banqueting hall being decorated with huge vases of gold and silver', or so Giustinian enthused.[30]

The diplomacy reached its formal conclusion in early October. First came the Universal Peace (2 October), which bound Christian princes from the emperor downwards to the ideal of perpetual peace and the practicalities of collective security. So comprehensive was the treaty that any conflicting arrangements were instantly annulled. Such had been the terms of many a treaty between the Italian states in previous decades, but this was the first attempt to apply that diplomatic model across Christendom as a whole. In terms of sheer scale it was without precedent and Thomas Wolsey was its only begetter. Like any triumph, it could not be sustained indefinitely and it also set a standard which not even Wolsey was able or likely to match again but, for the moment, he continued to pull diplomatic rabbits from his conspicuously red hat. On 3 October he celebrated Mass in St Paul's Cathedral in the presence of Henry and the various ambassadors, and Richard Pace, who succeeded Colet as dean later that month, gave a Latin oration on the ideal of peace. The day concluded with Wolsey hosting a banquet. Thereafter attention turned to the more specific Anglo-French aspects of the treaty of London. As Wolsey had long planned, the substance of this was the English cession of Tournai, which the French acquired at a cost of 600,000 crowns. Wolsey renounced his claim to the bishopric there and was compensated with an annual pension of £1,200, which rather dwarfed the Flemish pension he had been offered by Chièvres in 1517. There was also a Scottish dimension to the agreement, according to which Francis undertook not to support the Scots against their southern neighbours. In practical terms this meant that John Stewart, duke of Albany, the pro-French regent who had forced Margaret Tudor into temporary exile, was obliged to remain in France, even though the bulk of the Scottish nobility was anti-English and would have preferred him to return.[31] Aside from those treaty terms which had an immediate impact, there was also the highly symbolic betrothal of the two-year-old Princess Mary to the eight-month-old dauphin, which was formally celebrated at Greenwich on 5 October.

The venerable Richard Fox had lived through the English civil wars of the fifteenth century and been active in public life when his state was still of little consequence in the international arena, so was not indulging in unjustified hyperbole when he congratulated Wolsey on the achievements of those few heady days: 'undoubtedly, my Lord, God continuing it, it shall be the best that ever was done for the realm of England; and after the king's highness, the laud and praise shall be to you a perpetual memory'.[32] Such enthusiasm was not shared in Rome, where Leo ratified the treaty of London with understandable reluctance on 3 December. The upstart English cardinal had not only forced him to concede the quasi-papal legatine powers but had also usurped his role as the peacemaker of Christendom. He doubted that Wolsey's peace would last as long as his own projected five-year truce, but there could be no such consolation for the Englishman's audacious crushing of the very crusade he had been appointed to preach in the first place.

Leo's hopes of mounting a crusade received a still greater setback on 12 January 1519, when the emperor died at Wels in Upper Austria. Maximilian's lucrative second marriage, to Bianca Maria Sforza of Milan, was without issue, so all his heirs were descended from his first marriage, to Marie of Burgundy. More precisely, they were the children of his son, the Archduke Philip, rather than of his daughter, Margaret of Austria, whose marriages to the Infante Juan of Aragon and Castile and to the equally juvenile Philibert, duke of Savoy, left her with neither issue nor the desire to enter into a third matrimonial adventure. By way of contrast, the archduke's marriage to the Infanta Juana had been nothing if not productive: three daughters and two sons were born between 1498 and 1505, with a fourth daughter born posthumously in 1507. By the time of their imperial grandfather's death two of these siblings were already married: Eleanor to her uncle, the twice-widowed King Manuel of Portugal, and Isabella to King Kristian II of Denmark. Their eighteen-year-old brother Charles was now head of the house of Habsburg.

There was no rule, written or unwritten, which dictated that the seven imperial electors were obliged to elect the Habsburg candidate, for that dynasty had provided no more than the last four emperors, though their eighty-year monopoly of the honour certainly constituted living memory. Charles's election might have passed without much comment had he not broken with all precedents by being king of Castile and Aragon, and consequently *de facto* ruler of Naples, even if he had not received formal papal investiture with the Regno. As the ruler of at least one Italian state, Leo was more acutely aware than most monarchs of the dangers of one man doubling up as emperor and king of Naples: only Venice and the Papal States would be free from either his direct rule or indirect overlordship. When the concept of 'balance of power' has been applied to the Renaissance period, it has been done so most convincingly with regard to the states of Italy before the French invasion of 1494, the period in which Leo's father Lorenzo de' Medici was one of the peninsula's leading diplomatic players. Charles's election would mean a complete imbalance of power in the peninsula, regardless of its implications elsewhere. Francis I, with his passionate interest in Milan, cast himself as the only reasonable alternative to Charles and cultivated the electors accordingly, to the extent of promising Princess Renée as a bride for the margrave of Brandenburg's son. Even the English exile Richard de la Pole played a part in the process, being sent to Prague to solicit the vote of the king of Bohemia. Pope Leo's Medicean inclination towards France had been confirmed when his brother Giuliano married Filiberta of Savoy and was granted the dukedom of Nemours in 1515, and again when the pope's nephew Lorenzo, duke of Urbino, married Madeleine de la Tour d'Auvergne in 1518, though it did not necessarily follow that the pope regarded Francis as his ideal counterpart in the leadership of Christendom.[33] Wolsey, meanwhile, had put so much effort into cultivating both the candidates that he was not eager to jeopardize relations by being seen to favour one over the other. When Leo alluded to the possibility of a third candidate, Henry took this to be a serious reference to himself. As ever, Wolsey flattered his monarch but had to be more realistic about the near inevitability of Charles of Habsburg's election.

Making the most of their rarely used power, the seven electors made their votes available to the highest bidder and were not greatly exercised by either Italian or English concerns. Among the seven, only Duke Friedrich III of Saxony had been in power long enough to have voted in the last imperial election, that of 1493, and was, as the pope realized, the most electable of their number if both Charles and Francis were to be sidelined. The second most experienced ruler was Joachim I Nestor, margrave of Brandenburg since 1499, followed by another of the lay electors, Ludwig V, elector palatine of the Rhine since 1508. Then came the three ecclesiastical princes: Richard Greiffenclau von Vollrads, archbishop of Trier since 1511, Cardinal Albrecht of Brandenburg, archbishop of Mainz since 1514, and Hermann von Wied, archbishop of Cologne since 1515. By far the youngest of the electors was the thirteen-year-old Ladislas (also known as Lajos or Louis), king of Bohemia since 1516, who was betrothed to one of Charles's sisters. Two of the seven were already significant players in the Reformation story, for Albrecht was the prelate who charged Johann Tetzel with preaching the indulgence to which Luther took such exception, and Friedrich was Luther's lord and protector, but that was of no particular significance as the electors assembled in Frankfurt-am-Main and prepared to cast their votes. Richard Pace was Henry's man at the diet. He began by maintaining England's neutrality, but was then instructed to bribe the electors to vote for Henry, and finally to support Charles, the front-runner, rather than Francis. The voting itself was concluded rapidly and on 28 June Charles was elected unanimously.

In his frustration at this outcome, Francis turned to England and to the hope of realizing one of the provisions of the recent Anglo-French treaty, a personal meeting between the two kings. He wanted this to occur as soon as August or September, and asked Wolsey to engineer it, luring him with the promise of fourteen safe votes in the event of a conclave. Mathematically speaking, Wolsey's chances of election to the papacy were certainly increasing: three cardinals died in 1518 but only one was created, five died in 1519 and none were created that year. The debit side happened to include some of Francis's tame electors, confirming the lack of substance behind his rather desperate and rather impulsive offer. Wolsey had no desire to antagonize Charles so soon after the imperial election and therefore stalled, arguing that the arrangements for the Anglo-French summit would take until the summer of 1520 to complete. In the meantime, Francis consoled himself with a secret Franco-papal treaty concluded in September.

As ever, the filling of episcopal vacancies remained the stuff of Anglo-papal relations. Three vacancies were filled in 1518–19. First was St Asaph, for which Henry chose one of his favourite preachers, the Lancashire-born Franciscan Henry Standish, in preference to Wolsey's candidate. In August 1518, as we have seen, Wolsey himself acquired Bath and Wells after Castellesi's deprivation. In the same month the much-respected Hugh Oldham was succeeded at Exeter by that conspicuous son of Sutton Coldfield John Veysey, who had been president of Magdalen since 1507 and was therefore very much a known quantity to the cardinal. Standish and Veysey had further distinguished themselves by siding with the king in the course of the Hunne affair and now received their reward. Meanwhile, two other English bishops resolutely refused to die. Warham continued to stand between Wolsey and complete domination of the English Church, while the reputed octogenarian Edmund Audley stubbornly held on to the see of Salisbury, thereby preventing Campeggi receiving it as an induce-ment to favour English interests once he returned to Rome. While Campeggi waited for what we might reasonably call Audley's end, he received the use of Castellesi's Roman palace by way of compensation.[34]

Ecclesiastical reform has rarely been absent from the history of the Church, but it has manifested itself variously, according to the spirit of the age. One of the distinctive characteristics of early sixteenth-century reform was provided by the stinging satire of Erasmus and his followers, who aimed their barbs at clerical worldliness identified in anyone from popes downwards. The practical business of reform was certainly no laughing matter, as participants in the Fifth Lateran Council could attest. That assembly met for nine sessions spread over five years and reached its conclusion in March 1517. There was no shortage of ideas for reform of the Church and, in the course of the earlier sessions, the Venetian-born Camaldolese hermits Paolo Giustinian and Pietro Querini drew the up wide-ranging reform proposals known as the *Libellus ad Leonem X* (1513). For an English counterpart, we can select John Colet, whose sole surviv-ing sermon probably dates from 1510 and is a clarion call to the clergy to reject worldliness and lead lives of exemplary purity. The proposals of Giustinian

and Querini did not strike much of a chord in Leonine Rome, so did Colet
fare any better by preaching reform to the English episcopate? Archbishop
Warham was foremost among the English patrons of Erasmus, but the primate's
priorities were those of a lawyer, centred on clerical privileges, and left largely
untapped the opportunities for energetic, extensive and systematic reform.
In an English context, reform included the targeting of asset-rich but under-
manned monastic houses. John Alcock's suppression of St Radegund's convent
in Cambridge and its revival in 1496 as Jesus College provided a particularly
successful model of such reform in practice. Replicated throughout the country,
the opportunities were manifold. Thus Wolsey lobbied Rome for permission
to visit religious houses and reform them as required; on 27 August 1518 he
and Campeggi received a bull empowering them to do just that. Rome refused
to concede permission for parallel reform of the secular priesthood. At that
stage Wolsey's legatine authority was intended to last only as long as Campeggi
remained in England, so speed was essential if much impact was to be made.
Scores of visitations were ordered, both of houses which would otherwise have
been subject to episcopal visitation and of those, such as Westminster Abbey,
which were exempt from any episcopal intervention.

Monastic visitations provided just one dimension of the awkward relationship which developed between the legates and the episcopate. Archbishop
Warham inevitably bore the brunt of that jurisdictional awkwardness. Relations
between Warham and Wolsey reached their lowest ebb after December 1518,
when the legates summoned the English and Welsh bishops to meet them
at Westminster the following March to approve a set of legatine constitutions. Warham responded to this 'tyrannical' behaviour by summoning the
Canterbury convocation to meet in February. In episcopal terms this meant
all the English and Welsh bishops with the exception of the three from the
northern province, Ruthall of Durham, John Penny of Carlisle and Wolsey
himself. It was a clever move and one to which Wolsey apparently responded
by charging Warham with the remarkably flexible but, in these circumstances,
somewhat ironic accusation of *praemunire*. Whatever the substance behind
the charge, it was Warham who backed down and Wolsey's assembly that met,
albeit without Bishop Penny, who was too ill to travel but nevertheless sent
a message of support.[35] From the southern province Richard Fox enthused
about 'a more entire and whole reformation of the ecclesiastical hierarchy of
the English people than I could have expected'.[36] Little is known about what
transpired at the March meeting, though Fisher of Rochester may well have

taken the opportunity to comment negatively on the state of the Church and to single out for particular censure those clerics who were too much involved in temporal affairs, a charge most readily levelled at Wolsey and Ruthall, the keepers of the great and privy seals.[37] As for the legatine constitutions, much of their content has been lost. A second legatine council was planned for September, but had to be abandoned on account of an outbreak of the plague in London.

Cardinal Campeggi left England on 24 August, but his departure had been much anticipated by Wolsey, whose extraordinary legatine powers depended on the presence of his colleague. To lose them would leave his cardinalate as an empty honour, something he would never be able to use for its intended purpose as long as he remained in England, but it would also mean losing a clear opportunity to enforce organizational reform the English Church. Consequently, on 25 March, he made yet another audacious appeal to Rome, requesting the retention of those powers after Campeggi's departure. On 10 June Leo obliged by confirming his power to work alone, for a limited term, in the cause of monastic reform, but the pontiff was far from ready to concede Wolsey's ultimate desire, for a life appointment as legate *a latere*.

To what purpose did Wolsey seek, obtain and actively employ such unprecedented power over the Church in England? The personal attacks and charges of self-aggrandizement made by those prelates whose privileges he threatened and whose exchequers he effectively diminished are understandable, but should not distract us unnecessarily. Wolsey's service to his king was sufficiently well founded and well developed by 1519 that there can be little doubt that he regarded his legation as not only compatible with the chancellorship, but even a complement to it, part of a unified whole. This makes sense if we reflect that, in the sixteenth-century, 'nations' were no longer peoples vaguely unified by a common tongue, but were increasingly centralized political entities. The creation of a centralized nation-state is most readily associated with France in the century after the conclusion of the Hundred Years' War, *inter alia* with Charles VII creating the nucleus of a standing army, Louis XI curbing the independence of the nobility, Charles VIII and Louis XII bringing the duchy of Brittany into the realm, Francis I negotiating the concordat of Bologna. The French State and the French Church were both considerably larger than their English counterparts, making it highly unlikely that a single servant of the crown could dominate either of them, let alone both at once. With Lang as his right-hand man, Maximilian had endeavoured to reform the governmentally unwieldy Empire into a more centralized unit, but was frustrated by the princes and cities whose autonomy was thereby threatened. A convenient indication of the sheer scale of Wolsey's power in the 1510s is provided by the 226 dispatches sent by Sebastiano Giustinian between 1515 and 1519, culminating in the end-of-mission *relazione* which he delivered to the Senate on 10 September 1519.[38] When Giustinian arrived in England, he reflected, Wolsey had been in the habit of disguising his actions under the formula 'His Majesty will do so and so'. By 1519 he had dropped the disguise and had no qualms about asserting 'I shall do so and so'. So phenomenally industrious was he, the envoy asserted, that he personally transacted the equivalent amount of business as all the magistracies and councils of the Venetian republic combined. According to Giustinian, writing to the Council of Ten on 2 January 1516, English government was certainly in the process of being centralized, in the person of Wolsey, 'in whom the whole power of the State is really lodged' and 'who, for authority, may in point of fact be styled *ipse rex*'.[39]

In the summer of 1520 Wolsey had cause to deal with the affairs of three kings at once. In addition to his perennial responsibilities as chancellor of England, he acted as the king of France's plenipotentiary for the delayed Anglo-French summit, the preparations for which were as elaborate as those required for a military expedition. Relations between Francis and Charles had remained poor since the imperial election, so Wolsey took care to sustain parallel negotiations with Charles, who needed to prevent the possibility of France and England uniting against him. It was a delicate balancing act, but one which the cardinal managed with an assured touch. Charles was aged only twenty, but already faced challenges spanning half a continent. On 20 May he sailed from La Coruña in order to make his way to Germany for the next imperial diet, but his departure from Spain triggered a reaction against the absent monarch and the Flemish advisers he left to rule the kingdom. This was the revolt of the Comuneros, in which the cities of Castile raised an army and declared that 'when princes are tyrants, then communities must govern'. With the summit between Francis and Henry imminent, Charles was invited to meet Henry at Canterbury, where the English king was planning to keep Pentecost. Wolsey was effectively dictating terms to the emperor-elect, who had little choice but to obey. On 26 May Charles landed at Dover and was met by the cardinal, before Henry arrived and accompanied him to Canterbury. It was a brief visit, intended to assure the French that England's friendship was neither exclusive to them and nor to be taken for granted.

The nature of the Anglo-imperial discussions can only be surmised, but some of Wolsey's biographers have made much of Charles offering and Wolsey declining a Spanish bishopric around this time. There is some confusion about the precise course of events but, according to papal sources, Pedro Ruiz de la Mota was translated from Badajoz to Palencia on 4 July 1520 and was replaced by the archbishop of York on the same day.[40] With the exception of a small number of prelates appointed to titular sees in partibus infidelium and with suffragan responsibilities in England, this again made Wolsey the only Englishman in occupation of a continental bishopric, however reluctantly. His resignation of Badajoz can presumably be explained by a scrupulous desire not to be seen to favour Charles over Francis. That he subsequently received an annual pension of 2,500 ducats from the bishopric was not incompatible with such scrupulousness, for he was already in receipt of a French pension, but the next bishop was not papally provided until February 1521, leaving a period of seven months in which Wolsey was the only person who could claim that position.

At the end of May Charles sailed from Sandwich and made for Flanders, where he loitered close to the border throughout the following month. On the same day Henry, Katherine and their entourages crossed from Dover to Calais. The king was accompanied by 3,997 persons, the queen by 1,175. More than 2,800 horses were required for this highly ambitious expedition. Virtually the entire English socio-political elite made the journey, the presence of the duke of Buckingham confirming that being staunchly anti-French was no bar to participation. In addition to Wolsey, the English episcopal contingent included Warham of Canterbury, Ruthall of Durham, West of Ely, Booth of Hereford, Ateca of Llandaff and Fisher of Rochester. Indeed, this was the only occasion on which Fisher ever left his native shores.

On 4 June the royal party moved to the fortress at Guînes, on the edge of the Pale of Calais, where the monarchs took up residence for the duration of the summit. It was here that the ambition of Wolsey's plans became evident, for the castle was connected by a long gallery to a large temporary palace designed by the cardinal himself. Such temporary structures were certainly a feature of court culture in the Renaissance period, an example being the temporary palace constructed in piazza SS. Apostoli in Rome for a banquet in 1473 but, at 328 feet long, it was the sheer scale of Wolsey's palace that made it remarkable. The inspiration for the project presumably came from Hampton Court, for it consisted of a courtyard surrounded by lodgings, with a gatehouse in the middle of one side and a chapel projecting outwards from the opposite side.[41] Henry and Katherine had suites nearer to the chapel, while the other quarters were allocated to lodgings for Henry's sister, the ex-queen of France, and for Wolsey. Meanwhile, Francis and his court settled in the neighbouring town of Ardres, on the French side of the border. Contact between the two sides was initiated when Wolsey rode to Ardres and spent two days in negotiations there. His direct counterpart was the French chancellor Antoine Duprat, who had been in office since the beginning of Francis's reign, but who had only recently entered the clerical state, after the death of his wife, and had to wait until 1525 to be made an archbishop and until 1527 for a red hat. Preceded by his silver crosses and antique-style pillars, the Englishman therefore outranked and upstaged Duprat, but did not necessarily overawe him, for the French chancellor had effectively cut his diplomatic teeth by leading negotiations for the concordat of Bologna. According to the very nature of summitry, their discussions covered all manner of outstanding issues between the two states, including the proposed marriage between Princess Mary and the dauphin, the instability in Scotland, and the considerably wider problems in Franco-imperial relations.

On 7 June the two kings finally met, on the site outside Guînes that is still marked as the Field of the Cloth of Gold. There followed more than a fortnight of celebrations such as only the courts of the most *puissant* monarchs could enjoy: jousts and other feats of arms, banquets, a high Mass sung by the chapels of both monarchs, and even a dragon in the night sky made from fireworks attached to kites. Confirming his talent for being able to cope with numerous responsibilities simultaneously, this most spectacular of festivities allowed Thomas Wolsey to prove himself as accomplished as a master of ceremonies as he was as a diplomat.[42]

3

Papal Pretensions, 1520–3

In the spirit of the Universal Peace but without the ostentation of the Anglo-French summit, Wolsey devoted the first half of July 1520 to arranging no less carefully choreographed meetings between Henry and Charles, first on the border between English and imperial territory, then at Gravelines, on the imperial side, and finally at Calais. This time it was Francis who was left to kick his heels and speculate about deals being concocted behind his back. In the spirit of the increasingly intense rivalry between Charles and Francis, neither of whom had done more than pay lip service to the pacific ideals behind the treaty of London, Charles proposed a new bilateral alliance based on his own betrothal to the four-year-old Princess Mary, in defiance of both Mary's recently confirmed arrangement with the dauphin and his own with Charlotte of France. In reality, Charles could not afford to be sincere about either of these potential marriages, for he needed a bride who could enrich him with a dowry and bear his children somewhat sooner than either Mary or Charlotte. Still presenting himself as an honest broker, Henry informed Francis of Charles's dynastic proposals, but assured him that they had been rejected. While the French and imperialists seemed intent on finding excuses to play out their differences on the battlefield, Wolsey recognized that it was in England's interest to remain as neutral as possible, for as long as possible, to see which of the contending parties had greater need of the kingdom across the narrow sea.

While the potential campaigning season drew to a close, Charles made his way to Aachen, where he was crowned as king of the Romans (*Romanorum rex*) on 23 October. Thereafter, he was acknowledged as emperor-elect, the full imperial title (*Romanorum imperator*) still requiring coronation by the pope. Wolsey's information about Charles during this period came from one of his most astute diplomatic agents, Cuthbert Tunstal, who followed his quarry first to Aachen and then to Worms for the imperial diet, which opened at the end of January 1521. The diet's most significant business concerned Luther's teachings, publications and recent excommunication. The content and popularity of three major tracts published in 1520 underlined the fact that this was no ordinary heretic who could be dismissed as an aberration and quietly forgotten. *An den christlichen Adel deutscher Nation* ('An address to the Christian nobility of the German nation') patriotically reflected long simmering antagonism between Germany and Rome and called on the German princes to take a lead in reforming the Church. *De captivitate Babylonica ecclesiae* argued that Christians were effectively and wrongly imprisoned by Rome's eucharistic teaching. This was the text which Tunstal acquired in Worms and sent to Henry, who quickly responded by composing the thoroughly orthodox *Assertio septem sacramentorum adversus Martinum Lutherum*. Luther's third tract, *Von der Freiheit eines Christenmenschen* ('On the freedom of the Christian'), provided a triumphant solution to the problems identified in the other two: the essence of Christian freedom lies in the soul being justified through faith alone. Manuals and treatises poured from Luther's pen and provided good business for the printers, so that something akin to a revolution was taking place in the towns and cities of central Europe, a revolution which the secular authorities could hardly ignore. Luther's appearance before the diet took place in April. He offered a vigorous defence of his opinions and was then whisked away by the duke of Saxony, ahead of Charles's imperial ban and the diet's formal condemnation.

Meanwhile, the spread of Lutheranism in England was relatively easy to contain. Lutheran texts had begun to reach the country by 1519, but excited little interest until after 15 June 1520, when their author was condemned as a heretic and threatened with excommunication in the bull *Exsurge domine*. Writing from Rome, Silvestro Gigli sent Wolsey advance notice of this development. This was a specific condemnation of works by one author, teased out from the great tangle of ideas about reform of the Church which were then issuing from the printing presses. The universities were brimming with potential readers of the condemned texts, but it did not follow that such readers were also potential Lutherans. Of the two English universities, Cambridge caused more immediate concern, in part because of its proximity to the east coast ports through which Lutheran texts entered England and in part because of Erasmus' presence there between 1511 and 1513. Within the university, Trinity Hall was perhaps particularly vulnerable to ideas from the continent because it was essentially a college for men from East Anglia, having been founded in the fourteenth century by Bishop Bateman of Norwich 'for the promotion of divine worship and of canon and civil science and direction of the commonwealth and especially our church and diocese of Norwich.'[1] As such it was the Cambridge college most likely to interest Wolsey. In the early 1520s his closest Cambridge associate was his confessor and fellow Suffolk man Thomas Larke, who was master of Trinity Hall between 1520 and 1525. Two younger members of the college, both of whom went on to have significant dealings with the cardinal, provide a convenient illustration of the intellectual vitality and spiritual intensity of life in Cambridge around 1520. Although Stephen Gardiner of Bury St Edmunds was a doctor of both laws by 1522, his command of Latin and Greek gave him a humanist's appreciation of theology and he is known to have associated with some of the university's more advanced thinkers and future Protestants. In 1523 he met Wolsey on university business and acquired his patronage, succeeding Larke as master of Trinity Hall two years later. More than anyone else, Gardiner overcame what has been described as Wolsey's 'built-in disadvantage for Cambridge men'.[2] Like Gardiner, Thomas Bilney of Norwich was a Trinity Hall lawyer attracted to theological studies, with the distinction that his reading of Erasmus' Latin New Testament had the effect of sparking a spiritual conversion. Thereafter, Bilney was at the heart of 'evangelical' circles in Cambridge, but the membership and activities of such circles in the early 1520s is extremely difficult to trace. Future reformers such as Thomas Cranmer of Jesus College and Matthew Parker of Corpus Christi were as yet perfectly conventional in their piety, and Hugh Latimer of Clare College was not converted by Bilney until 1524. Another of Bilney's 'catches' was Robert Barnes, the thoroughly humanistic prior of the Augustinian friars in Cambridge. However, according to the Protestant martyrologist John Foxe, Barnes did not preach the message of the reformed religion until 24 December 1525.

By setting the English hierarchy's response to the Lutheran challenge in a wider geographical context, Peter Gwyn has effectively scotched the notion that Wolsey was 'soft on heresy' and too slow to realize the significance of the Lutheran threat: in his legatine capacity he banned the importation of Lutheran works into England early in 1521, which was between the burning of them in Louvain and Cologne in October and November 1520 and their condemnation by the Sorbonne in April 1521.[3] The first ban on the circulation of Lutheran books in Spain was issued on 7 April 1521, confirming that England was squarely in the mainstream among those lands where the German nationalistic appeal of Lutheranism simply did not apply. Luther's own burning of *Exsurge domine* in Wittenberg occurred in December 1520, thereby igniting his excommunication, which was not finally pronounced until 23 January 1521, in the bull *Decet*

Romanorum pontificem. It was indeed a protracted process, in which Wolsey's reaction was no more tardy than those of his counterparts elsewhere. Under the direction of Thomas More, one of the royal councillors closest to Wolsey, the English authorities were actually remarkably efficient at preventing the spread of Lutheran literature.[4] At the same time, many of the English bishops were already conditioned by fear of Lollardy, so adapted easily enough to meet the Lutheran challenge. In Cambridge that challenge was met by Bishop West of Ely and by John Fisher, who used his position as chancellor of the university to preach against the new heresy. The reformed religion did not begin to take root in Oxford until the mid 1520s, but a dynamic bishop of Lincoln nevertheless got there first. This was John Longland, a distinguished preacher who had been a Magdalen contemporary of Wolsey and proved himself particularly zealous in having booksellers' premises searched for heretical literature. Longland was papally provided to Lincoln in March 1521 and consecrated on 5 May. Exactly a week later, on Sunday 12 May, he was present at Paul's Cross to hear Fisher's two-hour refutation of the German heresiarch and to witness Wolsey's promulgation of *Exsurge domine* and the public burning of Luther's works. The king was absent due to illness, but Wolsey appeared as his faithful servant sought to represent Henry by holding in his hand throughout this highly symbolic event the unfinished text of the *Assertio septem sacramentorum.*

The following day, 13 May, it was the turn of the lords temporal to assert their authority, when the duke of Buckingham appeared before more than twenty of his peers in Westminster Hall to answer the charge of treason arising from his hopes of succeeding to the throne. The intemperate duke had not masterminded or participated in any definite plot to kill the king, but he had recalled his father's intention to murder Richard III, had talked of rebelling against Henry, and had been encouraged by the prophecies of the Carthusian Nicholas Hopkins, who appeared as a witness in the case. The other witnesses were members of the duke's household, including his chancellor, his confessor and his cousin Charles Knyvett, who had recently been dismissed from Buckingham's service. Knyvett argued that it was in the wake of the Bulmer trial in 1517 that Buckingham spoke meaningfully of his father's murderous intention towards an anointed king and expressed the opinion that Wolsey employed necromancy to maintain himself in royal favour. Disputes within the ducal household could have been dismissed as inconsequential had Buckingham not commanded substantial numbers of retainers in England and Wales and had the Tudor dynasty not been on the verge of extinction. The 'aged and sickly' but nonetheless clear-headed chief justice Sir John Fyneux was consulted on whether or not 'imagining' the king's death constituted treason, and he had no doubt that it did. On 16 May the peers reached their verdict and it fell to the duke of Norfolk, as lord high steward, to pronounce the death sentence. It was a duty that reduced even that battle-hardened warrior to tears, for Buckingham could hardly have occupied a place closer to the heart of the English aristocracy: his wife was Eleanor Percy, daughter of the fourth earl of Northumberland; his sister-in-law was Cicely Bonville, widow of Wolsey's early patron, the first marquis of Dorset; his daughters were married to Norfolk's son, the earl of Surrey, to Ralph Neville, fourth earl of Westmorland, and to George Neville, third baron Bergavenny, the last of whom we have already encountered in the 1516 investigation into illegal retaining. Most significantly of all, Buckingham's only son, Henry Stafford, was married to Ursula Pole, daughter of the countess of Salisbury and therefore a descendent of the house of York. This last was a match that Wolsey had encouraged, but it also had the unforeseen consequence of making the countess too closely connected to the traitor to be allowed to continue in her role as Princess Mary's governess, and she was thereupon deprived of this office until 1525.

In contrast to his presiding role at Paul's Cross on the Sunday, between the Monday and Friday of that week Wolsey was not directly involved in Buckingham's trial and execution, but it nevertheless suited contemporaries, including foreign ambassadors seeking to explain events in England for their home governments, to cast the cardinal as the hidden hand manipulating the duke's destruction, complete with speculation that Buckingham had been plotting to assassinate Wolsey.[5] According to this interpretation of events, Buckingham was the self-appointed figurehead of aristocratic opposition towards the upstart chancellor, and a man whose consistent anti-French views ensured his antipathy towards Wolsey's considerably more subtle foreign policy. Wolsey had no problem with law-abiding aristocrats and had sought to avoid a crisis by warning Buckingham to act and speak more cautiously: he was perfectly at liberty to say what he liked against the king's minister, but should take great care over what he said against the king. It was as the king's faithful minister that Wolsey was obliged to keep the duke under surveillance, and Charles Knyvett was one of the means he employed to do so. The speculation in which Buckingham indulged was about events after Henry's death and the imminence or otherwise of the king's demise. Henry, not Wolsey, was therefore the person most eager to see Buckingham's destruction, even though it did nothing to resolve the problem of the succession, for the queen was now aged thirty-five and highly unlikely to bear any more children.

Neither the containment of heresy nor the fall of Buckingham occupied much of the cardinal's time in 1521. On the other hand, at no other point in his career did diplomacy prove to be quite so time-consuming, as Wolsey vainly sought to prevent full-scale war breaking out between France and the Habsburgs. With Charles safely preoccupied in Germany during the winter of 1520–1, Francis planned to spend time in Milan, but this was frustrated first by the illness of his mother and proposed regent, Louise of Savoy, and then by an accident which put him out of action for a couple of months.[6] In the spring of 1521 proxy conflicts broke out on a number of fronts. To the north, Robert de la Marck, lord of Sedan (then a sovereign state), invaded the imperial territory of Luxembourg, but was chased out by Charles's commander Henry of Nassau, who invaded Sedan for good measure. To the south, Henri d'Albret, king of Navarre, took advantage of Castilian preoccupation with the revolting Comuneros to invade and reclaim that portion of the Pyrenean kingdom which had been snatched by Ferdinand of Aragon in 1512.[7] However, Henri's calculations backfired when royal and aristocratic forces scored their famous victory at Villalar on 23 April, leaving the Comunero cause completely defeated. While the English waited to see which way the wider Habsburg-Valois conflict would turn, Pope Leo effectively broke off his 1518 alliance with Francis and made a secret treaty with Charles on 29 May. Unlike Henry and Wolsey, Leo was obliged to protect the temporal interests of the papacy in Italy, while at the same time addressing the escalating troubles in Germany and, most significantly, leading the defence of Christendom as a whole, for the Ottomans were resurgent under their new sultan Süleyman. In all those respects, Leo found Francis to be an unreliable ally and decided that Charles represented by far the better option, even if this meant reversing his previous aversion to investing Charles with the kingdom of Naples. Although the papal-Habsburg alliance was not public knowledge, Francis was well aware of the forces, military and otherwise, being mustered against him and, on 9 June, called upon Henry to arbitrate between himself and Charles under the terms of the otherwise neglected treaty of London. This was what triggered the convening of the peace conference at Calais and the diplomatic initiatives to which Wolsey devoted his attention between August and November 1521. More immediately, Francis suffered simultaneous reversals in Spain and Italy. In Iberia, the French army overplayed its hand by venturing into Castile and was defeated in battle on 30 June, in consequence of which

Navarre reverted to Habsburg rule. Two days earlier the French garrison in Milan suffered three hundred fatalities when lightning struck the ammunition store, an incident which Leo interpreted as both divine retribution for a recent French incursion into papal territory and the spur he needed to publicize his anti-French alliance with Charles.

At this point Henry's instinct was to abandon any pretence of arbitration, throw in his lot with Charles and go to war against England's traditional enemy. Wolsey, on the other hand, was well aware that such an adventure was well beyond the king's means, best avoided or, at least, postponed for as long as possible. If England had no option but to declare war, it would have to be in defence of the treaty of London and, paradoxically, the cause of peace. The different strategies favoured by the king and his chancellor may well account for Wolsey's precaution of taking the great seal with him to the Calais conference. So flexible was the English policy ahead of these trilateral negotiations that, even among the principal players, Thomas Ruthall knew of the plan for an Anglo-imperial alliance while Cuthbert Tunstal apparently did not.

Wolsey arrived in Calais on 2 August and renewed his acquaintance with Chancellor Duprat. The imperial delegation was led by Charles's new chancellor, the Piedmontese lawyer Mercurino Arborio di Gattinara. Mandell Creighton rated Gattinara as 'equal to Wolsey in resolution and pertinacity', but lacking the Englishman's genius for 'far-reaching schemes' and concluded that 'his was the hand that first checked Wolsey's victorious career.'[8] Gattinara and his master were content to use the conference as a cover for their real design, which was to persuade Wolsey to sign the proposed Anglo-imperial alliance. Hardly had the negotiations opened in Calais than Charles sent an invitation to the cardinal to meet him at Bruges. The most difficult task was to persuade Duprat that the French were not being deceived, but Wolsey managed to convince him that this shuttle diplomacy was the only way to prevent Charles from rejecting any form of mediation and withdrawing from the conference altogether. At every point in the process Wolsey contrived to play for time, for it was still by no means certain which side would get the upper hand in the military sphere. In mid August he made a stately progress from Calais to Bruges, accompanied by more than a thousand attendants, and was met by Charles at the city gate. Neither dismounted when they embraced as equals, the 'butcher's cur' from Ipswich and the emperor-elect. The following day they attended Mass in the cathedral and knelt together on the same prie-dieu. In the thinking of the time, only the pope was the emperor's equal, but Wolsey had already proved in the treaty of London that he had usurped the pontiff's traditional claim to be Europe's peacemaker. Here was the confirmation.

There followed some hard bargaining, from which the treaty of Bruges emerged on 25 August. Charles secured Henry's promise to declare war on France, which Wolsey mitigated by encouraging the negotiation of a truce at Calais during the current campaigning season and by delaying any joint Anglo-imperial military campaign until March 1523, a delay subsequently extended to May of that year. Beyond that, the marriage of Charles and Mary was again envisaged, with much haggling over the details of the dowry. Naturally enough, the treaty of Bruges was unpublished, leaving room for further negotiations back in Calais. By the time Wolsey returned there on 28 August, imperial forces had besieged Mézières (now Charleville-Mézières), on the river Meuse, and he was obliged to respond in a manner befitting an impartial arbitrator. This he did by authorizing the usual autumn departure of the English merchant fleet to collect wine from Bordeaux. French suspicions were not allayed for long. On 9 September an imperial raiding party attacked Ardres, close to the Pale of Calais, which was enough to persuade Francis of some kind of collusion between Charles and the English. By way of response, though, Duprat was only half-heartedly instructed to leave the conference, because Francis hoped that a truce might still be negotiated. Indeed, just two days after the attack on Ardres, the French and English chancellors dined together and Wolsey used the opportunity to present a sequence of ingenious arguments to counter the impression that any anti-French deal had been struck in Bruges. As it was by no means clear which side would gain the upper hand by the end of the campaigning season, Wolsey remained in Calais, his efforts concentrated on the possibility of a truce, which was consistent with the longer-term plans agreed at Bruges, rather than on a full-scale peace with immediate effect. It was a wise decision, for there followed a period of French victories on various fronts, perhaps none more satisfying than the taking of Fuenterrabía, the fortress on the Spanish side of the river Bidassoa, by the French admiral Guillaume Gouffier, seigneur de Bonnivet. On France's northern border the imperialist siege of Mézières was also abandoned. Charles now had greater cause than Francis to seek a truce negotiated by the English cardinal, and the French king rebuffed proposals presented to him by Wolsey's agents, Bishop West and Charles Somerset, earl of Worcester. Seizing the momentum, Francis then sought to relieve the much-contested city of Tournai, which had been besieged by imperialists. Only when it was clear that he could not regain it before winter did Francis begin to talk of an eighteen-month truce. By November, Fortune had ceased to favour the king: some weeks before Tournai finally surrendered to its imperialist besiegers it was clear that the French initiative there had failed, and it was Charles's turn to stall regarding a truce. At that stage Wolsey complained to Francis that he was

> sore tempested in mind by the untowardness of the chancellors and orators on every side putting so many difficulties and obstacles to condescend to any reasonable condition of truce and abstinence of war, that night and day I could have no quietness nor rest, so that almost my appetite and sleep . . . are sequestrate from me.[9]

After months of confusion and delay, events moved fast in the second half of November. On the 19th imperialist troops broke into the city of Milan and forced the French commander, Odet de Foix, seigneur de Lautrec, into ignominious flight. It was not long before the under-resourced French forces withdrew from the entire duchy, leaving it in the hands of its imperial overlord. Just three days after the breakthrough at Milan, Duprat and the French delegation finally withdrew from the Calais conference. That, in turn, created the opportunity for their English and imperialist counterparts to sign the treaty initially negotiated at Bruges and much refined thereafter. This was done on 24 November. After nearly four months in Calais, relieved only by the brief foray to Bruges, Wolsey crossed the Channel again on the 27th. England's countdown to war against France had begun. Regardless of their conclusion, the cardinal's protracted negotiations had created a clear break with traditional diplomatic practice and caused at least one contemporary observer to question his motives. That observer was the poet John Skelton. In *Speak, Parrot* (1521) he alleges that Wolsey's principal motive at the peace conference was to cultivate the larger powers in the hope that they would secure his election to the papacy.[10]

Papal interests at Calais were represented not by the legate, Wolsey, but by the nuncio Girolamo Ghinucci, who had been sent to England in 1520 ahead of the Anglo-French summit at the Field of the Cloth of Gold and had, more recently, witnessed the burning of Lutheran texts in London. Ghinucci's association with Anglo-papal relations went back to the time of the Fifth Lateran Council and entailed collaboration with his fellow Sienese Silvestro Gigli. After faithfully executing Roman business for the Tudor monarchs since 1498, Gigli died on 18 April 1521. So thoroughly did he identify with the English cause that he was buried in the church of the English hospice in via di Monserrato (now the Venerable English College). Ghinucci offered himself as Gigli's natural successor in the see of Worcester, but Henry had different ideas and, on 21 May, wrote to Leo offering Worcester to the pope's cousin and England's cardinal protector Giulio de' Medici. There was no possibility of Giulio taking up residence in England, for he was needed in Rome as vice-chancellor of the Church and in Florence as archbishop and *de facto* ruler of what was now a republican state in name only. On the basis of that missive Giulio received papal preferment to Worcester on 7 June, but it meant no more to him than did the Hungarian bishopric of Eger, which he 'administered' between 1520 and 1523. Gigli had not been replaced as the English orator when Henry's *Assertio septem sacramentorum* was published in July, and it was Ghinucci who spied an opportunity to initiate a new chapter in relations between England and Rome by suggesting to Wolsey that a presentation copy of the king's anti-Lutheran treatise be given to the pope. Ghinucci was well aware that Francis had quashed the 1516 proposal that Henry be granted the title 'Defender of the Christian faith', but argued that the *Assertio* could effectively secure it at a time when relations between Rome and France were in a downward spiral.

Wolsey's close associate John Clerk was chosen to convey the presentation copy to Rome. Clerk was a graduate of Cambridge and Bologna, from where he gained his doctorate in canon law in 1510, before gravitating towards Rome and the patronage of Cardinal Bainbridge. Clerk's Roman experience also included service as chamberlain of the English hospice but, like Richard Pace, he found no reason to remain in the city after Bainbridge's death and made his way back to England. Wolsey's patronage brought him a succession of high profile preferments, including the deanery of the Chapel Royal in 1516 and that of St George's Chapel, Windsor, three years later. On 2 October Clerk presented the *Assertio* as the work of a loyal son of the Church, and an anti-French one at that. Much to Henry's satisfaction, the title 'Fidei defensor' was duly conferred towards the end of the month. Thus there was a clear convergence of imperial, papal and English interests, expressed in those clauses of the Anglo-imperial treaty which undertook to defend Leo against French aggression. As we have seen, far from being in immediate need of such protection, the pope had cause to rejoice at news of the French retreat from Milan. Thus were the secular powers disposed, for and against the papacy, when the forty-six-year-old pontiff died quite unexpectedly on 1 December.

The fourth conclave of the sixteenth century opened twenty-six days later. Over two hundred people – cardinals, conclavists and officials – crowded into the enclosure before its formal sealing. Indeed, Leo had created so many cardinals that not all could be housed in the temporary wooden cells constructed in the

Sistine Chapel. A quick result and a merciful release was presumably desired by many of the eminent prisoners. Of the thirty-nine electors, only eleven had previous conclave experience. The dean of the Sacred College was Bernardino López de Carvajal, who still hoped for the election of an 'angelic' pope. The other cardinals who survived from the pontificate of Alexander VI were the Venetians Domenico Grimani and Marco Corner, the Florentine Francesco Soderini, the Roman Alessandro Farnese and the Genoese Niccolò Fieschi. From the Julian pontificate came four other Italians, together with Matthäus Schiner. All but one of the twenty-eight electors who had been promoted by Leo were Italians, with names such as Pucci, Salviati and Ridolfi identifying the strong Florentine contingent and loyal Mediceans from elsewhere in Tuscany including Silvio Passerini of Cortona and the Sienese Raffaele Petrucci. The natural leader of this grouping was Giulio de' Medici, who had governed Florence on Leo's behalf, in addition to being its archbishop, but his leadership was countered by the cardinals' desire to avoid electing two Medici popes in direct succession. At the same time, a desire to perpetuate the recent convergence of papal and Habsburg interests meant that Giulio also went into the conclave as Charles's preferred candidate. His protectorship of England and administration of the see of Worcester made the prospect of his election not uncongenial to Henry and his chancellor. French interests were in the hands of sympathetic Italians such as Agostino Trivulzio, for none of the native French cardinals participated in the conclave. In addition to Wolsey, the other non-electors included the firmly non-curial cardinals Matthäus Lang, Albrecht von Brandenburg and Adriaan Florenszoon Dedel (Adrian of Utrecht). The ultimate absentee was Adriano Castellesi, who had not been reconciled with Leo after his alleged participation in the Petrucci conspiracy, but who nevertheless hoped to be admitted to the conclave. It was a vane hope, for he died in suspicious circumstances while making his way to Rome.

Accounts of the conclaves of 1521–2 and 1523 can easily become distorted by anglocentric speculation about Wolsey's chances of election, so it may be useful to separate facts and figures about the electoral process in Rome from any hopes and speculation experienced in England. Three scrutinies (ballots) was a reasonable average for sixteenth-century conclaves, but that of 1521–2 represented a sign of things to come by requiring eleven ballots in order to reach the required two-thirds majority.[11] Baldassare Castiglione's quip about the Holy Spirit deserting Rome on this occasion cannot be verified. The real distinction between this and previous conclaves lay in the sheer quantity of electors and therefore the number of candidates whose chances could only be tested by having their names put forward, scrutiny by scrutiny. For more than a week Giulio de' Medici advanced the cause of Alessandro Farnese, but he consistently failed to gain the twenty-six votes required for victory. The core of the opposition to Giulio's faction was provided by the Roman patrician Pompeo Colonna, who had papal ambitions of his own. The deadlock was finally broken on 9 January, when Giulio proposed the election of the absent Adriaan Florenszoon Dedel, who had been Charles's tutor in the Low Countries and was currently governing Spain in the absence of the emperor-elect. Colonna supported this surprising move and the Flemish bishop of Tortosa was duly elected as Adrian VI.[12] At sixty-two, Adrian was of an average age for a newly-elected Renaissance pope, neither a geriatric stopgap nor a match for the unusually youthful Pope Leo, but the cardinals had nevertheless managed to observe one of the unwritten rules of conclaves and elected a man whose character contrasted with that of the previous pontiff, for Adrian was as austere as Leo was indulgent and as parsimonious as Leo was generous. At last Carvajal had his angelic pope.

It is true that both Francis and Charles had made encouraging noises about supporting Wolsey's candidature in the event of a papal election but, aside from the pensions which they paid him anyway, in reality there was nothing else they could offer to a man who already enjoyed every privilege that king or pope could bestow. There is no need to speculate whether his age – just the 'wrong' side of fifty – was against him, for he was already too dominant, too powerful a player on the European scene to be entrusted with the keys of St Peter. What Charles needed was a compliant pontiff, not one who had already demonstrated ample confidence in his own ability to dictate the affairs of nations and who, even as a cardinal, had been declared to have seven times more repute than the pope.[13] Having served as Bainbridge's conclavist in 1513, Richard Pace was the Englishman best qualified to make Henry's electoral preferences known to the cardinals in 1521–2. His instructions had to be as clear and as comprehensive as possible; they presented Wolsey as a candidate favourable to both Henry and Charles, but acknowledged Giulio de' Medici's strong position and anticipated the likelihood of his election. The long-suffering Pace did not reach Rome until after Adrian's election, leaving John Clerk's report to his patron as the only English source for Wolsey's fortunes in the conclave. According to Clerk, the cardinal of England received nine votes in the first scrutiny, twelve in the second and nineteen in the third, but dropped out of the running after that. All things considered, they are highly respectable figures, but they do not come from a conclave insider, cannot be verified or corroborated, and were presumably designed to cast Clerk's patron in the best possible light. Campeggi suggested that Wolsey received as many as eight or nine votes in individual scrutinies, but other sources maintained that he featured in only one ballot and received no more than seven votes. The identity of Wolsey's potential supporters remains a mystery; the only electors who had actually met him were the vehemently anti-French Schiner and the former legate Campeggi. It should also be remembered that, until the reforms introduced by Gregory XV in 1621, electors were free to name as many or as few candidates as they liked in each scrutiny. When all these considerations are borne in mind, they highlight the fragility of Wolsey's candidature and therefore the exaggerated claims made about it in anglocentric historiography. In reality, the only sixteenth-century Englishman who stood any reasonable chance of being elected pope was Reginald Pole in 1549, again in the imperial cause, but the English break with Rome and Pole's rather underwhelming character have contributed to that episode being played down, while too much has been made of Wolsey's relatively unrealistic candidature.

Initially, Francis refused to recognize Adrian's election and the king's mother quipped that Charles might as well have elected himself.[14] For some months after his election the new pope displayed no sign of making the journey to Rome, so the nuncio Ghinucci, accompanied by the English envoy Thomas Hannibal, travelled to meet him in Spain. They were received by the pope at Zaragoza on 3 May 1522. Among the matters discussed on that occasion was Ghinucci's proposal that Giulio de' Medici resign the see of Worcester so that Ghinucci himself could be appointed to it. This did not meet with papal approval. Nor did Ghinucci's other proposal, that Wolsey be made legate *a latere* to England for life. Where Francis miscalculated was in assuming that Adrian would automatically perpetuate Leo's alliance with Charles and, by extension, with England. Instead, the new pope took seriously his responsibilities as universal pastor and sought to keep the papacy firmly neutral in relation to the Valois-Habsburg conflict. Unlike Leo, Adrian had no alternative sources of allegiance in Italy. That lack of allegiance, combined with his absence from the peninsula, created something of a vacuum and encouraged the renewal of hostilities rather sooner than might otherwise have been the case. Francis spent the winter of 1521–2 preparing to recover the duchy of Milan. William Knight was sent to prevent the French from recruiting Swiss mercenaries, but he failed in that regard and the Franco-Swiss forces were ready for action early in the season. It proved to be a brief campaign, effectively concluded on 27 April, when the French were defeated in battle at La Bicocca, near Milan, by a combination of German and Spanish forces under the command of Prospero Colonna, an uncle of Cardinal Pompeo. The military significance of this encounter was that it broke the reputation and confidence of the Swiss. Its political significance lay in the French loss of both Milan and Genoa and in Charles's installation of Francesco II Sforza as duke of Milan, though Francesco proved to be the last of that previously illustrious line. This latest French reversal emboldened the English to make a formal declaration of war against France towards the end of May, but there was no immediate military action. This coincided with Charles's second, longer and more spectacular visit to England, which he made *en route* from the Low Countries to Spain.

The chronicler Edward Hall relates that Wolsey rode from London to Dover between 20 and 26 May, accompanied by a vast train comprising two earls, thirty-six knights, a hundred gentlemen, eight bishops, ten abbots, thirty chaplains clad in velvet and satin, and seven hundred yeomen.[15] On Monday 26th he met Charles on the sands and, as in the previous year, accompanied him to Dover Castle, where Henry arrived the following day. Thereafter the imperial and royal parties made their progress through Kent. Archbishop Warham hosted Charles during an overnight stay at Canterbury and Bishop Fisher received him at Rochester. At Greenwich he was welcomed by Queen Katherine, made the acquaintance of his young cousin and prospective bride, Princess Mary, and was entertained in a suitably courtly fashion. This sort of showmanship was the aspect of kingship of which Henry was a genuine master. From 6 June it was the turn of London to celebrate with pageants in honour of his imperial majesty. On Whit Sunday Wolsey celebrated Mass at St Paul's and accompanied Charles and Henry to Westminster, where they admired Henry VII's chapel and were assailed by cries for mercy and pardon from the sanctuary men: 'The cardinal gave them a gentle answer which contented them for a time.' From London the festivities moved on to Southwark, Richmond and Hampton Court.[16]

The first phase of Wolsey's building works at Hampton Court had been completed by this date, the essentially traditional design of Base Court and the Great Gatehouse being finished off with Classically-inspired terracotta decorations sent from Italy by the sculptor Giovanni da Maiano. From Giovanni Wolsey commissioned three large terracotta scenes from the story of Hercules, which have since been lost, though eight of the original ten terracotta roundels survive on the exterior walls of the palace, though exactly which of the ten it is now impossible to say.[17] On 18 June 1521 Giovanni sent a demand for payment, confirming that all these commissions had been completed and installed by that date. As the roundels depict the heads of Roman emperors, they provided the perfect setting in which to receive Charles, the latter-day Caesar. Not inappropriately, this was also the point at which Skelton featured the extravagance of Hampton Court in two of his satirical jibes at Wolsey, *Colin Cloute* (1521-2) and *Why come ye not to court?* (November 1522). The former describes but does not actually name Hampton Court, with its 'turrets' and 'towers', 'halls' and 'bowers'; the latter rejects such reticence and directly asserts that Wolsey, the master and presiding genius of Hampton Court, had usurped the king's position and authority:

> Why come ye not to court?
> To which court?
> To the king's court
> Or to Hampton Court?
> Nay, to the king's court!
> The king's court
> Should have the excellence
> But Hampton Court
> Hath the pre-eminence
> And York Place
> With 'My lord's grace'
> To whose magnificence
> Is all the confluence
> Suits and supplications
> Embassies of all nations.[18]

From Hampton Court Charles continued on to Windsor where, on the feast of Corpus Christi, pageantry was meshed with diplomacy when he was installed as a knight of the Garter. Aside from the outward display, the Anglo-imperial relationship was confirmed in two more treaties, signed at Windsor on 19 June and at Richard Fox's palace at Bishop's Waltham on 2 July, which further defined the mutual commitment to the Great Enterprise against France.

Charles finally sailed from Southampton on 6 July, with a naval escort commanded by the earl of Surrey, who took the opportunity provided by his return voyage to raid the Breton coast and venture inland as far as Morlaix. Thus emboldened, in September Surrey led an expeditionary force out of Calais and into Picardy. It caused much destruction to no obvious purpose, but was nevertheless the sort of patriotic endeavour that delighted Skelton:

Yet the good Earl of Surrey
The Frenchmen he doth fray.
And vexeth them day by day
With all the power he may.[19]

Between 1520 and 1522 Surrey had been lord lieutenant of Ireland and a source of great vexation to Gerald Fitzgerald, the ninth earl of Kildare. Ireland had been convulsed by its own version of the Wars of the Roses, for the Fitzgerald earls of Kildare and Desmond were Yorkists while the Butler earls of Ormond were Lancastrians. Their dynastic feud continued into Henry VIII's reign, complicated by the fact that there were two claimants to the Ormond title, Piers Butler in Ireland and Thomas Boleyn, grandson of the seventh earl, in England. When Wolsey first turned his attention to Ireland, his priority was to contain the lawless activities of the earl of Kildare, who was the king's lord deputy but who could nevertheless frustrate the business of government because his estates lay just outside the Pale. The crown lacked the capacity to tame Kildare, but if Butler could do so it would be in the crown's interest as well as furthering his claim to the earldom. This convergence of interests was sealed by Butler sending his son, James, to join the cardinal's household. Thus the feud and the violence continued. Kildare was removed as lord deputy in 1519 and briefly replaced by Maurice Fitzgerald of Lackagh, who had the title of lord justice, until the arrival of the earl of Surrey early in 1520. It has been suggested that Wolsey sent Surrey to Ireland so that he would be far from England when his father-in-law, the duke of Buckingham, was tried for treason, but there is no conclusive evidence to support this assertion. That said, Surrey was certainly thinking dynastically when he sought to devise his own solution to Ireland's governmental problems. His sister Elizabeth happened to be married to Thomas Boleyn, one of the Ormond claimants, and had produced three children, George, Mary and Anne. In February 1520 Mary married William Carey, a member of the king's privy chamber, but Anne, who returned to England in 1521 after a lengthy sojourn at the French court, was eminently marriageable. Surrey's scheme was to marry his niece to James Butler, thereby uniting the interests of the two families who claimed the earldom, while promoting Piers Butler as the king's representative in Ireland. Butler duly became deputy lieutenant in December 1521 and lord deputy in March 1522, thereby freeing Surrey to return to court and to undertake the naval expedition mentioned above, but the new lord deputy's position was so weak that, within months, he pleaded for Kildare to be allowed to return from England to impose some sort of order on his lawless followers. When Kildare arrived in Ireland on 1 January 1523 it was with a new wife, Elizabeth Grey, daughter of the first marquis of Dorset. Meanwhile, the Butler-Boleyn match came to nothing.

The Irish episcopate during the period of Wolsey's prominence was largely composed of native-born clerics, though some of its more senior members were English. Wolsey's Hibernian counterpart was the Somerset-born Wykehamist Hugh Inge, who was bishop of Meath from 1512, lord chancellor of Ireland from 1522 and archbishop of Dublin from 1523.[20] The Meath appointment was combined with the responsibilities of being vicar-general to the primate of Ireland. Between 1513 and 1521 the primate was John Kite, a loyal friend of Wolsey who received the archbishopric of Armagh through the cardinal's intervention. Of these two men, the industrious Inge adapted better to the trials of life so far from the court, while Kite never acclimatized and made repeated appeals to Wolsey to be released from his 'exile'. When a suitable vacancy finally arose, it was the bishopric of Carlisle, one of the poorest in England. In order to retain his archiepiscopal dignity, Kite's translation to Carlisle was accompanied by his appointment to the archbishopric of Thebes *in partibus infidelium*. More prosaically, he was made treasurer to Thomas, Lord Dacre, warden of the western Marches against Scotland.

Again Kite found himself in lawless country, where he had to contend with banditry and simmering disputes between the leading families, in addition to cross-border incursions. He had not been there long when relations between England and France deteriorated sufficiently for Francis to call on the Scots to harass their southern neighbours. While the emperor-elect was being feasted and feted in southern England, the Franco-Scottish treaty of Rouen (signed in 1517) was ratified on 13 June 1521. The duke of Albany was sent back to Scotland with a contingent of French troops and arrived in Edinburgh in early December. As Queen Margaret had received scant support from her brother Henry, whose foreign policy priorities lay elsewhere, she now turned to Albany, her erstwhile rival, in the hope of securing a greater degree of control over her son and even a divorce form her unfaithful husband the earl of Angus. The earl, on the other hand, had created a favourable impression in England. Henry and Wolsey hoped that he might be able to steer the Scottish leadership in a pro-English direction and might even be reconciled with his wife. If the former hope was rather desperate, the latter was sheer fantasy. Margaret's situation did improve marginally with the return of Albany, who set about raising an army in 1522 for a cross-border invasion. In September he marched on Carlisle, which was poorly defended, but the memory of Flodden was still strong in the minds of his soldiers, who were reluctant to risk a similar massacre. Dacre offered a truce, which was gratefully accepted by the Scots. Albany could hardly have been more frustrated and responded by appointing a regency council, excluding Margaret from this new arrangement, and returning to France within a matter of weeks. At the apex of the English government there were widely differing reactions to this turn of events. Henry regarded Dacre's truce as a humiliating capitulation, but Wolsey was delighted that a dangerous distraction had been averted and entertained hopes of a permanent settlement being cemented by a marriage between the first cousins James V and Princess Mary.

While the English government geared up for the Great Enterprise against France in 1523, there could be little hope of the northern border remaining quiet. Wolsey was kept informed of preparations for another Scottish expedition by the duke of Albany, this time with the support of the English pretender Richard de la Pole. Dacre could not be entirely trusted, so command of the border region was given to the earl of Surrey, a veteran of many an Anglo-Scottish campaign. This time he set about 'frying' Scottish monks, with raids on the abbeys at Kelso and Jedburgh in the summer months. Although hopes of an English rising favour of the Yorkist claimant proved to be misplaced, Francis again sent the duke of Albany to the northern kingdom with a French army and an invasion plan. He besieged Wark Castle, on the English side of the river Tweed, but it was relieved by Surrey late in the campaigning season. Again, Skelton wrote a patriotic account of the episode, *The Douty Duke of Albany*, praising Surrey as 'our strong captain' and emphasizing the cowardliness of the Scottish regent. The fact that this and other poems were commissioned by Wolsey seems to confirm that Skelton's earlier anti-Wolsey satires were not intended for wide circulation, let alone for publication. Relations between Skelton and the cardinal developed further when Wolsey promised the poet ecclesiastical preferment, though nothing had come of that by 23 October 1523, when his *Garland of Laurel* was published and Skelton used the double dedication to Henry and Wolsey to remind the latter of his undertaking.

Archbishop Kite's translation to Carlisle was the last English episcopal promotion of Pope Leo's pontificate. Such business only resumed after Thomas Hannibal had followed Pope Adrian from Spain to Rome in August 1522 and assumed the usual range of curial responsibilities expected of the English orator. Thus, although Bishop Richard Fitzjames of London died on 15 January 1522, he was not replaced by Cuthbert Tunstal until 10 September, when normal curial operations had resumed. In contrast to Kite, who could easily be spared for the wilds of Armagh or Carlisle, Tunstal was a valued member of the king's council and a highly competent diplomat, all of which was regarded as compatible with diocesan responsibilities in London. Girolamo Ghinucci achieved his objective of indirectly succeeding Silvestro Gigli at Worcester in September, when Giulio de' Medici obligingly resigned the see but retained a 2,000-ducat pension from its revenues. Wolsey had good cause to be pleased with both the London and Worcester appointments, for Tunstal was so highly regarded that even Polydore Vergil – no friend of the cardinal – wrote that 'the city was anxious to have him on account of his splendid reputation for virtue', and Ghinucci could continue to provide loyal service in Rome.[21]

At that stage the cardinal still held the bishopric of Bath and Wells *in commendam* with the archbishopric of York, but was evidently in need of further income to maintain the dignity of his office and, more prosaically, to meet the needs of his substantial household. In England, only the bishoprics of Winchester, Canterbury, Durham, Ely, Exeter, Lincoln, Norwich and Salisbury offered the prospect of greater income than Bath and Wells, and none of those became vacant in 1522. During the previous century prelates in Italy, France, Iberia and elsewhere had found alternative sources of income in commendatory abbacies; appointments which allowed them to act as patrons to wealthy monastic houses and to take a proportion of the income, while otherwise leaving the communities to their own devices under the authority of their elected superiors. Cardinals frequently possessed a clutch of such abbacies at any one time. By the early sixteenth century the practice was in decline and commendatory abbots used their authority to reform communities before relinquishing their patronage. By way of illustration, the great Benedictine abbey of Montecassino received the patronage of commendatory abbots until 1504, when Cardinal Giovanni de' Medici entrusted it to the reformed congregation of S. Giustina. The greater monastic houses of England had not required such patronage, a point confirmed by the fact that, in Wolsey's time, twenty-six mitred abbots were entitled to sit among the lords spiritual in the House of Lords. Nevertheless, just as the practice of appointing commendatory abbots was waning in Italy, Wolsey introduced a curious and unique variation on the theme into England. In 1521 Abbot Thomas Ramryge of St Albans died, and was buried in style. The Ramryge tomb in the former abbey is comparable with those of bishops of the period, rather than those of Ramryge's fellow abbots. It is a highly personalized affair decorated with rams, just as that of Archbishop

Morton at Canterbury is decorated with tuns. If the abbot of St Albans could afford to operate in episcopal style, then his revenue was evidently substantial. The abbatial vacancy coincided with Wolsey's lengthy sojourn in Calais, where he was obliged to meet the substantial expenses of the peace conference. The king estimated that cost at £10,000 and suggested that this highly extraordinary expenditure be met by the equally extraordinary expedient of Wolsey becoming the next abbot of St Albans. The matter was passed to Thomas Hannibal in Rome, who ensured that papal provision obligingly followed on 8 November 1522, but Hannibal was also at pains to point out that Wolsey was entitled to claim revenues from S. Cecilia, his titular church in Trastevere. From the Roman angle, the arrangement at St Albans must have appeared to be yet another commendatory abbacy and consequently raised no curial eyebrows. In reality, it was decidedly odd, for the next claustral abbot was not elected until after Wolsey's death.

Second to the income, St Albans was of practical use to the cardinal because it provided him with two Hertfordshire manors, Tyttenhanger, a little to the south-east of St Albans, and the More (now Moor Park, home of a well known golf club), near Rickmansworth. Both residences were immediately subject to extensive building work, but whereas too little is known about Wolsey's contributions at Tyttenhanger to permit its reconstruction, the More is known to have been a small moated house which the cardinal enlarged by creating an outer shell of principal lodgings and, beyond the moat, a base court of guest lodgings on the Hampton Court model and a long gallery stretching far into the grounds.[22] As at York Place, he was expanding the work of Archbishop George Neville. More recently, the manor had been leased by Wolsey's close collaborator Bishop Ruthall, which perhaps accounted for his appreciation of its potential as a summer residence at those times when the king ventured to the north of London and Wolsey needed to communicate with him by the most direct route. In September 1523, for example, Wolsey was at the More when news reached him of the death of Pope Adrian. From there, in turn, he wrote to Henry at Woodstock.[23]

Before that, in the winter of 1522–3, the Anglo-Welsh episcopate was further reconfigured due to the deaths of Edward Vaughan and Thomas Ruthall. Vaughan had proved to be a conspicuous builder during his dozen years at St David's, but although his diocese was the wealthiest in Wales, it was still poor by English standards and was worth only one eighth of the richest see, that of Winchester. It was therefore of no immediate use to Wolsey, and could be spared to provide a refuge for Richard Rawlins, the aged and recently deposed warden of Merton College, Oxford. Ruthall's death on 4 February 1523 finally released a pearl of great price, the prince-bishopric of Durham. This prize – or at least its lucrative administration – the acquisitive and perhaps even needy cardinal claimed for himself, relinquishing Bath and Wells to his faithful lieutenant John Clerk, who was then master of the rolls, but who was shortly sent on his third diplomatic mission to Rome, where he duly received his episcopal consecration. On 26 March Wolsey received papal provision to the administration of Durham. Between 1523 and 1529, therefore, Wolsey combined the archbishopric of York with administration of the bishopric of Durham, and could rely for regional support on 'the flatteryng Byshope' Kite in Carlisle. The entire northern province was therefore even more firmly under his authority than was the southern province under that of Archbishop Warham, with the added distinction that Wolsey had never actually set foot in his province.

Between Clerk's departure from Rome in 1522 and his return to England in June 1523, Thomas Hannibal was the only English ambassador there. He dealt with the Durham appointment speedily enough, but his failure to persuade Pope Adrian to grant Wolsey's legatine powers for life presumably contributed to the cardinal's determination to replace him with a more reliable agent. Silvestro Gigli had set a high standard, which the relative newcomer Hannibal was not able to match. Wolsey's frustration over the permanence or otherwise of the legation is understandable because there is evidence to confirm that his legatine court was in existence by 1522, apparently operating at York Place. Its officials were known as auditors, foremost among whom was John Alen, a man of exceptionally forceful character and a canon lawyer who had previously served Richard Fitzjames in the diocese of Rochester and William Warham as a proctor at the Roman Curia. Alen acted as Wolsey's commissary-general from 1519 onwards, which meant that he had primary responsibility for putting into practice the legate's reforming, centralizing initiatives, not least by conducting legatine visitations. The purpose and activities of the legatine court begs many questions, for it seems to have heard the sort of cases that would otherwise have been sent from diocesan courts to be heard before the archbishop of Canterbury's courts of arches and audience. One area of acute conflict between them concerned testamentary jurisdiction, the proving of wills, which was a source of considerable income. On this issue a compromise was reached whereby the legate and the archbishop shared the work of testamentary administration in a joint-prerogative court and shared the fees as well.

Whatever the challenges of their working relationship, personal relations between Wolsey and Warham had improved by the early 1520s. In 1521, for example, the cardinal stayed in the archbishop's palace at Canterbury when on his way to meet Charles V at Dover. The following year Wolsey acknowledged their shared devotion to Warham's sainted predecessor Thomas Becket by sending him a jewel for the saint's shrine. In 1523, the cardinal invited the convalescing archbishop to spend time at Hampton Court, presumably before it had become too much of a building site once more. By the same token, there were jurisdictional conflicts between the legate and the English diocesan bishops, but it is equally true to say that many of those bishops remained personally loyal to Wolsey as their patron. By the spring of 1523 thirteen out of the twenty-one English and Welsh bishoprics were held either by Wolsey himself or by his clients, and another was held by his former patron Richard Fox, whose continuing admiration for Wolsey as minister and legate we have established.

Aside from the bishops, Wolsey needed the support of the nobility in order to sustain his position at the heart of the king's government. The Stafford duchy of Buckingham died with the third duke in 1521; Buckingham's son Henry Stafford never rose above the barony of Stafford. Though he remained loyal to his father's memory and later argued that the duke's death had been an act of revenge by Wolsey against Buckingham's defence of Queen Katherine in an incident at the Field of the Cloth of Gold, Henry Stafford did not constitute a great power in the land. As we have seen, Buckingham's brother, the earl of Wiltshire, had been a cause of concern to the king and therefore to his minister, but he died without issue in April 1523, at which his earldom became extinct. If the Staffords were a spent force, the Howard dukes of Norfolk were quite the opposite. Wolsey enjoyed a close working relationship with the aged second duke, but the latter took a considerably reduced role in public affairs even before resigning the treasurership in December 1522. Relations between the cardinal and the younger Thomas Howard, were consistently strained. During the second duke's lifetime, Surrey was kept occupied with missions far from court, including those to Ireland and the Scottish Marches, but tensions began to emerge when he inherited the treasurership and found that Wolsey left him little room for action or initiative. This was one nail in the cardinal's coffin but, fixed with one alone, the lid could still have been prized open. It was in the course of 1523, as we shall see, that relations between Wolsey and the duke of Suffolk took a decisive turn for the worse: a second nail.

Henry Algernon Percy, the fifth earl of Northumberland, was another of the magnates over whom Henry urged Wolsey to 'keep good watch' in *c.* 1520, and he never succeeded in freeing himself from suspicion in the eyes of the king and the cardinal, even though Wolsey took care to inform him that he was not suspected of colluding with the late duke of Buckingham. Surrey's presence in the northern Marches, which was very much Percy territory, provided confirmation of that lack of trust. However, in 1523 Wolsey acquired two causes to cultivate relations with the earl. Administration of the bishopric of Durham gave him authority over a diocese that stretched to the border and gave him control of the strategically important castle at Norham, with its commanding views over the Tweed. At the same time Wolsey sought to improve relations with the Percies by employing the fifth earl's heir, also Henry Algernon, as a page in his household. This arrangement would have passed without comment had the young man not fallen in love with the sophisticated, French-educated daughter of Thomas Boleyn. When Anne Boleyn returned to England at the end of 1521 it was after a brief sojourn at the court of Margaret of Austria in Brussels (in 1512–13) and a considerably longer period at the French court, in the households of Queens Mary and Claude. Anne had been back in England only a few weeks when she took part in the Shrovetide 'Chateau vert' pageant hosted by Wolsey at York Place on 4 March 1522. She played the part of Perseverance, while her married sister Mary was cast as Kindness. It was possibly on this occasion that Mary, rather than Anne, caught the king's eye as he assumed the entirely appropriate role of Amorus. Royal favours to Mary's husband, William Carey, suggest that he was first cuckholded around this time. Henry's liaison with Mary may have continued until 1525, but only malicious gossips suggested that her son Henry, born in March 1526, was not fathered by her husband. No such guarantee could be made for Mary's daughter Katherine (later Knollys), who appears to have been born around 1523. While Mary was preoccupied as the king's mistress, Anne received attentions from the younger Henry Algernon Percy, who defied arrangements for his marriage with Mary Talbot, daughter of the fourth earl of Shrewsbury, as well as Anne's with James Butler, by entering into some sort of understanding with her and being set upon matrimony. Thus young Percy also defied the king's will, for Henry had approved the Talbot match. Wolsey put himself *in loco parentis*, tried to talk him out of this 'tangle' with a 'foolish girl' and explained that a youth in his position could not marry without the consent of the father whose title he was set to inherit. Percy employed the Boleyn claim to the earldom of Ormond as proof of Anne's noble status, but Wolsey was not persuaded. The earl made his way down from Northumberland and proved to be of one mind with the cardinal on this matter, hinting that he could easily disinherit his eldest son if he was so disobedient as to marry Anne. Cavendish's report of these various encounters concludes:

> Wherewith Mistress Anne Boleyn was greatly offended, saying, that if it lay in her power, she would work the cardinal as much displeasure; as she did indeed hereafter. And yet was he nothing to blame, for he practised nothing in that matter, but it was the king's only device. And even as my Lord Percy was commanded to avoid her company, even so was she commanded to avoid the court, and sent home again to her father for a season; whereat she smoked: for all this while she knew nothing of the king's intended purpose.[24]

Percy married Mary Talbot early in 1524, suggesting that his liaison with Anne can be dated to some time in 1523. It is thought that matters came to a head in the spring of that year, around the time that Wolsey became bishop of Durham in March but before the parliament met in April. Such chronological niceties are lost in Cavendish's version of events, which attributes the king's determination to break up the relationship to his own designs on Anne, though in 1523 Henry had yet to turn his attention from the elder to the younger sister. It also suits the carefully crafted shape of Cavendish's biography to present Anne as Wolsey's nemesis and to interpret the Percy episode as the source of her – unjustified – determination to seek revenge on him.

In 1522–3 relationships between members of England's ruling elite were conditioned by the need to unite in a common patriotic cause and prepare the nation for the much-anticipated war against France. Wolsey spearheaded a nationwide audit of men and material resources known as the 'general proscription', supplemented by the raising of loans from both laymen and prelates. This was how he put into practice the lessons he had learned from making preparations for war in the previous decade. In terms of sheer scale it was a characteristically ambitious undertaking. In terms of fairness it accorded with the principles he adopted in his courts of law, for the tax assessments were calculated progressively, strictly on the ability to pay. Edward Hall's chronicle tells of how, in June 1522, Henry sought to borrow £20,000 from the citizens of London, but also of the reluctance with which many of them contributed to the king's war chest.[25] The relative wealth of the sees of London, Canterbury and Winchester was reflected in the clerical contributions, with Tunstal donating £333, Warham £1,000 and Fox £2,000. From the combined wealth of York and

Bath and Wells Wolsey himself was able to make the largest clerical contribution, £3,000.[26] By the spring of 1523 the Church had raised over £55,000 and the laity over £200,000 towards the so-called Great Enterprise, but this was insufficient to finance a major campaign and there was now no alternative but to summon parliament in order to raise a subsidy.[27]

The parliament met at London's Blackfriars, close to the king's residence at Bridewell, during the second half of April, was prorogued until 31 July and then sat again until its dissolution on 13 August. It passed few acts, for its sole significant purpose was to approve the subsidy, as was made clear in the opening speeches made by Cuthbert Tunstal in his capacity as master of the rolls and by Wolsey as lord chancellor. The fact that this was Wolsey's only parliament as chancellor can be regarded as a measure of his success as an international peacemaker, for it was the cost of wars which necessitated the calling of parliaments in order to raise extraordinary income for the crown. In such circumstances, it was perfectly conventional for the crown to request a larger sum than that for which it was prepared to settle and Wolsey adopted this approach with his request for a subsidy levied at 4s. in the pound, with a view of raising a total of c. £800,000. So well managed was this parliament that a non-noble and non-clerical member of the king's council, Thomas More, was elected as MP for the City of London and then selected by Henry and Wolsey to act as the Commons' speaker. Such management was perfectly conventional practice in order to facilitate the work of government. In the absence of a Commons diary, later generations of commentators have been much influenced by the account of this parliament included in William Roper's life of his father-in-law, which casts More as a hero, so therefore requires a villain, a role assigned to the heavily guarded figure of Wolsey hectoring the Commons with his demand for a hefty subsidy.[28] This interpretation has appealed to those historians intent on detecting deep-seated antagonism between crown and parliament, rather than the mutually supportive notion of crown-in-parliament, in contrast to which Gwyn concludes that the parliament of 1523 was actually extremely successful. The Commons could not approve the enormous sum requested by the crown, but they finally consented to the raising of a subsidy designed to raise £153,000 over a period of four years.[29]

Tradition dictated that the meeting of parliament was accompanied by that of convocation, the assembly of senior churchmen which assented to clerical taxation. According to the surviving summonses, the convocation of 1523 met in early June. There is no official, impartial record of its business, but a clerical subsidy was duly declared in the names of the provinces of Canterbury and York. Again, this accorded with traditional practice. However, just as appreciation of what transpired in the parliament has been strongly coloured by Roper's account, so appreciation of Wolsey's role in this clerical assembly has been distorted by the accounts of two unsympathetic contemporaries. Hall states straightforwardly: 'In this season the cardinal by his power legatine dissolved the convocation at St Paul's, called by the archbishop of Canterbury, and called him and all the clergy to his convocation in Westminster which was never seen before in England', but enlivened this with a couplet attributed to Skelton:

> Gentle Paul lay down thy sword
> For Peter of Westminster hath shaven thy beard.

Polydore Vergil, on the other hand, is in full vengeful mode as he presents a picture of the cardinal's egomania in action:

> Therefore the prelates and clergy met for some days in Wolsey's 'senate'. There sat Wolsey on a golden chair. At first he began to promise much concerning matters of religion, but then he began to deal with financial questions, on account of which the convocation had been summoned. But the man was 'headlong and erratic in his judgments', and when a little later he learnt that there were legal impediments to prosecuting the business in the province of Canterbury except under Canterbury's authority, he dismissed the prelate to St. Paul's Cathedral and himself returned to his own provincial convocation.[30]

Vergil tells of Bishops Fox and Fisher, together with the vicar of Croydon, Rowland Phillips, daring to stand up to Wolsey over clerical taxation. It is that version which inspired A. F. Pollard's damning statement about Wolsey treating convocation even worse than he treated parliament, but more cautious commentators have cast doubt over Vergil's version of events.[31]

Wolsey's administrative and organizational stills were well employed in preparing England for war against France, but not even he could conjure up resources which simply did not exist in a state a fraction of the size of her intended adversary. The longer Wolsey organized and the longer his fellow-countrymen endeavoured to prepare, the more the international scene changed from what it had been at the time of the cardinal's visits to Calais and Bruges. Events elsewhere did not oblige the English by remaining in suspended animation. The most dramatic action was seen towards the opposite corner of Christendom, where the Knights Hospitaller mounted another heroic defence of Rhodes in 1522. They had been based on the island since 1310 and had fended off a succession of Ottoman assaults from 1480 onwards, but their last defence collapsed on 21 December 1522, after which they retreated to Venetian-held Candia (Crete). News of this defeat reached Rome in February 1523, initiating a fresh papal appeal for united Christian action against the infidel. Princely ears were as selectively deaf as they had been on similar occasions in the past: Francis, one of the more powerful potential crusaders, demanded the restoration of Milan to France as the price of French assistance.

Pope Adrian sought to keep the papacy firmly neutral between France and the Habsburgs, but his resolve was repeatedly tested, whether by Cardinal Francesco Soderini's pro-French treachery or Gallic threats to set up an anti-pope.[32] By July 1523 Adrian was sufficiently exasperated to become party to an anti-French treaty signed by Charles, Venice and the Milan of Francesco II Sforza. Lorenzo Campeggi, the former legate to England, was entrusted with the papal negotiations in Venice. English foreign policy also changed in the course of 1523. Previously, England had been a sluggish ally, a disappointment to Charles and reluctant to put an army in the field against France. England's – that is, Wolsey's – caution was well founded: any invasion of France had to stand a good chance of reaching its objective, whatever that might be, or risk destabilizing the increasingly well-oiled machinery of government at home. What triggered the English *volte-face* was the treachery of the duke of Bourbon, the erstwhile constable of France. Bourbon can be regarded as the French equivalent of the third duke of Buckingham: not only was he of royal descent himself, but his wife, Suzanne, was the daughter of Anne and Pierre de Beaujeu, the daughter and son-in-law of Louis XI. The constable held the Bourbon title by virtue of his wife, but Suzanne died in 1521. King Francis and his mother, Louise, declared that Suzanne's extensive inheritance had reverted to the crown, which drove the constable into rebellion against his king. Bourbon sought aid from the enemies of France and they, in turn, were only too eager to nurture rebellion. In June 1523 William Knight, the English ambassador in the Low Countries, was ordered to visit Bourbon in disguise and offer him terms. Charles and Bourbon had already signed an agreement before Knight reached the duke, but this did not prevent Henry joining the others in a plan to aid Bourbon's rebellion by launching coordinated invasions of France, the English from across the Channel and Charles from Spain.

At the end of August the duke of Suffolk led an English army of 10,000 men across the Channel to Calais, his modest objective being the capture of Boulogne, in advance of the much-anticipated Great Enterprise in 1524.[33] Only when Suffolk had set out on this mission did Wolsey abandon his habitual caution and decide that Boulogne was too modest and potentially too expensive an objective, and that the element of surprise would best be employed by urging Suffolk to head straight for Paris, while Charles and Bourbon wreaked similar damage with their strikes in other regions of France. This time it was Henry's turn to be cautious. Military history was part of the education of princes rather than that of prelates, and military history showed that whereas English invasions of northern France could boast some degree of success, the mountain barriers of the south and east provided very effective defences. Nevertheless, Henry bowed to Wolsey's sudden enthusiasm for a lightning campaign, and Suffolk was ordered to abandon the siege of Boulouge and march on Paris. That was, indeed, the easy part: by October the duke was only fifty miles from the French capital, but where was the emperor and where was Bourbon? The attack from Spain had been contained easily enough, and the constable's nerve had completely failed him. In early September Bourbon could no longer sustain the pressure of rebelling against Francis from within the kingdom and fled in the hope of seeking imperial protection. Meanwhile Wolsey appeared to be waging war in the same manner as he orchestrated peace initiatives: ambitiously. He did so with precious little practical experience of anything beyond its organization, and his last-minute change of plan proved to be disastrous. Henry's caution was vindicated. As the weather turned colder, Suffolk's dispirited soldiers retreated into Flanders, and their commander became fixed in his resolve that this humiliating turn of events was entirely Wolsey's responsibility. Reflecting on the events of 1522–3, Peter Gwyn concluded that the English were deluded if they imagined that Charles ever seriously intended to conquer France; for the imperialists, the treaties of Windsor and Bishop's Waltham were merely temporary expedients, not a blueprint for dismemberment of a major power.[34]

If the cardinal of England meddled rather too much in military matters in the course of 1523, thereby adding the duke of Suffolk to his list of confirmed enemies, Pope Adrian's meddling in secular affairs probably caused him to pay the ultimate price. By allying with the enemies of France in July that year he not only confirmed Francis's initial impressions, but also compromised the ideal of papal neutrality, and that disappointment may well have contributed to his final illness and death, which occurred on 14 September.

A Renaissance pope's relative strength or weakness can be measured in the numbers of cardinals he created, for the power of each individual cardinal was enhanced if the Sacred College was allowed to dwindle in size and diminished in relation to papal power if it was allowed to increase. By that measure alone

Adrian was a weak pope, for he created only one new cardinal, his fellow-countryman Willem van Enckenvoirt, and that just four days before his own death. Meanwhile, four cardinals had died since the previous conclave: Matthäus Schiner, Raffaele Petrucci, Adrien Gouffier and Domenico Grimani, the last of whom is now best remembered as a distinguished cultural patron who bequeathed numerous works of art to the Venetian republic. Cardinals François Guillaume de Castelnau, Louis de Bourbon, and Jean de Guise were all in France at the time of Adrian's death, but Francis was convinced that this conclave would be a less one-sided affair than the previous one and ordered them to make their way to Rome as rapidly as possible. Thus thirty-six cardinals entered the enclosure on 1 October, though voting was delayed by pro-French Italians until the arrival of the Frenchmen, all of whom were conclave novices. This time, all the absentees were active or potential imperialists: Enckevoirt, Lang, Wolsey, Albrecht of Brandenburg, Eberhard von der Mark, and Afonso of Portugal. As before, Giulio de' Medici went into the conclave as the imperial frontrunner and therefore as the candidate most likely to win. He also drew the lot for the 'lucky' cell located beneath Perugino's fresco of Christ giving the keys to St Peter, so appeared to enjoy supra-imperial favour as well.[35] There was considerably less certainty about the identity of his principal rivals. Francis favoured Jean de Lorraine or the more experienced Niccolò Fieschi who, as a Genosese, was intermittently the king's subject and whose family had been represented in the French hierarchy since the later fifteenth century.

The French proffered Fieschi in the first scrutiny, while the imperialists tested the water with Carvajal, but both were well short of the twenty-seven votes required for victory. Indeed, the first ballot was generally regarded as an opportunity to vote for friends or for respected senior members of the College, rather than for the likely victor. Carvajal's seniority was confirmed by his death less than a month after the conclave closed. He was succeeded as dean of the College and as bishop of Ostia and Velletri by Francesco Soderini, but Soderini died in May the following year. Both distinctions were then enjoyed by Cardinal Fieschi, though only for less than a month, for he died on 14 June 1524. Cardinal Giocchi del Monte, another of the cardinal-bishops, acquired twenty-six votes in the next scrutiny, but Giulio refused to accede to him, not only denying him instant victory but also scuppering Giocchi del Monte's chances in subsequent ballots. From 13 October onwards the imperialists made their real intentions plain by voting for Cardinal de' Medici, while their opponents chose Alessandro Farnese in their latest attempt to block Medici's election.

After almost seven weeks of electoral deadlock, what finally broke the anti-imperialists was a fault line in the composition of the Sacred College that went back generations. Franciotto Orsini was one of the Medicean kinsmen with whom Leo had packed the College in 1517. In the context of the Italian Wars, the Roman Orsini dynasty had acquired French sympathies, making Franciotto a pro-French candidate for the papacy. The Colonna were Rome's Ghibellines, so acted as imperialist proxies. Leo had carefully neutralized the imbalance between the Orsini and their Colonna rivals by promoting Pompeo Colonna to the cardinalate on the same occasion as he raised Franciotto Orsini. There had been no Orsini pope since 1280, but the Colonna still cherished the memory of Pope Martin V (d. 1431) and Pompeo was the latest member of the family to harbour papal ambitions, so he went into this conclave among the *papabili*. When faced with prospect of voting for Franciotto to prevent Giulio becoming pope or for Giulio to prevent Franciotto from doing so, Cardinal Colonna instinctively chose the second option. Following his lead, members of his faction also cast their votes in favour of Giulio, who thereby secured the two-thirds' majority and was elected pope on 19 November, taking the name Clement. Colonna did not live long enough to enjoy another attempt at the tiara and sought what consolation he could by dressing in papal white.[36]

Although Adrian's death had been much anticipated among those eager for the tiara, Wolsey and the ambassador John Clerk had not indulged in such politicking. Indeed, news of Adrian's death did not reach Wolsey until 30 September, the day before the cardinals entered the conclave. His instructions to Clerk and Pace were dated 4 October and cannot be regarded as anything more than a formality. These made it clear that Wolsey expected Cardinal de' Medici to be elected and that the Florentine was therefore England's first choice. Only if the frontrunner stalled were the English envoys to advocate their patron as Charles and Henry's candidate, presenting him as a suitable contrast to Adrian's 'rigour and austereness', as a man who had demonstrated his commitment to peace among Christians and who now promised to build on this by launching a crusade against the infidel.[37] This message was not seriously aimed at the electors, but was designed to flatter the English king, whose projected role was to lead his fellow princes in the crusade. As in 1521, any English bid for the papacy was of greater interest to the king than to his cardinal, who had no such ambitions and sought only to remain in royal service. Wolsey's was the more realistic view: there was no serious chance of a second successive non-Italian pope elected *in absentia* being acceptable to the cardinals or to the people of Rome.

4

Heretics and Rebels, 1524–7

Among the most striking passages in Cavendish's life of Wolsey is his detailed enumeration of the cardinal's household. For scene-setting reasons it is placed towards the beginning of the text, though it surely reflects Cavendish's personal experience of the household during the 1520s. He recalls that the three principal officers were a steward, who was either 'a dean or a priest', a treasurer, who was a knight, and a comptroller, who was an esquire.

> Then had he a cofferer, three marshals, two yeomen ushers, two grooms, and an almoner. He had in the hall-kitchen two clerks of the kitchen, a clerk comptroller, a surveyor of the dresser, a clerk of his spicery. Also there in his hall-kitchen he had two master cooks, and twelve other labourers, and children as they called them; a yeoman of his scullery and two other in his silver scullery; two yeomen of his pastry, and two grooms.[1]

The tour then continues through the privy kitchen (where the cardinal's food was prepared apart from that of the main household), larder, scalding-house, scullery, buttery, pantry, ewery, cellar, chaundery, wafery, wardrobe of beds, laundry, bakehouse, wood yard, garner, garden, out through the gateway to the river, the stables and the 'almeserie'. In his chapel, the cardinal

> had there a Dean, who was always a great clerk and a divine; a Sub-dean; a Repeater of the quire; a Gospeller, a Psiteller; and twelve singing Priests: of Scholars, he had first, a Master of the children; twelve singing children; sixteen singing men; with a servant to attend upon the said children. In the Revestry, a yeoman and two grooms: then were there divers retainers of cunning singing men, that came thither at sundry principal feasts.[2]

By way of comparison the Chapel Royal employed thirty singing men and ten children. A reduced version of the full chapel accompanied Wolsey to Calais in 1521 and on his French embassy in 1527, but even the former consisted of a dean, sub-dean, ten chaplains, ten gentlemen lay clerks and ten choristers.[3] Cavendish does not name individual musicians employed by the cardinal, but a number of them can be detected in a miscellany of sources. From at least January 1517 until the cardinal's fall, Richard Pygott was the master of

Wolsey's choristers. By the Christmas season of 1517–18, Pygott had already made such an impact that the king had cause to suspect Wolsey's chapel choir of being superior to that of the Chapel Royal, despite the latter's direction by the more experienced William Cornysh, and accordingly devised a sight-reading competition for both ensembles. Wolsey's choir gave the better performance, but soon lost its star chorister to the king by way of a diplomatic gesture on the cardinal's part.[4] Among the few known compositions by Pygott, the one with the clearest connection to Wolsey is the antiphon *Gaude pastore*, written in praise of the cardinal's patron saint, Thomas Becket. In addition to Pygott, two other composers are known to have enjoyed Wolsey's patronage: John Mason, formerly of Magdalen, who was one of Wolsey's chaplains by 1521, and Avery Burnett, one of his gentleman choristers in 1527.[5] Thus Wolsey nurtured native English talents, while his curial counterparts tapped into a more extensive, supranational network of itinerant musicians, illustrated by Cardinal Ippolito d'Este's employment of the Fleming Adriaan Willaert from 1515.

Moving on from the chapel, Cavendish next introduces his readers to the more public figures of the two crucifers and two pillar-bearers, who carried the symbols of Wolsey's archiepiscopal and legatine authority. Then he moves up the social hierarchy by accounting for the chamberlains, the gentlemen ushers – of whom Cavendish himself was one of twelve, and Thomas Heneage was an earlier example – and the gentlemen waiters. They lead on to the lords who resided in the cardinal's household, with particular attention devoted to the earl of Derby. This was Edward Stanley, whose father, the second earl, had died in 1521. Wolsey thereupon secured his lucrative wardship and is alleged to have plundered the Derby estates, which were concentrated in the north-west of England. Apprenticeship in Wolsey's household was not the exclusive preserve of young noblemen with northern power bases, but it certainly made strategic sense for the cardinal to cultivate them in such a way as to complement his ecclesiastical dominance of the northern province, a point underlined by the presence of Henry Algernon Percy, the future sixth earl of Northumberland, as a page in Wolsey's household in the early 1520s.[6] When all the departments of the household are accounted for, Cavendish concludes that it consisted of about 500 people.[7] A tax assessment of 1524 provides a more precise figure: 429.[8] Only the royal households were more numerous than that of the king's wealthiest subject, though it may be more meaningful to compare Wolsey's establishment with that of his clerical peers. According to information compiled in 1509, the households of twenty-six curial cardinals contained an average of 154 *familiares* each.[9] Curial cardinals distinguished their 'familiars' from the more menial members of their households. Contemporary lists of familiars are headed by the cardinals' closest associates, such as secretaries, treasurers and chaplains, but also include the names of clerics from all quarters of Christendom who required patronage in Rome. The households of curial cardinals were therefore much more heavily clerical than Wolsey's, the composition of which reflected his peculiar combination of secular and ecclesiastical responsibilities. Returning to England, Archbishop Warham's household was only half as large as that of his fellow primate.

By the 1520s, Warham's Otford and Wolsey's Hampton Court were perfectly capable of accommodating vast numbers of people. During that decade, the cardinal turned his attention to enhancing the principal lodgings at his Thames-side palace. For his personal use he created a set of lodgings between Base Court and the long gallery, with views towards the river. For the royal family he built a four-storey stacked lodging, comprising apartments for Princess Mary on the ground floor, for the king on the first floor, and for the queen on the second and third floors. These were all conveniently located near to the cardinal's new, generously proportioned chapel, where Henry, Katherine and Mary could see themselves depicted in the east window.[10] Thus Hampton Court was very much a royal palace well before Wolsey's disgrace, even if the king made highly infrequent use of it in during the cardinal's lifetime. As Simon Thurley has dispelled another misconception by pointing out that, although Henry spent time there in 1525 and permitted Wolsey to use nearby Richmond, which he did for Christmas that year, this did not amount to a straight swap.[11] The cardinal's second phase of building at Hampton Court was completed by 1528. This included the basic shell of the room now known as the Wolsey Closet, although its decorative elements were not assembled until the nineteenth century and none of them actually date from Wolsey's time.

That second phase of building at Hampton Court coincided with the construction of Cardinal College (now Christ Church), though Wolsey's Oxford patronage went back to 1518 and therefore presents a story of continuous development from Richard Fox's foundation of Corpus Christi College the previous year. In the wake of that foundation and with a view to reforming the English Church through the educating of priests along Erasmian lines, the cardinal announced his intention to fund six public lecturers, who would be based at Corpus. Priority was given to Latin and Greek literature through the appointment of John Clement, a former pupil of Lily, as the first lecturer in the humanities. Erasmus hailed Wolsey's achievements in a letter to the cardinal in May 1519:

> The study of the humanities, hitherto somewhat fallen, is rebuilt; the liberal arts, still struggling with the champions of ancient ignorance, are supported by your encouragement, protected by your power, gilded in your reflected glory, and nourished by your magnificence, as you offer princely salaries to attract outstanding scholars to come and teach.[12]

In 1520 Clement was succeeded by another protégé of Lily, Thomas Lupset, who came with the distinctions of having assisted Erasmus in editing the New Testament and of having inherited Colet's library. After Lupset left Oxford for Padua he was succeeded in 1523 by a scholar of even greater distinction, the Valencian Juan Luis Vives. Vives' English contacts began during Wolsey's visit to Bruges in 1521, when he made a point of meeting Thomas More, and continued through the teaching of English students at Louvain, but it was Queen Katherine who invited her fellow countryman to England. So enticing was the prospect of following the example of Erasmus that Vives turned down a chair at Alcalá in order to do so. This litany of distinguished names confirms that Wolsey was fully committed to promoting the humanist cause in the universities and, by extension, to favouring Erasmian reform by means of a highly educated priesthood. Aside from the humanities, it is known that he appointed the schoolmaster Thomas Brinknell as his Oxford lecturer in theology in 1519, but the other proposed lectureships seem to have remained unfilled.

Another frustration was encountered when the cardinal took as authoritarian an approach to the university as he did to the State or the Church and proposed a revision of its statutes. As in the Church this brought him into conflict with Warham, but in this case the latter effectively saw off the threat to his authority. Thereafter, Wolsey's educational enthusiasm was channelled into the more conventional act of founding a college within the university, albeit on a grander scale than those of William of Wykeham, Henry VI and Henry Chichele, William Waynflete, Hugh Oldham, and Richard Fox. Thus Hugh Trevor-Roper describes Wolsey as 'the last of the great medieval prelates', who 'wished to eclipse his predecessors in munificence, as he had already eclipsed them in power, wealth, and ostentation'.[13] The decision to found Cardinal College was made in 1523. Following the example of John Alcock's suppression of St Radegund's and foundation of Jesus College in Cambridge, Wolsey fixed on the Augustinian priory of St Frideswide, adjacent to Corpus, for the site of his college and obtained a papal bull in April 1524 authorizing its suppression, but the Alcock model then had to be extended to include the suppression of more than twenty such houses in various southern and midland counties in order to raise the funds for the building campaign and to create revenues of £2,000 per annum.[14] From July 1524 the conveyancing skills of the London lawyer Thomas Cromwell were employed in the acquisition of the monastic houses and their various manors. Although it was through the former gentleman usher Thomas Heneage that Cromwell entered the cardinal's service, his closest collaborator in this project was John Alen, Wolsey's tough 'enforcer'. Cromwell and Alen's over-zealous approach to this work was a cause of concern, even to the king, who nevertheless went on to employ the former in a similar capacity when it came to the widespread dissolution of monasteries in the 1530s.

With the church of St Frideswide remaining in place as the chapel of Cardinal College and continuing to honour Oxford's patron saint, Wolsey's buildings were erected around a vast cloister between the church and the north-south thoroughfare of St Aldate's.[15] The foundations were dug in just ten days. Erection of the buildings began in January 1525, with Bishop Longland of Lincoln preaching at the laying of the foundation stone, and cost an estimated £22,000 between then and the cardinal's disgrace in 1529. During that time Wolsey employed three master masons, all of whom had worked for him before: Henry Redman at York Place, John Lebons and William Johnson at Hampton Court.[16] The college statutes specify that Cardinal College was to consist of a dean and sub-dean, sixty canons (graduates) and forty petty canons (under-graduates), figures which may be contrasted with those for the more exclusive Corpus, with its president, twenty fellows and twenty scholars.[17] The first dean was John Hygdon, a Magdalen contemporary of Wolsey and president of that college since 1516, who moved to Cardinal College in 1525. Hygdon has been described as an 'overstrict disciplinarian', a characteristic which was presum-ably regarded as a virtue by his patron.[18] Promising young scholars from both universities were invited to join this substantial new foundation. Among those who achieved subsequent distinction, Thomas Cranmer and Matthew Parker were invited to migrate from Cambridge, but neither of them joined what has been called the 'Oxford gravy train'.[19] Wolsey's commitment to the six public lectureships was revived within the collegiate structure, the statutes specifying that the college lecturers were to be in theology, humanity (that is, Latin and Greek), canon law, civil law, philosophy and medicine.[20] The statutes detail the personnel of the college chapel and provide an indication of Wolsey's musical priorities, including polyphony, together with a number of his particular devotions, including that to St William of York. For his choirmaster Wolsey sought nothing less than the best: John Taverner was headhunted by Longland at Tattershall College in the Lincoln diocese. After some negotiation over his terms and conditions, Taverner moved to Oxford before the beginning of the academic year in 1526, and duly obliged his patron, the archbishop of York, with the composition of his antiphon to St William. In other respects, the contents of the statutes were not realized, for they state that numerous schools were to be founded throughout the country, from which pupils would proceed to Cardinal College. This was a characteristically ostentatious development from William Wykeham's foundation of one feeder school for his Oxford college and William Waynflete's creation of two such establishments for Magdalen. In the event, only Cardinal College at Ipswich came into being.

Wolsey's Oxford foundation was intended to be a bastion of religious orthodoxy, the cardinal's most overt response to the threat of heresy. Ironically, this aim was defeated by the importation of some of the brightest young men from Cambridge, who brought with them a certain enthusiasm for 'evangelical' religion. It was also unfortunate that Taverner and some of his choir members were from Lincolnshire, where Longland was particularly suspicious of Lutheran texts entering through small ports such as Boston. From 1526 Cardinal College was unwitting host to a Lutheran cell, but it was not until February 1528 that half a dozen clerical members of the college were arrested on account of their heterodox beliefs. Taverner was among those caught up in the investigation but, in a curious reversal of benefit of clergy, his lay status meant that he was not considered to be as dangerous as the clerics, a view with which Wolsey concurred when he was informed of the proceedings.

Cambridge heterodoxy remained a much greater cause for concern, especially to John Fisher as chancellor and Nicholas West as diocesan. In 1525, for instance, West played a particularly prominent role in the anti-Lutheran cause, not only by insisting that a newly instituted parish priest swear an oath renouncing Lutheranism, but even more publicly by confronting Hugh Latimer as he preached in Great St Mary's. At West's appearance in the church, Latimer is said to have changed his subject and inveighed against the worldliness of prelates. West then challenged Latimer to denounce Luther, which Latimer promptly asserted he could not do because of the ban on Luther's works. Thus provoked, the bishop declared that Latimer smelt 'of the pan', indicating that he would yet fry for his heresy. Thereafter Latimer lost his licences to preach in the diocese and the university, but these decisions were reversed when his appeal was heard in Wolsey's legatine court, thereby contributing to the impression that the cardinal was lenient towards heretics. Such an impression is only created by knowledge of the subsequent history of the Reformation. In the 1520s, these matters were not clear cut, for it was also in 1525 that West licensed the evangelical Thomas Bilney to preach in the Ely diocese, a decision which enabled Bilney to undertake two preaching tours of the region. On 24 December that year attention turned to the Augustinian friar Robert Barnes, who did not expound Lutheran theology from the pulpit of St Edward's church in Cambridge, but did raise the stakes by denouncing clerical abuses and corruption, with particular reference to Wolsey. One anticlerical sermon in a university city was still a far cry from the radical Reformation which was in evidence in Germany by the mid 1520s, but the Peasants' War of 1524–6 provided a model of what could happen when Luther's message of Christian freedom from the shackles of the hierarchical Church was combined with social revolt against the established order. The English authorities could take no chances.

Barnes was arrested on 5 February 1526 and conveyed to London, accompanied by a loyal friar from his community, the future biblical translator Miles Coverdale. Tried in Wolsey's legatine court, he put up so convinced and spirited a defence of his anti-clerical position that Bishop Clerk declared that he would see him fry for it. However, the centrepiece of Foxe's characteristically vivid account is the direct confrontation between Barnes and Wolsey, when the friar challenges the cardinal over his ostentatiously unchristian manner of living and argues that the gold of the two processional crosses habitually carried before him might be sold in order to aid the poor. It was not Wolsey the prelate who replied to this charge, but Wolsey the minister of the crown:

> Whether do you think it more necessary that I should have all this royalty, because I represent the king's majesty's person in all the high courts of this realm, to the terror and keeping down of all rebellious treasons, traitors, all the wicked and corrupt members of this commonwealth; or to be as simple as you would have us?[21]

The Barnes case happened to coincide with a government crackdown on suspected heretics in London. On 26 and 27 January Thomas More led raids on the Hanseatic community resident in the Steelyard. The suspects detained on those occasions appeared before the same legatine tribunal as Barnes, again without having first been dealt with in a diocesan court. The two cases finally came together on 11 February in Wolsey's second set-piece anti-Lutheran event at Paul's

Cross. As in 1521, Lutheran books were burned and Fisher preached a roundly anti-heretical sermon, in which he lavished praise on Wolsey and other heresy-hunting bishops. This time there were also faggot-bearing penitent heretics on display: Barnes and five Hansa merchants. Barnes had preached an Erasmian rather than a Lutheran sermon on Christmas Eve, so his public recantation of heresy was not technically accurate, but it happened in order to satisfy Wolsey's need to show how the authorities would deal with if confronted by any real live English heretics. Thereafter, Barnes was sent first to the Fleet prison and later to his order's London friary. This proved to be an inadequate form of house arrest, for he became a centrally located seller and distributor of the vernacular New Testament translated by the Lutheran sympathizer and self-imposed exile William Tyndale, a translation published in Cologne and Worms in 1525–6 and firmly proscribed by the English government, on whose behalf Wolsey sought Tyndale's extradition from the Low Countries. When Barnes' clandestine book trade came to light he was sent to reside with the Austin friars in Northampton, where his last dealing with the cardinal proved to be the most audacious of them all. In 1528 he faked his own suicide in elaborate detail, leaving a note for Wolsey, a pile of clothes on a river bank, and instructions to the mayor of Northampton urging him to search for his body, upon which a second letter to the cardinal would be found. In reality, he escaped to the continent and found refuge among the Lutherans of Wittenberg.

The manner of Barnes' escape suggests that his social and religious convictions were matched by a healthy sense of humour, squarely in the satirical tradition of Erasmus, but a number of his contemporaries were already moving well beyond the Erasmian template. As the evangelical religious reformers increased in numbers and in confidence, Wolsey became more vulnerable to their coded attacks, in part because of his anti-Lutheran measures, but also because he was effectively a lightning rod for criticism of the royal government. For example, during the Christmas season of 1526–7 the cardinal heard of a masque pro-duced at Gray's Inn by one John Roo, a sergeant-at-law, which alleged that the public weal was being ruled by 'dissipation and negligence . . . . misgovernance and evil order'. In contrast to Skelton's unpublished satires, this appeared to be a semi-public expression of discontent with the government, which Wolsey took so seriously that he had Roo committed to the Fleet. Among the masquers was a young lawyer called Simon Fish, who held sufficiently advanced religious ideas that he fled into self-imposed exile in the Low Countries rather than risk investigation.

The legatine powers under which Wolsey became involved in the Barnes case were granted to him for life on 21 January 1524. Such a move had been strongly resisted by Popes Leo and Adrian, who conceded a series of fixed-term legations, but the second Medici pope had longer experience of English affairs, had expressed approval of the legation for life prior to his papal election and made it a reality within a few weeks of the conclave. Armed with renewed powers, the cardinal-legate fixed his attention on London, where his commissary-general, John Alen, conducted visitations of parish churches and religious houses during the Easter and Trinity terms of 1524. In the spring of that year three of the bishops who were among Wolsey's closest collaborators – Booth of Hereford, Longland of Lincoln and West of Ely – redefined their formal relationships with the legate by entering into 'compositions' with him. In other words, they bought back their episcopal rights in order to avoid future legatine interference in these dioceses. This course of action was duly taken by bishops who were more inclined to be critical of Wolsey, including Nix of Norwich and Sherborn of Chichester.

One distinction that can easily be made between these conscientious pastoral bishops and some of their continental counterparts is that they did not create clerical dynasties and did not treat bishoprics as though they were family property.[22] If anything, legal – and Kentish – dynasticism was more prominent in England in the mid 1520s. Sir John Fyneux, the venerable chief justice of king's bench, was predeceased in 1524 by his son-in-law John Roper, the attorney-general. Roper had already set up his eldest son William in a profitable legal career, so divided his property among all three sons, according to Kentish custom. William challenged his father's will and thus came to the attention of Wolsey a second time, the first having been over his temporary enthusiasm for evangelical Christianity. In ordinary circumstances the will would have been proved in the joint prerogative court from which Wolsey and Warham gained equal fees, but in this instance it seems that William Roper took his dispute with his younger brothers to Wolsey's legatine court. Warham was naturally aggrieved at this apparent undermining of his authority, but Wolsey was now so adept at dealing with the primate's wounded pride that one letter explaining the details of the case appears to have mollified him. That was not the end of the matter, for William was even more zealous in the cause of primogeniture than he had briefly been about Protestantism and finally had the matter settled in his favour by an act of parliament in 1529, by which time his father-in-law More had succeeded Wolsey as lord chancellor.

In view of the fact that the precise activities of Wolsey's legatine court remain difficult to trace, greater scholarly attention has been devoted to his commitment to monastic reform, again undertaken in his legatine capacity. This appears to have increased in the course of the 1520s, at least if measured by the occurrence of his interventions in abbatial elections: at Wigmore in 1518, Newcastle and Taunton in 1523, Barlinch and Chester in 1524, St Augustine's at Bristol, Glastonbury and Milton in 1525, Athelney, Fountains, Pershore and Selby in 1526, Chester again in 1527, Haltemprice, Peterborough and Wilton in 1528, Bruerne, Butley, Rievaulx and Wherwell in 1529.[23] These instances represented but a small proportion of the total number of religious houses, male and female, dotted across the map of England and Wales, but it was enough to lead Pollard to the seriously misleading conclusion that 'any kind of election' was 'abhorrent' to the cardinal.[24] More detailed analysis of Wolsey's abbatial appointments reveals many a story of the legate bringing authority and order to divided and sometimes disorderly communities.[25] He did so by means of agents such as William Benet, an auditor of the legatine court, who was chosen to direct the elections at Taunton, Barlinch and Glastonbury, all of which were in the diocese of Bath and Wells. In 1525 Glastonbury, England's richest monastery, was not disorderly but it did require a successor to Richard Bere, who had been abbot since 1493 and whose death marked the end of an era. The community was indeed divided about how to proceed and positively invited an election by compromise – that is, by an influential outsider – and insisted only that the new abbot should be chosen form among their number. With Bishop Clerk of Bath and Wells being then in Rome, Wolsey was that influential outsider. Glastonbury being a Benedictine house, he turned for advice to the most senior Benedictine of his acquaintance, Abbot Islip of Westminster, who had recently visited Glastonbury and recommended that Richard Whiting fill the vacancy. In this instance, legatine intervention resulted in the appointment of a future martyr, whose death at Glastonbury Tor in 1539 has made him the object of a cult. Wolsey's interventionist dealings with monastic houses, whether or not they were exempt from episcopal jurisdiction, were consistent with those of his fellow bishops, not least Longland who, in 1526, asked Wolsey to send a legatine commissary to conduct a visitation of the disorderly, but exempt, Cistercian house at Thame. When this failed to reform the community's manner of living, Longland secured Wolsey's support for the election of a new abbot. Peter Gwyn has concluded that Wolsey's approach to monastic reform, like his dealings with the nobility, was tactful and calculated not to cause offence.[26]

Much to the annoyance of bishops since the thirteenth century, all the mendicant orders were exempt from episcopal authority. Thus, for example, when Longland was concerned about the inappropriate behaviour of the Dominican prior of King's Langley in 1528, he could remonstrate with him privately but could take no official action against him and had no option but to call upon the legate to authorize a visitation. For the most part, as Gwyn concludes, exercised his legatine authority tactfully, but it was a notable exception to that rule which has attracted most attention. In January 1525 John Alen and Bishop Henry Standish went to Greenwich to conduct a legatine visitation of the Observant Franciscans, only to discover that nineteen of the friars had absconded. The nineteen were therefore considered to be guilty of apostasy and declared excommunicate. Some of them were apprehended when the visitors returned to Greenwich, and a number were detained at various locations in London, including York Place. Others fled to the continent. The Greenwich case was exceptional and noteworthy in at least three respects. First, between 1524 and 1526, the Observants enjoyed a two-year exemption from legatine supervision. Second, Pope Clement wrote to Wolsey in 1524 arguing against the proposed visitation because the friars were needed in the fight against heresy. Third, the choice of Standish, a Conventual Franciscan, as visitor was at least insensitive and at most deliberately provocative.[27] However the blame is apportioned between Wolsey, Alen and Standish for the manner in which the Greenwich visitation was conducted, it certainly stoked up clerical resentment against the legate, resentment that received formal expression at his fall but also informal expression in the work of the Franciscan William Roy. In the course of 1525 Roy made his way from Greenwich to Cologne, where he assisted Tyndale with his vernacular translation of the New Testament. Tyndale and Roy then fled up the Rhine to the Lutheran city of Worms, where the 'bare text' was printed in 1526. The timing suggests that Roy's flight to join the English reformers on the continent was directly provoked by the legatine visitation of Greenwich.

While interventionist pastors like Bishop Longland lectured religious communities on how they failed to live up to the standards of their pious predecessors, the consequences of one particular worldly desire continued to haunt Wolsey throughout the mid 1520s, as provision had to be made for his son Thomas and daughter Dorothy. The latter was in her early teens and was placed with the nuns of Shaftesbury. Thomas presented a greater challenge. When the lecturer Thomas Lupset left Oxford for Padua, presumably in 1522, it was as tutor to Wynter, who was then about twelve years old. In Padua their path crossed that of the king's cousin Reginald Pole, who represented the social apex of the English nation at what was effectively the university of Venice. In 1523–4 Wynter seems to have been back at Louvain, to have visited England in 1524–6, and then to have lived a spendthrift existence in Paris for the remainder of his father's life.[28] Uninspiring though the young man's character may have been, Wolsey was bound by social convention to provide for Wynter as best he could. In 1523 he was made archdeacon of York. During his brief English sojourn he also acquired the deanery of Wells, the archdeaconries of Richmond and Suffolk, the chancellorship of Salisbury, the provostship of Beverley, and a host of other benefices, including the rectory of Winwick in Lancashire, a church associated with both the Stanley earls of Derby and with the Leghs, the family into which Wynter's mother had married.

At the same time as Thomas Wynter was showered with benefices, the king was also making provision for his illegitimate son, Henry Fitzroy. On 7 June 1525 the six-year-old boy was elected a knight of the Garter. Eleven days later, as Edward Hall relates, he was brought into his father's presence at Bridewell and created earl of Nottingham. Immediately, he was brought back in again and elevated to the dukedoms of Richmond and Somerset. Richmond recalled Henry Tudor's earldom before the battle of Bosworth and Somerset was the duchy granted to Henry VII's third son, Edmund, who died in 1500. The implication was clear: Fitzroy was the king's heir in all but law. Wolsey also had a use for this new embodiment of royal authority, as warden of the northern Marches and nominal president of a revived council of the north, in which capacities the boy was sent to live in Yorkshire from August 1525 to June 1529. This provided the secular counterpart to the ecclesiastical hierarchy headed by Wolsey as archbishop of York. Indeed, Richmond's chancellor was Brian Hygdon, who was Wolsey's vicar-general from 1514, dean of York from 1516, supervisor of abbatial elections such as that at Fountains in 1526, and brother of Dean John Hygdon of Cardinal College. Another active member of Richmond's council was Thomas Magnus, archdeacon of the East Riding and one of Wolsey's most loyal lieutenants in the north. Thus the absentee archbishop ensured that Yorkshire became a microcosm of his vision for governance throughout the realm: the rule of law was maintained by a viceregal figurehead and a team of able clerical judges and administrators. Far from being revolutionary, this vision and the means to realize it were entirely traditional. If there was a distinction, it lay in the ability of the clerics and their determination to enforce the law on behalf of litigants for whom the London courts were too distant.

The council of the Marches of Wales was designed to offer similar legal provision for the principality and the neighbouring English counties, but there Wolsey enjoyed no position corresponding to his northern archbishopric and was less able to create a cadre of able and reliable lieutenants. The king's flagrant promotion of Henry Fitzroy in the summer of 1525 effectively undermined the position of Princess Mary, and was therefore countered by sending the nine-year-old to head the Ludlow-based council, as the eldest sons of Edward IV and Henry VII had done before her. Although she was not formally invested as princess of Wales, it was tacit recognition of her superiority over the illegitimate Richmond. Among the four Welsh bishops Standish of St Asaph was clearly the most dynamic, and among those English bishops whose dioceses covered the adjacent counties Booth of Hereford's prior experience of the council might have suggested him as a suitable president of the same in its reconstituted form, but Bishop Veysey of Exeter was chosen in preference to either of them. Veysey's principal qualification was that he had been vicar-general of Coventry and Lichfield for a few years either side of 1500, but that was not long enough to ensure command of the Wales and its Marches, the relative lawlessness of which was little tamed during Wolsey's lifetime.

Completely untamed was Ireland, where the hostility between Ormond, the lord deputy, Kildare and their followers paralysed any attempt to impose order. Wolsey accused Inge, the lord chancellor, of colluding with Kildare in order to prevent Ormond exercising authority in the king's name, but any collusion was effectively justified when three English commissioners were sent to Ireland in 1524 to restore order by composing the differences between the feuding earls and recommended that Kildare be restored as lord deputy. Butler was promptly ousted. Kildare proved to be a stronger deputy, but his strength was as controversial as Butler's weakness. In 1525, for example, he gained particular notoriety by ordering the crucifixion of the archdeacon of Leighlin, whose own contribution to the general state of lawlessness was that he had murdered his bishop. The next phase of the Geraldine-Butler feud focused on Ormond's accusation that Kildare was an accomplice of his kinsman James Fitzgerald, who was in league with the French. Both earls were summoned to England: Kildare lost the deputyship for the third time, being replaced by Richard Nugent, who was given the title of lord justice. Again Wolsey made a distinction between the rival earls when he interceded to ensure that Butler was exonerated.

English policy towards Scotland continued to favour the anglophile minority among the Scottish nobility, in the hope of breaking the kingdom's links with

France. After the aborted invasions of England in 1522 and 1523, the duke of
Albany made what turned out to be his final retreat from the northern kingdom,
thereby creating a power vacuum, which the redoubtable Queen Margaret filled
by declaring an end to the regency and having the twelve-year-old James V
crowned in July 1524. The following autumn Henry and Wolsey sought to
capitalize on this opportunity by sending two carefully chosen emissaries to
Edinburgh: Thomas Magnus was trusted by Margaret and had long experience
of Anglo-Scottish diplomacy, and Roger Radcliffe was a gentleman of Henry's
privy chamber who could assure the young king of his uncle's interest and
support. They were empowered to propose an alliance incorporating a marriage
between James and his first cousin Mary, and to reconcile Margaret with her
estranged second husband, the earl of Angus, who had found a congenial refuge
at the English court. The first proposal floundered in the Scottish parliament,
which was determined to retain the French alliance, and the second encountered
even fiercer resistance from a queen determined to have her marriage annulled
so that she could marry her latest paramour. The weakness of Margaret's position was underlined when Angus returned to Scotland early in 1525 and became
a leading figure in what was still a regency government. At that point Francis
reminded his allies of the terms of the treaty of Rouen and offered his daughter
Madeleine as James's consort. Although they were finally married in 1537 and
the sixteen-year-old Madeleine spent the last few weeks of her life in Scotland,
nothing came of the notion in 1525 because Francis was spectacularly defeated
in battle at Pavia on 24 February and spent the following year languishing in
Spain. During this humiliating imprisonment, an Anglo-Scottish peace was
signed, concluded on the English side by the earl of Westmorland, together with
Wolsey's trusted northern agents, Brian Hygdon and Thomas Magnus.

Elsewhere, John Clerk's third stint as English orator at the Roman Curia
lasted from 1523 to 1525 and featured the final securing of legatine powers
for life. Until June 1524 Clerk was assisted by Thomas Hannibal, who then
returned to England and his new responsibilities as master of the rolls, bringing with him the papal bulls relating to the foundation of Cardinal College.
The much anticipated death of Bishop Edmund Audley of Salisbury finally
occurred on 23 August that year, providing Clerk with what proved to be his
last opportunity to steer an appointment to an English or Welsh bishopric
through the consistorial process. After waiting for more than half a decade,
Cardinal Campeggi received the administration of the see on 2 December.
At that point, this redoubtable papal trouble-shooter was in the middle of a

twenty-one month legation to the German lands, Bohemia, Hungary, Poland and Scandinavia, the essential purpose of which was to stem the spread of Lutheranism. Campeggi had succeeded Giulio de' Medici as cardinal protector of England and Ireland, so it was perhaps fortunate for Wolsey and Clerk that his lengthy absence from Rome happened to coincide with a lull in one of the staples of a protector's activity.[29] In contrast to the regular episcopal turnover that had occurred throughout Wolsey's career to date, there were no further English or Welsh vacancies until the death of Richard Fox in 1528, though a handful of Irish vacancies were filled in the meantime, mostly with native Irish prelates.

Although he was elected as an imperialist in November 1523, Pope Clement soon learned the same lessons as his predecessors about the need to balance imperial and French interests in Italy, the nature of which was succinctly expressed by Charles when he declared, 'My cousin Francis and I are in complete accord: he wants Milan and so do I.' In the spring of 1524 Francis was frustrated in that cause when his under-resourced and demoralized army retreated over the Alps, leaving Charles and his lieutenants without serious rivals in the peninsula.[30] The duke of Bourbon had found military employment in the imperial cause and, on 25 May, another anti-French treaty was signed between Charles and Henry, this time with a view to supporting Bourbon's invasion of France from the southeast, ousting Francis and installing Henry of England on the throne of St Louis. Bourbon's campaign fared well in the rural areas of Provence, but in September he encountered such fierce resistance from the defenders of Marseille that he was forced into retreat back into Italy. In contrast to the previous campaigning season, this time there was no genuine attempt at a coordinated attack on the kingdom of France and it was Bourbon's turn to despair of his allies. England's carefully harvested resources had been expended on Suffolk's failed expedition and Wolsey certainly had cause to repent his experiment with an aggressive foreign policy. Nor was Charles able to offer the sort of financial support that came England's way whenever she happened to be allied with France. Richard Pace was the English agent accompanying Bourbon. In his opinion, the ex-constable's attack failed because Wolsey had not sent sufficient men and equipment. He speculated that the cardinal was actually in league with Francis and determined to scupper the expedition by some means or other. By September, therefore, Francis was sufficiently confident of his success against Bourbon in the south that he contemplated destabilizing the English by sending Richard de la Pole, that thorniest of white roses, on another insular expedition, this time possibly to Ireland. In the event, that notion was overtaken by the French king's highly ambitious plans for a new intervention in Italy. This time Francis was so determined to succeed south of the Alps that there was no insular sideshow and the duke the Albany was sent not to Scotland, but to Naples, with a view to drawing the viceroy, Charles de Lannoy, and his troops away from Lombardy. The king himself concentrated on besieging the former Sforza power base of Pavia, which the imperialists chose to defend in preference to Milan itself. The stand-off at Pavia continued throughout the winter.

On 5 January 1525, little more than thirteen months after his election, Clement sought to counter Habsburg dominance in Italy by entering into an anti-imperial league with Francis and the Venetians, thereby placing papal and Florentine resources at the disposal of the French. Charles interpreted this as treachery by his former ally and resolved to exact revenge on the pontiff. While Clement was driven into a French alliance as a matter of immediate necessity, Habsburg suspicion rightly extended to the English chancellor, whose disillusionment with the Anglo-imperial alliance was quite distinct from the power struggle in Italy but nevertheless prompted him to inch ever so subtly back towards the French. During the night of 23–4 February imperial forces, led by the duke of Bourbon and the marquis of Pescara, broke into the walled park north of Pavia where the French army was encamped. The French were not taken entirely by surprise, but their reliance on armoured cavalry proved to be their undoing, as the concealed imperialist infantry, armed with arquebuses, were able to pick off French knights in their glinting armour. Francis fought as bravely as chivalric culture required but, at some point before midday on 24 February, accepted defeat and surrendered to the viceroy. Although this outcome marked the end of Sforza ambitions to regain control of Milan, the battle continued by proxy when pro-French Orsini and pro-imperial Colonna supporters took to the streets of Rome, and Clement had to face the consequences of having backed the loser.

A fortnight after the battle, news of the decisive French defeat reached Madrid and London, but what Charles and Henry could not yet know was each other's immediate reactions to this devastating event. Charles had the relief that comes with victory, but also the knowledge that his victory was rather too complete to offer the basis for a lasting settlement. Henry's initial reaction was unfeigned delight at the death of Richard de la Pole, one of the French commanders, with whom the last lingering Yorkist claim to the English throne also expired, but Pavia suddenly opened up the tantalizing possibility that France was now his for the taking. Wolsey had long experience of adapting to changing circumstances, and overcame his recent disillusionment with the imperial alliance to the extent of celebrating Mass in St Paul's Cathedral to mark the defeat and capture of Francis, the man regarded by many of his compatriots as England's natural enemy. Also present were the papal nuncio and the imperial, Scottish, Venetian, Milanese and Florentine ambassadors, only one of whom, the imperialist de Praet, actually represented an overtly anti-French power. Indeed, so fragile was the anti-French alliance that Charles wrote to de Praet on 26 March, a fortnight after the Mass, speculating about a suitable punishment for Wolsey, whose enthusiasm for the imperialists was known to have waned. The cardinal had made his reputation by commanding the minutiae of diplomacy between the three larger powers of north-west Europe, but the overwhelmingly imbalanced consequences of Pavia created a situation the like of which he had not previously experienced. Should the English seek to correct that imbalance or did Pavia really give them the opportunity to make good their claim to the French throne? Without taking time to sound out opinion at the imperial court, the king and his councillors opted for yet another invasion of northern France and then, on 26 March, commissioned Bishop Tunstal and Sir Richard Wingfield to inform Charles of this development. This was a severe miscalculation, for the dismemberment of France was simply not on the imperial agenda.

More immediately, the invasion plan was scuppered by serious opposition at home, for it could only take place at short notice through the raising of non-parliamentary taxation. On 21 March commissioners were sent out to collect this so-called 'Amicable Grant'. This new policy was adopted with too much haste and too little thought: the levy was set at too high a rate; it followed too soon on the parliamentary subsidy of 1523; there was no guarantee that it would yield results in France.[31] Crucial to the smooth running of Wolsey's earlier years in office was the peace policy which avoided the need for extraordinary taxation, parliamentary or otherwise. Then came the Great Enterprise and the parliamentary subsidy, but there was absolutely nothing to show for so much national effort. The initial signs of popular discontent with the Amicable Grant were apparent in Kent in the first week of April and spread to East Anglia during the following month. This was a region used to flexing its economic muscles and had recently been targeted by Richard de la Pole as the area most likely to support his attempt to overthrow the Tudor monarchy. At the height of the rebellion ten thousand people gathered in Lavenham to protest against the levy and had to be dispersed by the dukes of Norfolk and Suffolk. On 14 May the government finally admitted defeat: the commissioners were withdrawn; there was to be no invasion of France that year. This was not only the first significant regional rebellion of Henry's reign; it was the first of the Tudor period to occur so close to London. The king was naturally troubled by so extensive a reaction against the policy which he had advocated as the means of realizing his dream of wearing the French crown, but he sought to defend himself in the eyes of his subjects by blaming his chancellor for such a serious error of political judgement. It was a dishonourable but not an unreasonable course to take, for the rebels had no hesitation in recognizing Wolsey as the source of their woes. As we have seen, Wolsey had ample experience of acting as the lightning conductor for criticism of government policy, but when the king himself found it expedient to side with those critics it left the cardinal looking much more vulnerable than usual. In order to minimize the impact on the government as a whole, he accepted the blame for the contentious policy. It was a noble gesture, but one that could not conceal a fundamental miscalculation about the ability and willingness of the king's subjects to pay for another foreign policy adventure so soon after the damp squib that was the Great Enterprise. The episode was effectively concluded on 30 May with the king's formal pardon of his rebellious East Anglian subjects, but this avoidable crisis was a reversal which left Wolsey's reputation permanently tarnished.

The English government was already repenting its hasty invasion plan when Tunstal and Wingfield arrived in Toledo to propose that very scheme to Charles. Many a Renaissance ambassador feigned illness to avoid conveying unwelcome news, but these English envoys were at least spared further diplomatic pain by falling genuinely ill with dysentery. After a few weeks, Wingfield died and was buried in the church of San Juan de los Reyes. King Francis did not arrive on Spanish soil until 19 June and did not reach Madrid until August, where his honourable confinement lasted for the next six months.

The battle of Pavia has been likened to that of Agincourt 110 years earlier for the scale of the French defeat, but the greatest difference lay in the aftermath of the two battles, for the kingdom was effectively dismembered after Agincourt but, far from being an easy target for English opportunism, after Pavia it remained intact and well governed by the regent Louise of Savoy. Her government took a particularly strong line with the ecclesiastical reformers associated with Bishop Guillaume Briçonnet of Meaux, men who had previously enjoyed the protection of both Francis and his sister Marguerite. By way of illustration, it was at this point that the distinguished scholar Jacques Lefèvre d'Étaples,

. Magdalen College Tower. In contrast to his later career as a prolific builder – at Hampton Court and York Place, the More and Tyttenhanger, Ipswich and Oxford, Southwell and Cawood – few material remains can be associated with Thomas Wolsey's early life. Arguably the most significant source of inspiration for those various projects was the building of Magdalen College, Oxford, for William Waynflete, Wolsey's indirect predecessor as bishop of Winchester and lord chancellor. During Wolsey's ascendancy Magdalen men were promoted to numerous positions in government service and in the English ecclesiastical hierarchy, and provided the cornerstone of his patronage of the university, not least the foundation of Cardinal College. Before his own career took off, Wolsey served his college as bursar and as master of its school. There is, however, no means of verifying the popular assertion that the tower – seen here – provided an early indication of Wolsey's later architectural extravagance.

2. Henry VIII, Charles V and Leo X, and Wolsey. In theory, if not always in practice, the pope and the emperor exercised joint headship of Christendom. Between the imperial election of June 1519 and the papal interregnum of December 1521, the pope was Leo X, head of the Florentine Medici family, and the emperor was Charles V, the young head of the house of Habsburg. Much to Leo's frustration, the Italian peninsula seemed to count as little more than an attractive battlefield on which the various secular powers played out their rivalries, while the political initiative came to settle in that corner of north west Europe, where the territorial interests of the emperor and the kings of France and England converged. Thus it was that Francis and Henry met at the Field of the Cloth of Gold in June 1520, and Wolsey led lengthy negotiations at Calais and Bruges in the second half of 1521. Many of the leading figures of the period may be seen in this fanciful image, which includes proof that Wolsey has not always been depicted as a man of ample proportions.

3. Parliament Roll of Arms. In the parliament of 1515 the clergy were headed by Archbishop William Warham of Canterbury, the newly promoted Archbishop Thomas Wolsey of York, Bishop Richard Fox of Winchester, Bishop Thomas Ruthall of Durham and Bishop Richard Fitzjames of London. The arms of the first four may be seen on this portion of the Parliament Roll, Warham's clearly distinguished by the pallium, symbolic of his primatial dignity. Wolsey's arms contain numerous emblems, including two choughs, the symbol of Warham's martyred predecessor and Wolsey's patron saint, Thomas Becket.

4. Henry VIII letter. The undated letter in which Henry VIII, addressing 'Myne awne good Cardinall', instructs Wolsey to 'make good wache on the duke off Suffolke, on the duke off Bukyngam, on my lord off Northe Omberland, on my lord off Darby, on my lord of Wylshere and on others whyche yow thynke suspecte'. Concluding with the assurance that it was 'Wryttyen with the hand off your lovyng master. Henry R', it demonstrates the close working relationship between the king and his chancellor.

Left: 5. Pope Clement VII – portrait by Sebastiano del Piombo. According to his fellow Florentine Francesco Vettori, Pope Clement VII – seen here in a portrait by Sebastiano del Piombo – 'endured a great labour to become, from a great and respected cardinal, a small and little-esteemed pope'. Recent scholarly rehabilitation has effectively reversed this assessment, emphasising his refusal to comply with his captors' demands after the sack of Rome in 1527. He resisted Wolsey's proposal for an alternative 'papacy' in Avignon, thereby scuppering the English cardinal's attempt to secure the annulment of Henry VIII's marriage.

Top right: 6. Herbert Beerbohm Tree as Wolsey. Since the early seventeenth century the Wolsey of history has been somewhat obscured by the Wolsey of literature, which reached the stage in Shakespeare and Fletcher's *King Henry VIII*. Here the lordly prelate is played by Herbert Beerbohm Tree.

Bottom right: 7. Christ Church portrait of Wolsey. Sampson Strong's 'portrait' of Wolsey, which hangs in the hall of Christ Church College, Oxford, dates from c. 1600 and captures the appearance of the cardinal's college when the chapel had already become a cathedral church but before Wren created the iconic Tom Tower.

whose French translation of the New Testament predated Tyndale's English translation, was forced into exile in the free imperial city of Strassburg. The regent was no less forceful and effective in her diplomatic initiatives, the object of which was to secure the release of her son. To this end she sent an embassy to Spain in April 1525. Charles and Gattinara made exorbitant demands and were particularly keen to gain possession of the duchy of Burgundy, but the French delegation was under instruction to permit no territorial losses in any of the kingdom's border regions. In a parallel move, Louise set about a considerably easer task, that of breaking the already fragile Anglo-imperial alliance, to which end Jean Brinon and the Genoese friar Giovan Gioacchino da Passano were sent to England. Having been rebuffed by Charles, the English had good cause to be highly receptive to such overtures, not least because they feared isolation in the event of the Franco-imperial negotiations resulting in a peace settlement. Moreover, what Louise initiated was precisely the sort of diplomatic engagement in which Wolsey excelled.

On 30 August a new comprehensive Anglo-French agreement was signed at Wolsey's Hertfordshire manor of the More. First, the two nations agreed to make peace and to enter into a defensive alliance. This created the context for what mattered most to the French: English support for the release of Francis from his Spanish captivity. What mattered most to the English was the promise of a substantial French pension for Henry, to be paid in annual instalments of 100,000 écus, up to a final limit of two million écus. As was conventional in such arrangements, a number of the king's servants were also recipients of French largesse. Other treaties signed on this occasion dealt with various outstanding issues, including the settlement of maritime disputes and the terms for peace along England's border with Scotland.[32] There were certainly risks involved in these agreements, but they could be contained as long as peace with France did not mean war with the Habsburgs and as long as English trade with the Low Countries was untroubled. Thereafter a new diplomatic chapter opened. Sir William Fitzwilliam and John Taylor were sent as English ambassadors to France in October, and heard the bishop of Besançon laud Wolsey as the 'legate of God' who counselled peace.

Wolsey spent the Christmas of 1525 at Richmond, while Henry stayed at Eltham. It had been a bruising year and one that witnessed significant changes in the relationship between the king and his minister. In the wake of popular hostility towards the Amicable Grant and elite discomfort with the new Anglo-French alliance, Henry began to take a more mature approach to the responsibilities of kingship and to cast about for other councillors to advise him. The threat to Wolsey's dominance was clear and he responded in characteristically grand style: if Henry wanted domestic reform, he could have it in abundance, with attention to detail such as only his most experienced councillor could supply. The result was the Eltham ordinances, which were promulgated in January 1526. These measures revised the household ordinances of Edward IV's reign and were more far reaching than the reforms of 1519, which had seen the temporary expulsion of the 'minions' from Henry's privy chamber. They set out thoroughgoing reform of the king's household in the name of financial retrenchment. As the preamble explained, such reform was long overdue:

> the king's highness soon after his first assumption of his crown and dignity royal was enforced and brought unto the wars, wherein his grace ... hath much travailed and been occupied in such wise as many of the officers and ministers of his household being employed and appointed to the making of provisions and other things concerning the wars, the accustomed good order of his said household hath been greatly hindered and in manner subverted.[33]

The text then moves on to various types of expenditure incurred by the court, including food ('bouche of court') and salaries, and details the persons entitled to receive lodging there. Hundreds of royal servants were to be redeployed, and members of the royal household obliged to undertake the duties for which the king paid them, instead of delegating them to others.[34] Even the mealtimes are stipulated. Wolsey's hand is quite literally all over this document, for it contains numerous corrections made by the cardinal himself. While the ordinances introduced a new source of friction in relations between the cardinal and the courtiers over whom he otherwise exercised little or no control, they nevertheless made sound financial sense in the wake of the Amicable Grant. Additionally, they provide evidence of Wolsey's concern about the king's financial circumstances and his eye for detail in matters far removed from the glamour and sophistication of international diplomacy.

Embedded in the ordinances is a list of the king's councillors, men whose duty is defined as hearing the complaints of the king's subjects. Some are given by name, others by the office they held in the king's household. Of the seven clerics listed, four were at least of episcopal rank: Wolsey himself as chancellor, Tunstal of London, who had been keeper of the privy seal since 1523, Clerk of Bath and Wells, and Longland of Lincoln. By any reckoning, these were the bishops closest to and most trusted by the cardinal. The other clerics were the king's secretary Richard Pace, the dean of the chapel royal Richard Sampson, and the king's almoner Richard Wolman. Sampson had recently returned from three years in Spain as ambassador to the imperial court and Wolman had served as Wolsey's vicar-general at Bath and Wells. Pace was the odd man out, for his relationship with the cardinal was characterized by mutual suspicion: Wolsey had ensured that Pace, in spite of his secretarial duties, was long preoccupied by foreign embassies, while Pace had become convinced that his mission to the duke of Bourbon was being actively undermined by Wolsey's pro-French interests. Pace returned to England in November 1525, but was replaced as secretary the following August, when William Knight assumed that role. Pace had a history of mental and physical illness, but it nevertheless suited the cardinal's detractors to maintain that Wolsey had driven a distinguished man of letters into insanity.

The ordinances also name thirteen laymen, seven of whom were peers. Precedence is given to the dukes of Norfolk and Suffolk. Thomas Howard, earl of Surrey, had succeeded to the former title on 21 May 1524. Suffolk held the office of earl marshal. Next come two marquises, for Thomas Grey, marquis of Dorset, had been joined in 1525 by another royal cousin, Henry Courtenay, the son of Princess Katherine, countess of Devon, who became marquis of Exeter. Courtenay was a noble in Charles Brandon mould, distinguishing himself in feats of arms and as one of the gentlemen of the privy chamber, a position from which Wolsey failed to oust him in 1526. The offices of steward of the household and lord chamberlain were held by the earls of Shrewsbury and Worcester. George Talbot, fourth earl of Shrewsbury, had diplomatic experience and had seen action in France and along the Scottish border, but perhaps most importantly he provided a calmer head and a steadier hand than did a number of the other nobles on the list. Charles Somerset (originally Beaufort), first earl of Worcester, was the illegitimate son of Henry Beaufort, second duke of Somerset, and provided one of the last surviving elements of continuity with the invasion of Henry Tudor in 1485. He was chamberlain from 1509 but did not long survive the promulgation of the Eltham ordinances, for he died in April 1526. Quite distinct from the lord chamberlain was the lord great chamberlain, an office which happened to be in abeyance between 1513 and 1526, on account of the misdemeanours of the fourteenth earl of Oxford. The de Vere earls had been hereditary great chamberlains since 1485, but John de Vere, the fourteenth earl, was a man of numerous personal excesses, who maltreated his wife, mismanaged his estates, and caused his father-in-law, the second duke of Norfolk, to ask Wolsey to intervene in his affairs. In 1526 the title passed to this earl's second cousin, another John de Vere but a man of considerably more sober character. Returning to the noble councillors listed in January 1526, there appears the name of Lord Sandys. The Hampshire gentleman William Sandys was much trusted by both Wolsey and Bishop Fox of Winchester and was consequently created Baron Sandys in 1523 in recognition of his manifold services to the crown.

The non-noble councillors listed in the ordinances were Sir William Fitzwilliam, treasurer of the king's household and future earl of Southampton, who was quite distinct from the Sir William Fitzwilliam who served as Wolsey's treasurer and high chamberlain, Sir Henry Guildford, comptroller of the household, Sir Thomas More, chancellor of the duchy of Lancaster and highly valued as Wolsey's eyes and ears at court, Sir Henry Wyatt, treasurer of the king's chamber and a Tudor partisan since the early 1480s, the vice-chamberlain, and Sir William Kingston, captain of the guard and constable of the Tower, a man of such steadying influence that Wolsey chose him as one of the knights who replaced the privy chamber 'minions' in 1519.

All this was mere window dressing, for nothing changed in reality. As the ordinances state quite openly, some of these councillors, led by Wolsey, had commitments in London during the legal terms, so could not be in daily attendance upon the king, whose court tended be at Greenwich, Windsor or at other locations further from the capital. In the light of this, the text continues, if circumstances permit, the king should be attended by Wolman, Clerk, Pace, More and Sampson. If even that proved impractical, then at least two of them should reside at court. Thus, far from reviving the council as a whole, as Wolsey's critics desired, the ordinances effectively confirmed the dominance of the chancellor and his closest associates. They effectively bought Wolsey time for, in spite of the reversals of 1525, he retained his accustomed dominance and authority in the king's government until the second half of 1527.

While Wolsey effectively outflanked his rivals in Henry's household and council, Francis I held the fate of nations in his hands and did so with nothing less than what his admirer Baldassare Castiglione celebrated as *sprezzatura*. By the terms of the treaty of Madrid, signed on 14 January, he made a series of territorial concessions to Charles in the Low Countries, Burgundy, Lombardy and Naples, and promised to resist the temptation to indulge in any more military adventures in Italy. It was arranged that the king's sons François, the dauphin, and Henri, duke of Orléans, would take their father's place in honourable captivity, and

Francis duly crossed the Bidassoa into French territory on 17 March. This occurred just a week after Charles finally took himself out of the marriage market and into a state of greater financial security by marrying his first cousin, the twenty-two-year-old Infanta Isabella of Portugal. At no point did Francis entertain the slightest intention of ratifying the decidedly one-sided treaty of Madrid and it took him just two months to assemble a new anti-imperial league, which came into being through the treaty signed at Cognac on 22 May. As the heart and soul of this league, Francis sought revenge for the defeat at Pavia and the humiliation of his imprisonment. Clement readily abandoned the ideal of papal neutrality in order to counter the sheer scale of Habsburg power in Italy, and used his influence as head of the house of Medici to commit his fellow Florentines to making significant financial contributions to the league. Among the less powerful signatories was Francesco Sforza, who was motivated by the hope of restoration to the duchy of Milan. The Venetians certainly preferred Sforza to any imperialist alternative, such as the duke of Bourbon, and sought to prevent Charles controlling their western border as he did their northern one. Thus they contributed to the composite army which assembled in Lombardy under the command of the papal kinsman known as Giovanni *dalle bande nere* from the black bands worn by his soldiers in mourning for Leo X. Giovanni distinguished himself in a series of minor skirmishes, but did not have the opportunity to make his mark in any more significant encounter.

As on previous occasions, the English were concerned by the serious imbalance of power proposed by the treaty of Madrid; they feared that Francis had been defeated as decisively at the negotiating table as he had on the battlefield, and took steps to prevent ratification. According to the Venetian ambassador in France, it was the English envoy John Taylor who persuaded Francis not to ratify the treaty.[35] Wolsey and Taylor ensured that Henry was cast as 'protector' of the league of Cognac, a role designed to provide diplomatic flexibility and the opportunity for the king and his minister to emerge once more as an 'honest brokers' but, crucially, it was also one that involved no financial commitment to a military campaign in distant Lombardy, much to the disappointment of the various allies. The Anglo-French alliance deepened in August 1526 when the two parties agreed that neither of them would make a separate peace with the emperor. This was the treaty of Hampton Court, for which the French delegation was led by Giovan Gioacchino da Passano.

It was a measure of Wolsey's commitment to the league and his appreciation of the diplomatic centrality of the French court that Taylor was replaced in the summer of 1526 by the cardinal's close confidant John Clerk. Clerk was something of a linchpin for Wolsey's diplomatic initiatives and served a second term in France in 1528. In the context of this latest alliance, however, it was Anglo-imperial diplomacy that represented the greater challenge. From late 1525 the resident English ambassador to the imperial court in Spain was Edward Lee, a Magdalen man who migrated to Cambridge, but also a safe pair of diplomatic hands and much appreciated by Wolsey without being among his closest associates. Lee soon required assistance and an opportunity to supply this arose late in 1526 when Girolamo Ghinucci arrived in England as papal nuncio, charged with seeking support for a Clementine initiative to negotiate peace between Francis and Charles. From London, Ghinucci headed to the French court, where he was not detained for long, and then to Spain, where he provided Lee with suitable support. In the spring of 1527 they were joined by a diplomatic novice who was presumably recruited as a Cambridge contact of Lee: Thomas Cranmer. Pursuing Charles V across the wide expanses of Castile was certainly an unlikely way to cement the relationship between the next archbishops of Canterbury and York, for such Cranmer and Lee proved to be.

Military commitments may have been well beyond the means of the English king and his minister, but this did not mean that there were no significant military encounters anywhere in Europe during the summer of 1526. By far the most important was the battle of Mohács (29 August), near what is now the border between Hungary and Croatia, where the Ottoman sultan Süleyman scored a stunning victory over the forces of the young Hungarian king Lajos (Ladislas/Louis), who was killed in the encounter. The Ottomans went on to take Buda, the Hungarian capital, while a succession dispute erupted between rival claimants to the crown. Although Lajos left no legitimate offspring, he did leave a young widow, Charles V's youngest sister, the circumstances of whose widowhood contributed to her brother's future activities in the anti-Ottoman cause throughout the Mediterranean region. That season also saw a particularly violent outbreak of factional violence in Rome, where Colonna forces made a surprise attack on the Borgo and on the Vatican itself, with a view to capturing Pope Clement, who fled along the wall linking his palace to the fortress of Castel S. Angelo. Just as this episode was something of a rehearsal for the imperial sack of Rome eight months later, so was the scale of the devastation wreaked by the invaders, who sought spoils in the Vatican and neighbouring palaces. The pope was forced to concede a four-month truce in northern Italy, and suffered a further reverse when Giovanni *dalle bande nere* died at Mantua on 30 November from wounds received a few days earlier.

Throughout the winter of 1526-7 Clement's position looked increasingly desperate, so that even his fellow Florentines talked of cutting loose from the sinking barque of Peter. In January 1527 Bourbon's mainly Spanish army left Milan with a view to putting military pressure on the pope and inducing him to abandon his league with France. A confessional element was introduced into the peninsular power struggle for the first time when the duke's army joined forces with a contingent of predominantly Lutheran landsknechts commanded by Georg von Frundsberg. Bourbon's composite army was shadowed by the forces of the league, among whose leaders was the historian Francesco Guicciardini, though it was Francesco's brother Luigi who wrote a detailed account of this campaign.[36] His story is one of two armies traversing muddy plains, fording rivers and taking minor fortresses. At times there was doubt about their objectives, but the overall direction was southwards and no battle was sought. By this stage in the Italian Wars there had been a distinct shift away from cavalry and towards infantry, especially in the usually victorious imperial armies. This entailed a marked increase in the sheer numbers of men to be paid, but also greater disorder and destruction if no payment was forthcoming. Bourbon encouraged his men with the prospects of booty in Florence, though the Lutheran elements were more enthused by the idea of attacking the papal capital.

Even before Bourbon left Milan, Wolsey sent Sir John Russell and Sir Thomas Wyatt ('the elder' and the poet, son of Sir Henry) as extraordinary ambassadors to Rome, where they liaised with the resident envoy, Gregorio Casali (Sir Gregory Casale), were received by Clement on 8 February and presented the pontiff with a gift of 30,000 ducats from his English ally. It was hardly enough to turn the military tide in Italy. The pope hoped to avert an attack on Rome by negotiating a truce with the viceroy of Naples, Charles de Lannoy. The English envoys vainly sought to prevent Clement agreeing to Lannoy's terms, which included papal acceptance of Bourbon as duke of Milan, and the truce was signed on 15 March, much to the disappointment of Clement's various anti-imperial allies. Two of those allies inched closer to one another when French ambassadors arrived in England that month and set about negotiating what became the treaty of Westminster (30 April), according to the terms of which 'perpetual' peace was declared between the two kingdoms, and Princess Mary would marry either Francis himself or his younger son, the duke of Orléans, depending on whether Charles opted for war or for peace with France. In the event of peace, the French king, whose first wife had died in 1524, would marry one of Charles's sisters. Although Mary remained England's only serious contender in the dynastic marriage market, the spring of 1527 also saw Henry Fitzroy touted as a potential husband for either the pope's niece Caterina de' Medici, on whom the French and Scots had also set their sights, or for the Infanta Maria of Portugal. In addition to the dynastic dimension, a second summit meeting between the English and French monarchs was proposed, to be followed by another universal peace negotiated by Wolsey.

On 28 March Bourbon's astrologers informed him that the omens were now favourable and, in defiance of the recent truce, he ordered a definite southward march through the Romagna. The imperial army had merely to pass near Florence to inspire an anti-Medicean uprising on 26 April, but order in the city was soon restored by forces loyal to the pope. Meanwhile, Rome was gripped by an increasing sense of foreboding. In her account of this period Judith Hook quotes a Sienese prophet who appeared among the faithful outside St Peter's on Holy Thursday (18 April) addressing Clement as 'thou bastard of Sodom', and predicting that 'for thy sins Rome shall be destroyed', and that within fourteen days.[37] The first defensive measure taken by the pope was designed to shore up his position in the Papal States and among the Italian powers: five new cardinals were created on 3 May.[38] As we have seen on previous occasions, most particularly that from which Wolsey himself emerged with a red hat, the creation of cardinals could be a sign of papal weakness, which makes it particularly telling that Clement's first creation did not take place until this moment of crisis. His choice fell on two Florentines, a Genoese, a Mantuan and a Venetian: Benedetto Accolti, archbishop of Ravenna, Niccolò Gaddi, bishop of Fermo, Agostino Spinola, bishop of Perugia, Ercole Gonzaga, bishop of Mantua, and Marino Grimani, patriarch of Aquileia. Gonzaga and Grimani were replacements for their late uncles, Sigismondo Gonzaga and Domenico Grimani. While Venice was now represented in the Sacred College by both Marino Grimani and Francesco Pisani, Venetian secular power was personified in the formidable Andrea Gritti, who was doge from 1523 to 1538, and continued to offer one of the last vestiges of Italian independence from Habsburg rule. Needless to say, Milanese and Neapolitans were conspicuously absent from the list of new ecclesiastical princes.

Practical efforts to defend the eternal city were hampered by Clement's faith in the papal-imperial truce and did not begin until 4 May, the same day as Bourbon's army arrived in the area. The imperial assault began at dawn on 6 May. Bourbon led from the front, but his white garments made him an easy target for the papal gunners in Castel S. Angelo and he was killed in that initial assault. The English ambassadors had left the city with just days to spare, but so narrow was Clement's escape from the Vatican into the nearby fortress that it was said he would have been taken prisoner in his palace had he 'tarried for three creeds more'. Lorenzo Campeggi was among the cardinals who joined the pope in that stronghold, while the staunchest imperialists congregated at the Palazzo Colonna, on the opposite side of the city. For a week after the city's inadequately defended walls were breached, its citizens suffered the most violent sack of any city in the Renaissance period. The Spanish and German attackers numbered some 30,000; their victims were too numerous to be counted. Beside the human tragedy, there was also considerable material damage to churches and houses, libraries and archives, the extent of which can be only partially appreciated by comparing the paucity of fourteenth- or fifteenth-century Roman buildings with those constructed by post-1527 generations. Even the arch-imperialist Cardinal Pompeo Colonna wept when he viewed the devastation and tried to use his influence to negotiate Clement's safe delivery from Castel S. Angelo. That was not obtained for seven months, while the imperial occupation of the broken shell of a city lasted until February 1528.

The shockwaves from the sack of Rome were felt throughout Europe. Most immediately, the government of the Papal States broke down without pontifical leadership. In Florence Medicean government collapsed as early as 17 May and a constitutional revolution took place by the end of the month. Thus began the Last Republic, in which Christ was declared king of Florence, and the spirit of Girolamo Savonarola was revived in sumptuary legislation, book censorship and the suppression of carnival. Northern Italy witnessed a different sort of spiritual revival when Clement's close associate Gian Matteo Giberti retreated to his Veronese diocese after the sack and became so conscientious a diocesan bishop that he was later championed as a model by equally thoroughgoing reformers at the Council of Trent. In the cultural sphere, Rome's loss was Mantua's gain when the architect and painter Giulio Romano obtained Gonzaga patronage; Rome's loss was Venice's gain when the architect and sculptor Jacopo Sansovino endeavoured to create a 'new Rome' in the lagoon for the Gritti-led regime. Beyond Italy, the sack was a public relations disaster for Charles V, whose defenders resorted to the claim that it was nothing less than the wrath of God on the unreformed papacy and argued that it could have been avoided if the pope had heeded the warnings of men like Erasmus. From 21 May, Charles also had the consolation of a legitimate son, the future Philip II of Spain, but nevertheless perpetuated a Neapolitan tradition when, in the wake of the sack, he arranged the betrothal of his four-year-old illegitimate daughter to the papal nephew Alessandro de' Medici.

While the Tiber turned red with blood, Henry hosted festivities at Greenwich to celebrate the new Anglo-French treaty. News of the sack did not reach England until 1 June, and was followed by the realisation that Clement was effectively a prisoner of the imperialists. Wolsey's response was imaginative, decisive and took full advantage of the new Anglo-French alliance, for he proposed that all the cardinals free to do so should meet with him in the papal territory of Avignon to assume the governance of the Church for the duration of the pope's captivity. There was arguably more substance to this quasi-papal ambition than there had been to the alleged conclave bids of 1521 and 1523, but it met with no particular enthusiasm in any other quarter, least of all from Clement, who roundly rejected any further diminution of his authority. What Wolsey certainly required by the summer of 1527 was papal annulment of his king's marriage to the aunt of the emperor-elect, a concession that Clement, the imperial prisoner, was in no position to grant, but which could conceivably have been achieved by a some sort of temporary papal substitute figure with a suspicious resemblance to the cardinal of England.

5

A Great Fall, 1527–9

On 11 March 1527, less than two months before the sack of Rome, Pope Clement VII annulled the marriage of Margaret Tudor, the dowager queen of Scotland, and her second husband, Archibald Douglas, earl of Angus. The technicality on which Margaret finally secured her much desired objective was that her unfaithful husband had been betrothed to his mistress, Lady Jane Stewart of Traquair, and that his pre-contract with her invalidated his marriage with the widowed queen. This freed Margaret to marry her favourite, Henry Stewart, which she did in April 1528. South of the border, King Henry consistently supported his brother-in-law Angus against his sister, who secured the annulment thanks to the intervention of her erstwhile rival the duke of Albany. Albany was uncle by marriage to Caterina de' Medici and consequently enjoyed relative ease of access to the second Medici pontiff.[1] Crucially, the circumstances of Pope Clement's French alliance in 1526–7 made him all the more receptive to Albany's appeals. A case of considerably greater political significance than that of Margaret Tudor was the annulment of Louis XII's marriage with Jeanne de France in 1498, which freed him to marry this predecessor Charles VIII's widow, Anne of Brittany, thereby observing the terms of the late king's will and preventing her duchy reverting to its previously independent state. For the purposes of the dispensation which Louis required from Pope Alexander VI, he claimed that he had been coerced into marriage by Jeanne's father, Louis XI, and that it had never been consummated because of his aversion to her alleged physical deformities. Jeanne put up a dignified defence, expressing her desire to perform all the duties of a wife and a queen, but an ecclesiastical tribunal sitting in France found in the king's favour. Jeanne devoted the six years of her enforced retirement to the foundation of a religious order and received posthumous recognition by means of beatification in the seventeenth century and canonisation in the twentieth.[2] Her posthumous reputation is therefore not unlike that accorded to the uncanonized Katherine of Aragon in English Catholic culture.

When the future Queen Katherine was widowed in April 1502, neither government had any qualms about her perpetuating the Anglo-Spanish alliance by marrying the new heir to the English throne. A papal dispensation would be required because, as sister- and brother-in-law, the prospective bride and groom were well within the prohibited degrees of affinity, but that was not an insuperable barrier. Pope Alexander VI had consistently obliged the Spanish monarchs across a range of ecclesiastical and jurisdictional matters, including the marriage in 1500 of the Infanta Maria to her widowed brother-in-law King Manuel of Portugal. Henry and Katherine were betrothed in June 1503, but Alexander's death in August, followed by that of Pius III in October, meant that Julius II, a pontiff with no obligations to Spain or England and every reason to force the monarchs to cultivate his favour, inherited the matter of the dispensation. He stalled. In 1505 a bull arrived in England which may have been backdated to December 1503. This document allowed for an element of doubt over whether or not Katherine's marriage to Arthur had been consummated, as the young prince had given people to imagine that it had been and as the princess resolutely maintained it had not. Richard Fox recalled in 1527 that Prince Henry declined to marry because he was still under the canonical age, though Fox also maintained that the prince did so under direction from his father, who still had matrimonial ambitions of his own. In 1509 rumours that Henry's conscience was troubled by the prospect of marrying his brother's widow were rapidly scotched when he wedded her less than two months after his accession. According to Fox, the young king was not coerced into this act.

From 1514 onwards there was intermittent talk in diplomatic circles of the marriage foundering on the rock of consanguinity. This was supplemented in the early 1520s by Henry's somewhat superficial appreciation of scriptural scholarship, gained in the course of composing the *Assertio septem sacramentorum*. The king was troubled by Leviticus 18, which prohibits sexual intercourse between various close relatives and is followed in chapter 20 by penalties for those who transgress in such matters, including childlessness for the man who marries his brother's wife (Lev. 20:21). Henry believed that these were not merely rules for the Jewish people, but divine laws binding on Christians, and was convinced that the pope did not have the power to sanction the breaking of such laws. He refused to accept the argument that the injunction might be against a man marrying the wife of his living brother, rather than forming a union with his widowed sister-in-law. Nor was his conscience assuaged by Deuteronomy 25:5, which positively obliged a man to marry his late brother's widow and have children by her. After eighteen years of marriage Henry and Katherine had one daughter, the memory of numerous stillbirths and infant deaths, and no prospect of any more children. Whether or not they were living under the Levitical curse, there were serious implications for the future of the realm. From time to time the king discussed his problem with learned men. In 1525, for example, he raised the matter with Richard Pace, who sought to assuage the royal scruples with reference to a work by the Hebraist Robert Wakefield which argued that Leviticus was cancelled out by Deuteronomy. When Henry's unease about the inability of a papal dispensation to validate his union resurfaced in the spring of 1527, the crucial difference was that he had identified a younger alternative consort in the person of Anne Boleyn, of whom he had been enamoured for more than a year.

The first formal step towards the annulment of the king of England's marriage occurred in early April 1527, when Fox, the venerable and now blind bishop of Winchester, was obliged to testify concerning the nature of Queen Katherine's first marriage, with a view to determining the validity or otherwise of her second. It was no coincidence that the examination of Fox took place during the weeks of negotiations for the treaty of Westminster, for French officials had already raised concerns about the possibility that Princess Mary might not be of legitimate birth.[3] If that were the case, she would hardly be a suitable bride either for Francis or for his second son. Equally, if the marriage was invalid and the princess illegitimate, Henry had even greater need to rid himself of Katherine, contract a valid union and father legitimate heirs. In the context of the Anglo-French diplomatic initiative and the signing of the treaty of Westminster on 30 April, the dilemma was given added piquancy by Katherine's Spanish origins and her kinship with the emperor-elect.

Wolsey's first formal involvement in the case occurred on 17 May, when he and Archbishop Warham sat in a secret tribunal at York Place to determine the validity of the marriage. Like Fox, Warham had been heavily involved in the negotiation of the original Anglo-Spanish match; unlike Fox, he apparently shared the king's doubts about the Julian dispensation. For Wolsey it was not exclusively a legal matter, as he envisaged an opportunity to weave Henry's matter of conscience into England's foreign policy, replacing a Spanish queen by a French one, presumably Princess Renée, who had now reached the eminently marriageable age of sixteen. Though the details of what transpired in the York Place hearing are a matter of conjecture, the fact of its existence was soon known to Katherine and to the imperial ambassador in England, Íñigo López de Mendoza. It is not altogether certain when each of the English and Welsh bishops first became aware of or involved in the debate over the king's 'Great Matter', but some declared a fixed allegiance at an early stage of the proceedings. On Henry's side was his confessor, Longland of Lincoln, who cultivated support for the king's cause among the academic community in Oxford, while Fisher of Rochester, the most respected theologian on the episcopal bench, championed the queen's cause and, with it, that of papal authority. Bishop West of Ely was not only an ally of Fisher in seeking to stem the tide of heresy in Cambridge; he was also one of Katherine's chaplains and acted in her interest. Tunstal of London and Clerk of Bath and Wells were both active in the king's service, but it did not follow that they automatically supported Henry with regard to the annulment. Indeed, much to Henry's disappointment, both of them sided with the queen. What was not apparent in 1527 was how these divisions of opinion on interpretations of scripture and the dispensing power of the pope would subsequently become confused with attitudes towards ecclesiastical reform and acceptance or rejection of evangelical Christianity.

The proceedings at York Place were adjourned on 31 May so that expert legal opinion might be sought, but hardly had that happened than news arrived in England of the sack of Rome and Clement's imprisonment in Castel S. Angelo. Wolsey was fully aware of the implications of this for the annulment, but Henry was undaunted and, on 22 June, informed Katherine in person that they were not legally married and must separate immediately. The queen responded with an assured defence of her marital status, placing particular emphasis on the fact that her first marriage had not been consummated and was therefore no impediment to the second one, regardless of the papal dispensation. No less aware of the wider ramifications of the case, she reinforced her position with a written appeal to her imperial nephew, insisting that he apply pressure on the pope to have Wolsey's legatine powers revoked and the case heard in Rome. Throughout all the diplomatic and legal wrangling that ensued, Charles proved to be a consistent defender of his aunt's honour. Thus the battle lines were drawn. Wolsey was intimately involved from the outset, but his only hope of realizing Henry's objective lay in reviving his influence over the affairs of Christendom to an extent comparable with that of some six or more years earlier. It was a tall order.

As we have seen, Wolsey set about his task in typically ebullient fashion, proposing an assembly of cardinals in Avignon, quasi-papal authority for himself and, incidentally, the resolution of Henry's marital difficulties. This he did in the context of his embassy to France between July and September, a mission designed to cement the treaty of Westminster, with the ground work undertaken by John Clerk, who had been English ambassador in France since the summer of 1526. This expedition features prominently in Cavendish's biography of Wolsey, for the author took evident pride in serving so princely a master, a man who rode out of London 'like a cardinal, very sumptuously, on a mule trapped with crimson velvet upon velvet, and his stirrups of copper and gilt.'[4] At Canterbury he stayed in the prior's lodging at Christ Church and celebrated the translation of his patron saint, Thomas Becket, on 7 July, specifically enjoining the monks to pray for Pope Clement in his desperate plight. Repeating the precaution taken in 1521, Wolsey took the great seal with him as far as Calais, but then left it there in the care of John Taylor, who had replaced Thomas Hannibal as master of the rolls as recently as 27 June, while he ventured into French territory, accompanied by such valued lieutenants as Cuthbert Tunstal and Stephen Gardiner. Feted as *cardinalis pacificus*, Wolsey journeyed southwards through Picardy, stopping at Abbeville, scene of the Tudor-Valois marriage of 1514, and at Picquigny, where an Anglo-French peace had been signed in 1475, in order to rendezvous with Francis at Amiens. First to greet the cardinal were the king's mother, Louise of Savoy, and his sister, Marguerite, who had been queen-consort of Navarre since the previous year. The next day Francis himself came to escort the cardinal of England into Amiens, their accompanying train of French and English gentlemen so numerous that it extended for two miles. Writing decades after the event, Cavendish was still dazzled by the splendour of the occasion, delighting in the rich liveries and the honours paid to his master. Just as the emperor-elect and the English cardinal had shared a prie-dieu in Bruges in 1521, so Francis acknowledged Wolsey's status as Henry's vicegerent by sharing pieces of the same host when they attended Mass in Amiens Cathedral.[5]

In the weeks that followed, Wolsey was much occupied by negotiations with Chancellor Duprat and other French councillors, negotiations that resulted in a treaty signed at Amiens on 18 August. This ratified the peace terms of the recent treaty of Westminster, confirmed the proposed marriage between Mary of England and Henri, duke of Orléans, and made provision for war against Charles, if he displayed no obvious commitment towards peace. If the French had any scruples about Mary's legitimacy, either Wolsey assuaged them or the parties were realistic about the slim chance of such a marriage ever coming to pass. More immediately, Francis and Henry sealed their amity by exchanging chivalric orders, Francis becoming a knight of the Garter and Henry a knight of Saint-Michel, though a projected summit along the lines of the Field of the Cloth of Gold was not realized. In that there was no further Anglo-French conflict until 1544, Wolsey's peace strategy enjoyed a measure of success, though he could hardly have foreseen that this would leave the island nation free to expend its energies on doctrinal disputes and the destruction of its ecclesiastical fabric. Cavendish's position as a gentleman usher meant that he was not privy to the cardinal's diplomatic business, but his account of one particular day during the French mission nevertheless reveals much about Wolsey's immense capacity for work and provides a vignette of how the cardinal balanced his secular responsibilities and spiritual commitments, even to the neglect of his own person.

> The next morning after this conflict he rose early, about four of the clock, sitting down to write letters into England unto the king, commanding one of his chaplains to prepare him to mass, insomuch that his said chaplain stood revested until four of the afternoon; all which season my lord never rose once to . . . , nor yet to eat any meat, but continually wrote letters, with his own hands, having all that time his nightcap and kevercheif on his head. And about the hour of four of the clock, at afternoon, he made an end of writing, commanding one Christopher Gunner, the king's servant, to prepare him without delay to ride empost into England with his letters, whom he dispatched away or ever he drank. And that done, he went to mass, and said his other divine service with his chaplain, as he was accustomed to do; and then went straight into a garden; and after he had walked the space of an hour or more, and said his evensong, he went to dinner and supper all at once; and making a small repast, he went to his bed, to take his rest for that night.[6]

So thoughtfully constructed is Cavendish's *Life* that his account of the splendours and diversions of the French court quite deliberately gives way to intimations of Wolsey's fall from power. Opposition to his mission, and in particular to his presumed desire for two Anglo-French dynastic marriages – between Henry and Renée, as well as between Mary and the duke of Orléans – issued from the French presses in the course of the summer. Irritatingly, items of value were stolen from Wolsey's privy chamber; ominously, a cardinal's hat and a pair of gallows were found engraved in a window during his sojourn at Compiègne.[7]

In 1521 the cardinal had been able to risk a lengthy absence from England because he was at the height of his power and lacked significant rivals for the king's ear and in the king's service. By 1527 his reputation had been weakened by reversals such as the implosion of Great Enterprise and popular opposition to the Amicable Grant, but the key distinction lay in the emergence of Anne

Boleyn as a power at court and, consequently, in the increased prominence of her father, who had been made Viscount Rochford in 1525, and of her maternal uncle, Thomas Howard, duke of Norfolk. The king's brother-in-law, Charles Brandon, duke of Suffolk, also took this opportunity to assert himself. Once Henry had spied a means to satisfy his conscience with regard to Katherine while, simultaneously, creating a fresh opportunity to father a legitimate male heir, the balance of power began to shift against the cardinal and towards the emerging Boleyn faction. An early sign of this rebalancing came in April 1527, when Henry assured the French ambassadors that he wanted to communicate with their king about matters of which Wolsey knew nothing.

The king went further once Wolsey was out of the country, first by poaching Robert Wakefield from the opposition camp and employing him to set out the scholarly argument in favour of the annulment, and then by dispatching his secretary, William Knight, on a mission to Italy to obtain a papal dispensation for a second marriage, regardless of the fact that the first had not been annulled. Although the details of the request were intended to be kept secret from Wolsey, the cardinal already knew of them when Knight met him in Compiègne and Wolsey immediately tried to regain some control over the situation by assuring the king that such a mission would be more appropriate for an old curial hand like the bishop of Worcester, Girolamo Ghinucci. Far from being deflected by the word of his chancellor, by this stage Henry had convinced himself – or had been convinced by those who favoured Anne's cause – that his relationship with Katherine was no marriage in law, that Princess Mary was therefore illegitimate, and that the only thing standing between him and marriage with Anne was a more specific dispensation, in effect one which permitted him to marry the sister of his former mistress. Knight received a second commission and a second draft dispensation to that effect, and the most Wolsey could do by way of damage limitation was to seek to postpone any meeting between Knight and the pope. Thus he told the secretary to stall by heading towards Venice rather than Rome.

It was sage advice, for there was no realistic chance of Knight having an audience with Clement in the confines of Castel S. Angelo, let alone of persuading the pope to grant so audaciously anti-imperial a request. On 5 June Cardinal Pompeo Colonna used his influence as Rome's leading imperialist to broker a deal between Clement and Charles, under the terms of which the pope was obliged to pay a ransom of 400,000 ducats to secure his freedom and that of his fellow captives in the Tiber-side stronghold. Throughout the following six months the pontiff made herculean efforts to raise the money and to pay the ransom in instalments, a feat made all the more challenging by the continued imperial occupation of Rome and Clement's complete lack of control over the Papal States. Among the money raising initiatives which he found most distasteful was the creation of cardinals on 21 November. Four cardinals, all of them from Leo X's mass creation of 1517, died during the months of Clement's confinement: Scaramuccio Trivulzio and Ercole Rangone in August, Ferdinando Ponzetti in September, and in October Francesco Armellini, who was head of the Camera Apostolica, the now emaciated financial arm of the Curia. In numerical terms these losses were compensated twice over by Clement's creation of the eight new cardinals, but their geographical origins alone provide another telling reflection of his need to placate Charles, for six out of the eight were subjects of the emperor-elect: Antonio di Sanseverino, Gianvincenzo Carafa, Andrea Matteo Palmieri and Sigismondo Pappacoda were all Neapolitans, Enrique de Cardona was the Aragonese archbishop of Monreale in Sicily, and Girolamo Grimaldi came from a family of Genoese bankers who had recently made a substantial loan to the cash-strapped pope. The only French cardinal was the chancellor Antoine Duprat, who was valued far too highly by Francis to be spared for papal service. The eighth man was Pirro Gonzaga, bishop of Modena.

On 7 December another new cardinal was created: the Franciscan minister-general Francisco de Quiñones was promoted after he acted as an intermediary between Clement and Charles. However, that day was far more notable as the one on which the pope finally escaped – in disguise – from Castel S. Angelo and fled from Rome under Gonzaga protection, leaving Cardinal Campeggi as his legate in the ruined, desecrated city. The next day Clement arrived in the natural hilltop fortress of Orvieto, where he remained until the following summer, although the imperial occupation of Rome lasted only until February 1528. Clement's escape effectively scotched Wolsey's notions about using the pope's captivity as a cover beneath which to resolve Henry's marital problems with a minimum of fuss. On 20 December the Sacred College was further augmented by the addition of the Venetian patrician Francesco Corner, a secular-minded man who entered the Church after the death of his brother Cardinal Marco. Taken collectively, the fifteen cardinals created by Clement in emergency circumstances between May and December 1527 did nothing to convince the Church's critics that they could hope for reforming initiatives from this pope; in terms of their their wealth and dynasticism they provided a measure of his desperation.

Among the first envoys to appear in Orvieto was William Knight, who received his delayed audience on 23 December. He presented Henry's draft dispensation, but it failed to impress the grand penitentiary, Lorenzo Pucci. The alternative document with which Knight was provided on 1 January gave permission for Henry to marry someone to whom he was as closely related as he was to Anne Boleyn, by virtue of his previous relationship with her sister, but only providing his marriage to Katherine was yet proved to be unlawful.

Meanwhile, Knight's predecessor as Henry's secretary, Richard Pace, had become an early victim of the annulment campaign. As we have seen, Pace's enthusiasm for Wolsey as *quasi alter deus* did not survive his mission to the duke of Bourbon in 1524, but it seems that his fate was sealed when Wolsey returned from France in September 1527 to discover that Pace had been voicing opposition to the cardinal's policies and support for Queen Katherine. As the king's former secretary and an experienced diplomat, Pace was exceptionally well informed and well connected: his criticisms carried the weight of a genuine insider. However, he also had a history of physical and mental illness, which was clearly borne in mind when deciding how to deal with him. There is considerable uncertainty over the details of the case but, on 25 October 1529, immediately after the cardinal's fall, the imperial ambassador Eustace Chapuys reported that Pace had just been freed after two years of imprisonment. For most of that period he appears to have been in the care of Bishop Skeffington of Bangor, but this was not enough to restore him to health and he retired from court in 1530. There is no proof that Wolsey did mistreat this distinguished man of letters, but the case nevertheless illustrates the challenges he faced in trying to solve Henry's marital difficulties. The cardinal had previously been celebrated as a champion of learning by no less a scholar than Erasmus, and yet the annulment campaign effectively made him an enemy of any men of letters who dared to side with Katherine and against Henry. As this case illustrates, it was not only at the diplomatic level that Wolsey was effectively destroyed by the effort of serving his master in this most delicate of tasks.

Thus far we have observed a division between Oxford, where John Longland sought theological and legal support for the annulment, and Cambridge, where Nicholas West and John Fisher were influential in the queen's cause, but the academic division was by no means so clear cut. There was a strong reaction in Oxford against Longland's lobbying, while Wolsey's agent Stephen Gardiner used his influence as master of Trinity Hall to cultivate support for the annulment in Cambridge. Towards the end of 1527 Thomas Cranmer returned to Cambridge after his Spanish embassy and had the potential to act as another academic advocate for the annulment. There was still no indication that Cranmer would yet be swayed by men of an evangelical persuasion, but such men refused to be silenced either in the university or in the surrounding region.

In the first half of 1527 that charismatic fisher of men Thomas Bilney of Trinity Hall set out on a preaching tour of East Anglia, accompanied by one of his converts, Thomas Arthur, a fellow of St John's. Their route took them to London and their message was one of iconoclasm and rejection of the cult of saints. It was a heady brew that caused controversy wherever they went and left a trail of destruction as their converts put the message into practice. The advocates of such disorder did not go unnoticed by the secular authorities; the fact that those advocates were clerics who appeared to be preaching heresy made it a matter for the ecclesiastical authorities. More specifically, as Wolsey argued when the trial of Bilney and Arthur opened at Westminster in late November, it was a matter which ought to be dealt with by the legate.[8] This point was disputed by Bishop Tunstal, in whose diocese much of the preaching and iconoclastic activity had taken place. Some sort of compromise was duly effected, according to which the proceedings resumed on 1 December in the London palace of Bishop Nix of Norwich, with Bilney and Arthur facing a panel composed of Tunstal, Fisher, Longland and West. Prior to the relocation, Wolsey had established all that his legatine responsibilities required him to know: that Bilney was not preaching specifically Lutheran doctrines. Indeed, so idiosyncratic was Bilney's brand of evangelical Christianity that it was conveniently difficult to categorize. It fell to the bishops to question him about his preaching on pilgrimage, images and cults, questioning that resulted in a stand-off between Tunstal and the accused, who sought to employ all his persuasive powers and not a few legal technicalities in the hope of breaking the bishop's tender conscience. On 7 December Bilney and Arthur apparently confessed their heresy, though Thomas More found Bilney's form of words so curious that he doubted the confession was genuine. After performing his penance, Bilney lost his licence to preach and remained in prison until 1529; Arthur's fate is less certain. The Bilney case raised many questions – about the nature of his heresy, the source of the accusations against him, the authority under which he was tried, the conviction or otherwise behind his abduration – but elicited few definite answers. However, the man and his beliefs came into sharper focus in 1531, when the sense of guilt caused by his confession led him to leave Cambridge for Norwich and London, seeking martyrdom by distributing Tyndale's works and preaching the reformed gospel with a vengeance. As a relapsed heretic he duly met that end in the Lollards' Pit outside Norwich on 19 August 1531. Thomas Arthur died of natural causes over a year later.

Wolsey's role in the Bilney case was something of a cameo, thereby contributing to the misleading impression that he was soft on heresy, but it did not quite end with the conflict of episcopal and legatine jurisdiction. The trial of Bilney and Arthur soon became the subject of a Skelton poem, *A Replication against Certain Young Schollars Abjured of Late*,[9] which was commissioned by Wolsey, published by the ever-reliable Pynson, and appears to have been part of a governmental campaign against heresy that also included More's *Dialogue Concerning Heresies* (1529). In the light of Skelton's earlier satires at Wolsey's expense, one cannot help thinking that his tongue was firmly in his cheek when he dedicated the *Replication* to Wolsey as 'honorificatissimo, amplissimo, longeque reverendissimo Christo patri' (the most honourable, most mighty, and by far the most reverend father in Christ). Whatever the precise impact of Skelton's verse, it is true that a number of religious radicals chose to go into exile around this time, suggesting that anti-heretical actions by the legate and the bishops were actually achieving their purpose. As we have seen, Robert Barnes fled to the continent in 1528, and was followed towards the end of the year by his loyal associate Miles Coverdale, who devoted the next few years of his life to building on Tyndale's achievement by translating both the Old and New Testaments into English.

A war of words requires two sides and is best fought with weapons of comparable strength. By the late 1520s Skelton's satirical verse was no longer the novelty it had been when he first aimed his pen at the cardinal, and the art of 'Skeltonics' was ripe for adoption by other writers. In 1528 it was the style adopted by Tyndale's sometime associate William Roy and another former member of the Franciscan house at Greenwich, Jerome Barlow, when they met in Strassburg and pooled their wits in 3,700 lines of anti-clerical verse published under the alternative titles of *Rede me and be not Wrothe* or *The Burial of the Mass*. Their principal targets were Wolsey and Tunstal, who were singled out as the chief persecutors of religious radicals in the London area and as the patrons of Skelton's *Replication* and More's *Dialogue* respectively. Roy took particular delight in knowing that his works were among the publications which Wolsey was most keen to suppress and, from the safely of his exile, he used the poem to taunt the cardinal as the 'English Lucifer' and 'Antichrist's chief member', and to portray him at considerable length as tyrannical in government and lustful by nature. Not content with taunting Wolsey in print, Roy did so in person by returning to England in the winter of 1528–9 and again later in 1529, after which he disappears from the historical record.

Roy's return to England coincided with the publication at Antwerp of a shorter and more overtly popular work in which Wolsey was attacked more obliquely in a general assault on the worldliness of the clergy. This was the *Supplication for the Beggars* by Simon Fish, the evangelical young lawyer who had participated in the Gray's Inn masque and then thought it prudent to retreat to the Low Countries for his own safety. Fish soon returned to London and, in the manner of Bilney and other reformers, devoted himself to the clandestine distribution of banned texts, thereby bringing him to Wolsey's attention. It was around the time of Bilney and Arthur's trial that Fish made his second flight to the continent, where he wrote the *Supplication*. Of the various options on the ecclesiastical menu, the one selected by Fish was the existence of purgatory and the practice of praying for the souls therein, which he interpreted as an income-generating scam devised by grasping clerics. While churchmen got rich, the poor starved and the sick went untreated. According to Fish, only the king could help his people, by defending them from the greed of the Church. Thus Fish cleverly divided the king from his minister, subtly reflecting the divisions which had indeed emerged between them by the beginning of 1529. Thomas More was again employed to counter the accusations made against orthodox religion and the established order, his *Supplication of Souls* appearing in October 1529. Fish died of plague in 1531.

Until the middle of 1529 satirical attacks on Wolsey were not only part of a clear anti-clerical tradition; they were also attacks on the establishment, ecclesiastical and secular. From the moment that the Blackfriars trial collapsed in July 1529 and Wolsey finally lost the king's confidence, the dynamic changed and the socio-political establishment turned on the cardinal. This development has been traced by Greg Walker in his study of the *Enterlude of the Vertuous and Godly Queene Hester*, a dramatic reworking of the scriptural book of Esther, in which emphasis is placed on the villainous figure of the chancellor Aman, who plots against the Jews, misleads the Persian king Asseweras, and is executed by order of the monarch. Walker dates the piece to the second half of 1529, when the Lords' articles were being prepared against Wolsey, and argues that it was intended for a courtly audience.[10] The last notable anti-Wolsey satire to be published in the cardinal's lifetime was William Tyndale's *The Practice of Prelates* (1530), a classic of the traditional anti-clerical genre which, far from appealing to triumphant courtiers dancing on Wolsey's political grave, attacks the 'tricks' of the entire western Church, from the pope downwards, but reserves special condemnation for Wolsey – transparently disguised as 'Wolfsee', the 'shipwecke of all England' – whose worldliness is boundless and whose villainy is deviously concealed by his eloquence:

> . . . utterly appointed to semble and dissemble, to have one thing in the heart and another in the mouth, being thereto as eloquent as subtle, and able to persuade what he lusted to them that were unexpert; . . . this wily wolf, I say, . . . shewed himself pleasant and calm at the first . . . . came unto the king's grace, and waited upon him, and was no man so obsequious and serviceable.[11]

From the time of the diet of Speyer in 1529 those reformers identified thus far as 'evangelicals' began to be known as 'protestants'. The distinction did not matter to Wolsey, to whom they were all 'heretics'. For Tyndale and like-minded writers, whatever their designation, the cardinal's fall from power in 1529 was a fitting reward for his glaring defects of character, his ambition, his covetousness, his self-aggrandizement. For our purposes, such a moralizing explanation cannot suffice, for the cardinal had consistently displayed all those 'defects' throughout his time in government and yet had retained the king's favour, more or less untroubled, for nearly two decades. For an appropriately twenty-first-century explanation of Wolsey's fall, perhaps we should not even be content with the power politics of the 'divorce', but fix instead on the weather. Contemporary annalists noted that rain spoilt the celebrations held to mark the Anglo-French peace of April 1527. Indeed, it rained so heavily in April and May that the English harvest that year was the third worst of the sixteenth century. This resulted in grain shortages which peaked in the spring of 1528. Wolsey rose to the logistical challenge this presented, supervising the distribution of grain, but this development also happened to coincide with other sources of discontent arising from the French alliance.[12]

The connection between rain, harvest failure and disease was felt most acutely in Italy, where approximately one quarter of the Florentine population died of plague in 1527–8. Hard pressed though it was, the Florentine government continued to bank-roll the anti-imperial league of Cognac, for the French alliance was a something of a Florentine default position. In the second half of 1527 this was a reasonable choice, because an army commanded by Lautrec arrived in Lombardy in August on a mission to restore Pope Clement to power in Rome. Lautrec's rapid advance – together with diplomatic pressure from the Venetian Gasparo Contarini and Gregorio Casale for England – inspired Alfonso d'Este, duke of Ferrara, to join the league. Alfonso's reward came in the shape of marriage with Princess Renée in 1528, though he found this to be a mixed blessing when she proved to be a convinced Protestant. Lautrec was ordered to march on Naples and the initiative in Italy lay firmly with Francis. At this rate, the French would soon achieve dominance in the peninsula, would restore the Florentine pope to his rightful position and he, in turn, would express his immense gratitude for English financial support by granting Henry's annulment. Thus Wolsey could speak confidently about the French alliance and the prospects for peace when he made a formal speech in star chamber on the opening day of the Michaelmas term. Thus could he entertain the French ambassadors at Hampton Court in November, confident that the Italian tide had turned in favour of their master.

In the wake of the sack, Rome was no longer the diplomatic hub of Europe. That distinction fell to the peripatetic imperial court in Spain, at which England was represented by Edward Lee, the permanent ambassador, with recent assistance from Girolamo Ghinucci and Thomas Cranmer. The combination of the sack and the realization that King Henry wished to be rid of his Spanish consort made Lee's position challenging enough, but worse was to follow at the beginning of 1528, when he was required to join his French counterpart in declaring war on Charles. Not only did England lack a convincing *casus belli*, being drawn into a potential conflict simply as a consequence of the French alliance, but there was no English enthusiasm for a war against the nearest Habsburg target, the Low Countries, with which a large proportion of England's trade was undertaken. Indeed English merchants were arrested there and in Spain, as were Lee and Ghinucci: English trade and English diplomacy were unravelling together, while an annulment of the royal marriage appeared to be more elusive than ever. Nor was there any unanimity in the king's council, with the duke of Norfolk espousing a pro-Habsburg position in order to provide a deliberate counterweight to Wolsey's vocal advocacy of the cheap but unpopular French alliance, even though that made Norfolk an unintentional ally of Queen Katherine against the interests of his niece, Anne Boleyn.

Any military action would have been entrusted to the duke of Suffolk as earl marshal, but England had not been preparing for war and there was no possibility of even a half-hearted campaign until well into the season. However 'phoney' the war, it was decidedly unpopular with London's mercantile community, adding to their long-term opposition towards Wolsey's fiscal policies, and in the cloth-producing regions of East Anglia and Kent, where it coincided with the full impact of the previous year's harvest failure and sparked considerable unrest in March. The imperial regent Margaret of Austria prepared to defend the Low Countries against an attempted English invasion, supplementing this with a propaganda campaign which sought to divide Englishmen by being aimed principally against Henry's unpopular chief minister. From April onwards Wolsey sought a negotiated settlement with the authorities in the Low Countries, and then attempted to salvage his reputation by throwing his energy into gaining as favourable a deal as possible, ably assisted by Bishop Tunstal, a veteran of diplomacy in that region, and Sir Brian Tuke. A truce was agreed at Hampton Court in June. The 'crisis' itself had lasted for a matter of weeks in the first few months of 1528 and was resolved by the application of the cardinal's accustomed vigour, but he was also its most obvious casualty, a man who no longer dictated the affairs of nations and was now obliged to dance to tunes not of his own composition.

Even as the weakness of the cardinal's position became apparent, his ability to talent spot was confirmed during a mission to Pope Clement by two of his Cambridge protégés, Stephen Gardiner and Edward Fox, both of whom duly survived their patron's fall and proved to be so invaluable to the king that they joined the episcopate in 1531 and 1536 respectively. In 1528 Fox was the cardinal's secretary. He and Gardiner reached Orvieto in March and devoted a number of weeks to intense negotiations with Clement and leading canonists, with a view to obtaining a decretal commission which would give prior papal authorization to any legatine decision made in England on the validity or otherwise of Henry and Katherine's marriage. They served their monarch assiduously and succeeded in breaking the deadlock on the question of the annulment but, by 13 April, all that Clement was prepared to concede was another dispensation for a marriage between the king and the sister of his former mistress, together with a general commission – rather than a decretal commission – which contained too many loopholes to meet the king's requirements. Fox returned to England with the documents, which initially sparked royal elation, until Wolsey spotted their technical limitations. Gardiner remained in Italy and tried to hasten events by visiting Cardinal Campeggi in Rome, for it was generally accepted that any trial in England would be conducted by both Wolsey and Campeggi, thereby reviving their earlier legatine double act. Much to Henry's frustration, Campeggi was incapacitated by gout and had no immediate intention of travelling anywhere.

Disease of one sort of another dictated events across the political canvas in the summer of 1528. In June there was an outbreak of the sweating sickness in London.[13] Wolsey declared a premature end to the legal term, moved to the healthier environment of Hampton Court and then apparently succumbed to the disease himself, for the wording of the letter he wrote to Henry on 5 July suggested that it might be his last communication with the monarch.[14] Anne Boleyn was another victim. Her case provided a useful insight into Henry's priorities, for he was intent on avoiding infection at all cost, travelling from place to place and refusing contact with anyone who had been in contact with the disease. This was also a reminder of why Wolsey remained in office in spite of recent reversals: while Henry fled to Grafton in Northamptonshire, his chancellor carried on the business of government. By August, the French ambassador Jean du Bellay, bishop of Bayonne, was able to report that Wolsey was tired and demoralized by recent events, that he was anticipating an opportunity to retire from royal service and devote himself to spiritual matters, perhaps along the lines established by Archbishop Warham and Bishop Fox.[15]

If the cardinal really was considering retirement, it was in the context of securing his legacy, spiritual, architectural and educational. By the summer of 1528 Cardinal College, Oxford, had been operational for three years, but relatively little progress had been made with regard to Cardinal College, Ipswich. In May 1526 Ghinucci dispatched the papal bull authorizing its foundation and exploratory visits to Ipswich were paid by Thomas Cromwell in November 1527 and the duke of Norfolk in March 1528. Building could only commence when the necessary funds became available from the suppression of a number of small monastic houses. To this end, the pope authorized the closure of a number of East Anglican priories, including the Augustinian house of St Peter and St Paul in Ipswich, together with the transfer of others from the Oxford foundation. The foundation stone was laid on 15 June 1528 by John Holt, Tunstal's suffragan in the London diocese, and local masons were contracted to build with Caen stone imported by the cardinal's cousin, Mr Daundy: Wolsey envisaged a college chapel of the Eton and King's type rising near the banks of the Orwell. Next, Dean John Hygdon led a reform commission charged with amending the statutes of both colleges, and by the end of July Wolsey's almoner William Capon, master of Jesus College, Cambridge, had been appointed as dean of the Ipswich college, which was dedicated to St Mary, with a view to him presiding over a community of twelve priest fellows, eight clerks, eight boy-choristers, a grammar master, an usher, fifty scholars and twelve bedesmen.[16] This spate of activity came ahead of the new academic year, which began on 1 September and saw William Goldwin employed as the grammar master. Hitherto, Wolsey's interest in the teaching of Latin grammar had been confined to his brief experience of schoolmastering and his involvement in the education of Thomas Wynter and Henry Fitzroy. Now he could take the example of John Colet and William Lily at St Paul's School and apply it more widely. First, he chose Lily's *Rudimenta Grammatices* as the grammar to be taught at Ipswich. Then, if an inference may be drawn from the title page of the 1529 reprint, he used his influence to prescribe the use of Lily's book 'for all English schools'. It was certainly characteristic of the cardinal to do nothing by halves. The fledgling institution prospered in the course of its first academic year and building work progressed apace in the summer of 1529. Thereafter there were no further years of prosperity, for the cardinal's Humpty-Dumptyish 'great fall' put the college in jeopardy before the end of 1529.[17] It was dissolved in 1530, the small brick watergate being all that survives on the site, though the school was salvaged and duly became Ipswich School.

It seems that provision was made in 1528 for Wolsey to be buried in the chapel of his college at Ipswich, but no steps were taken towards erecting his tomb there.[18] In the final months of his life he recognized the likelihood that he would be buried in his cathedral church at York, though he never actually set eyes on the building. By then, the option of burial in Cardinal College, Oxford, had effectively been lost. Wolsey inherited an English tradition of episcopal tombs encased in gorgeously decorated chantry chapels, of which that of Richard Fox at Winchester provided a recent example, but in matters architectural the cardinal had already proved himself to be more of a leader than a follower, a patron of Italian craftsmen and godfather to the Classical revival in England. Work on Wolsey's tomb is known to have taken place between 1524 and 1529, and was entrusted to a Tuscan sculptor Benedetto de' Grazzini da Rovezzano, who made his name creating tombs in Florence, including that of the *gonfaloniere di giustizia* Piero Soderini in S. Maria del Carmine. The wall-mounted Soderini tomb is typical of Italian funeral monuments of the period, but the grandest monuments of the day were free-standing, such as those created for Pope Sixtus IV in St Peter's, Rome, or for Henry VII and Elizabeth of York at Westminster Abbey. Indeed, Benedetto was positively instructed to surpass Pietro Torrigiano's work at Westminster, and the inventory of effigy, escutcheons, saints, nine-foot tall pillars, angels, *putti* and assorted other items produced for the Wolsey monument suggest that he was equal to the challenge.[19] Had all those elements been assembled, Wolsey's tomb would indeed have surpassed those of England's kings and ranked among the largest such structures in Christendom. As the surviving components illustrate, it would also have been the most glaringly Classical tomb in England and a complete contrast to Fox's Gothic chantry with its haunting cadaver.

At Wolsey's fall King Henry appropriated parts of the tomb for his own future use, but that project also fell through. Nor did that great enthusiast for Italian culture Charles I succeed in being buried in Wolsey's sarcophagus. It remained empty until 1808, when it was transferred from Windsor to the crypt of St Paul's Cathedral and received the body of Horatio Nelson. The use and re-use of works of art was entirely in the spirit of Renaissance culture, much of which was intended to be temporary in nature.[20] This makes it all the more difficult to assess Wolsey's significance as a cultural patron. His building work at Hampton Court has in some measure been obscured by later accretions; at the More, which the French ambassador Jean du Bellay rated as a finer building than Hampton Court, the evidence of his patronage has disappeared entirely. His collections of plate and tapestries became the things of legends, but such collections were easily broken up.[21] As 'antique' as both those collections, but even more ephemeral, was the cardinal's patronage of drama, which included a performance of Plautus's *Menaechmi* as part of an evening's entertainment for distinguished guests at York Place in January 1527, an occasion on which the king made one of his 'unexpected' but entirely contrived appearances. In terms of a cultural legacy, there is no doubt that Wolsey's focus was firmly set on his Oxford college, whether in terms of building its fabric, recruiting its community of scholars or encouraging the creation of a suitable library, as he did in 1526 when he requested Girolamo Ghinucci to send from Rome suitable books and manuscripts, among which Greek works would be particularly appreciated. Across the cultural spectrum, therefore, Wolsey's patronage was conventionally motivated, but fashionably expressed in the language of the Classical revival; above all, it was entirely in proportion with his public profile.

Half a continent away from a pensive Thomas Wolsey brooding at Hampton Court over his plans for educational and sepulchral commemoration, Marshal Lautrec's army cut a spectacular swathe through the Italian peninsula during the spring and summer of 1528 and reached the city of Naples in July. Progress then ceased when it was decimated by a combination of dysentery, typhus and malaria, Lautrec himself dying in mid August. The war in southern Italy fizzled out in a matter of weeks and the French also abandoned their temporary gains in Liguria. This turn of events confirmed the limitations of Florentine reliance on French protection, but it also confirmed the wisdom of Pope Clement, who could have acceded to Henry's demands over the annulment and in the hope that French arms would protect him from imperial wrath, but instead he wisely prevaricated in order to avoid another lesson as painful as that of the sack of Rome. Clement finally returned to the papal capital in October. Charles, who still held the dauphin and the duke of Orléans as hostages, was left in a position of uncontested strength in the peninsula. Their male kinsmen having brought international relations to such a difficult pass, it fell to Louise of Savoy and her sister-in-law Margaret of Austria to begin the process of seeking out a path towards peace between France and the Habsburg states. It was a process that began before the end of 1528.

The French collapse in Italy occurred while Cardinal Campeggi was *en route* from Rome to England, where he arrived on 9 October. Not only had he been provided with the decretal commission which Wolsey was convinced was the only means of clinching the result so desired by Henry, but also had strict instructions from Clement to make the investigation spin out as long as possible and bring it to no definite conclusion, instructions that were confirmed in subsequent correspondence from Rome. Katherine played her part to that same end by introducing news that a papal brief of 1504 had recently surfaced in Spain, a document which was conveniently out of the reach of her opponents, and by resolutely refusing to follow the example of rejected wives who had entered the religious life. Her defiance succeeded in increasing the ranks of her supporters, both elite and popular. Wolsey's opinion of the queen is difficult to discern, for he was not inclined to let personal views obscure or confuse his official opinion as the king's loyal servant.[22]

On the other hand, according to George Cavendish, relations between Wolsey and Anne Boleyn had been permanently soured by his frustration of her love affair with Henry Algernon Percy in the early 1520s.[23] In reality, the breach occurred later in the decade and was characterized first by the steady rise of the Rochford/Norfolk interest in 1527, and then accentuated by the disputed abbatial election at Wilton the following year. Abbess Cecily Willoughby died on 24 April 1528. In the absence of the bishop of Salisbury, Cardinal Campeggi, the administration of the diocese fell to the vicar-general, Thomas Benet, and, beyond him, to Wolsey as legate. In line with previous legatine interventions, they sought to ensure the election of the best candidate. Benet reported to Wolsey that the prioress, Dame Isabel Jordan, was best suited to lead the community and, conveniently, had the support of the majority of the nuns. However, there was an alternative candidate in the person of the immensely well connected Dame Eleanor Carey, sister of Anne Boleyn's brother-in-law William Carey. It was at the height of his campaign on behalf of Dame Eleanor that William Carey suddenly died, on 22 June. At some point during the summer, Wolsey interviewed the candidates in person and heard from the lips of Dame Eleanor herself the evidence of her unsuitability: she had given birth to two children, fathered by different priests, and had recently had a relationship with yet another man. Wilton was clearly ripe for reform. Writing of the matter, Henry assured Anne: 'I would not for all the world clog your conscience nor mine to make her ruler of a house who is of such ungodly demeanour, nor I trust, you would not that neither for brother nor sister I should so stain mine honour and conscience.'[24] In the hope of placating his beloved, Henry promised that a third candidate would be found, but Wolsey ignored this royal intervention and insisted that Dame Isabel was the person most able to institute reform of the Wiltshire convent. A stand-off ensued until November, when Wolsey's support ensured that Dame Isabel was confirmed as the new abbess, but it cost the cardinal dearly in terms of his relations with the woman he labelled as Henry's 'night crow'.[25]

However impressive Wolsey's record in ensuring that the best candidates became heads of monastic houses, he still had an obvious blind spot when it came to the secular clergy: Thomas Wynter, the teenager who held the deanery of Wells, the archdeaconries of York, Richmond and Suffolk (exchanged for Norfolk in 1528), and numerous other benefices, and whose income from all these sources was for the most part pocketed by his father.[26] In the summer of 1528, as the Wilton case was in train, Dean John Constable of Lincoln died and Bishop Longland sought to pre-empt Wolsey's installation of his absentee and under-age son by urging the appointment of George Heneage to the vacancy. It was a shrewd move, in part because Heneage was mature, well educated and well placed as an existing member of the Lincoln chapter, but also because his elder brother Thomas, the cardinal's former gentleman usher, was so highly regarded by Wolsey that he had recently been placed in the king's privy chamber to spy for the cardinal and provide a means of communication with both Henry and Anne. George Heneage became the new dean.

Aside from the reluctance of bishops to meet the unproductive expense of Thomas Wynter from their diocesan revenues, the later 1520s also witnessed an emphasis on appointments to sub-episcopal benefices because the English bishops continued to exhibit a marked propensity to live and breathe. On 5 October 1528 that pattern was broken by the death of the octogenarian Richard Fox. His long working relationship with the cardinal was perpetuated even in death, his will accurately anticipating that Wolsey would be his successor at Winchester and therefore dictating that he receive more of Fox's plate and tapestries than would any alternative prelate. There was certainly no question of the king having an alternative candidate for England's wealthiest see and Wolsey was papally provided to the administration of Winchester on 8 February 1529, though it doubtless added to the sense of poetic justice when he proved able to hold so rich a prize for a very brief length of time. Not even Wolsey could reasonably retain control of York, Winchester and Durham for long, and the most northerly of those sees was resigned in April, though Cuthbert Tunstal was not translated from London to Durham until March 1530. In the meantime, temporal income from the bishopric and the use of Durham Place were granted not to a prelatical pluralist but to Anne Boleyn's father, Viscount Rochford. In January 1530 Rochford – who was by then earl of Wiltshire and Ormond – also took Tunstal's place as keeper of the privy seal, an appointment which marked the end of the line of clerical keepers and the beginning of lay dominance of that office. Temperamentally, Tunstal would have been no replacement for the fallen chancellor, but Henry was not prepared to risk the emergence of a new clerical statesman in succession to Wolsey.

By 1528–9 Wolsey's enthusiasm for reform of the English Church was undiminished and Pope Clement obliged him by sending a bull authorizing the suppression of further religious houses with less than a dozen members, together with one for a reconfiguration of England's diocesan boundaries, according to which a number of monastic churches would attain cathedral status. Elements of this scheme duly emerged in the later years of Henry's reign, when even the larger monasteries were dissolved and new bishoprics were established in Chester, Peterborough and elsewhere, but the spirit of such far-reaching reforms was way beyond anything that Wolsey countenanced. By that stage, of course, England's ecclesiastical composition had become a curious medley of traditional and innovative influences. By contrast, so zealous was Wolsey's zeal for orthodoxy that, in June 1529, he even proposed that the English universities become exempt from any episcopal oversight and come under legatine jurisdiction, but his fall from power meant that nothing more was forthcoming on that subject. One way or another, the momentum of the legation was lost, because the cardinal's attention was increasingly preoccupied with the annulment.

A notable feature of this last phase of Wolsey's legation was sustained criticism of his chief agents, John Alen and Thomas Cromwell, expressed by writers as diverse as the religious radical Simon Fish and the king's secretary William Knight. Cromwell's acquisitiveness and Alen's aggressive prosecution of his master's reform programme won Wolsey no friends and provoked widespread discontent, but in 1528 an opportunity arose in which Alen's particular combination of talents could do no obvious harm and might even succeed in furthering the cause of sound governance. Wolsey sent him to Ireland. By the end of 1527 the island was nominally governed by Richard Nugent, Baron Devlin, while the powerful earl of Kildare was detained in the custody of the duke of Norfolk, and Kildare's rival, Piers Butler, sought to prosper at court. On 23 February 1528 Butler renounced his claim to the earldom of Ormond and accepted that of Ossory. Royal government continued to be hampered by feuds among the principal families and their allies. In May 1528 Devlin was kidnapped and in August Henry defied Wolsey by sending the new earl of Ossory back to Ireland as lord deputy, but his prospects of imposing order were no greater than they had been during his first stint in that role: the Butlers were still no match for the Fitzgeralds, with or without Kildare. Ossory's appointment was made the day after the death in Dublin of Archbishop Hugh Inge and that was what created the opportunity for John Alen. If Wolsey could not influence the king's choice with regard to the deputyship, then he would seek to impose order in Ireland by other means. Alen would become his *alter ego* across the sea. He succeeded Inge in two capacities, as archbishop and as lord chancellor of Ireland, but also enjoyed the additional distinction of being Wolsey's vice-legate.[27] Even at this late stage in his career, the cardinal's ability to grasp an opportunity remained undiminished and Alen took that opportunity to throw his considerable energies into replicating Wolsey's centralizing achievements in secular and ecclesiastical administration. It was a Sisyphean task.

Within months of Alen's arrival in Ireland an entirely new approach to the island's government was attempted when Wolsey's royal charge, the young duke of Richmond – at around the time of his tenth birthday – became lord lieutenant and nominal head of an executive board designed to follow the model already adopted in Wales and the north of England. This was envisaged as yet another means to counter Geraldine dominance and effectively enhanced the position of the Irish chancellor and vice-legate. Less than four months after Richmond's appointment, though, Wolsey's fall from power brought the loss of Alen's vice-legatine authority. Their shared governmental initiatives died in 1541; James V survived her by only fourteen months. With the death of James and the advent of another minority government, Angus returned from his English exile in 1543 and went on to devote much of his considerable energies to fighting his erstwhile protectors, dying in 1557. In that final phase of his life, Angus proved that, in him, Wolsey had backed both a survivor and a winner.

When we return to Wolsey's own career and chart its progress in the course of 1529, we find a story of spiralling decline, as the irresistible force of Henry's determination to have his marriage declared null and void met the immoveable object that was Charles V's hegemony in Italy. Thomas Wolsey was crushed in the collision. Eric Ives charts that downward spiral from a point not later than the middle of January, when Anne concluded that Wolsey was not to be trusted in the matter of the annulment, but that is merely to consider insular developments.[29] Elsewhere, the year began with Pope Clement falling seriously ill. Despairing of his life, on 10 January he named as a cardinal his eighteen-year-old great nephew Ippolito, the illegitimate son of the late Giuliano de' Medici, duke of Nemours. Ippolito had been nominal head of the Florentine state prior to the sack of Rome and was an equally nominal archbishop of Avignon. This provided ammunition to those who suspected the Medici of attempting a dynastic takeover of the papacy and has also done nothing for the subsequent reputation for Renaissance cardinals, for Ippolito was not merely young; he was dissolute and more of a natural soldier than a natural prelate. At some point in January Clement also gave the hat to Girolamo Doria, another widower who had taken the death of his wife as the opportunity to enter the clerical state. Girolamo's promotion was an overtly political statement, for his father was the great Genoese admiral Andrea Doria, who had defected from French employment in 1528 and restored his city's independence, albeit under imperial protection.

It was February by the time that news of Clement's illness reached England. In contrast to 1521–2 and 1523, when he entertained neither the desire nor the expectation of donning the tiara, in 1529 Wolsey had genuine need of election as supreme pontiff, for it seemed to offer the guarantee of a conclusion to the annulment saga which in a manner favourable to his king. It was a measure of Wolsey's desperation when he sent Gardiner an annotated list of the Sacred College, with a view to lobbying for his election, only for Clement to recover and live for another five years. A revived Clement found that the imperial threat persisted and sent further messages to Campeggi about delaying any decision

were scuppered in 1530 when the executive board was abandoned, Sir Willia
Skeffington was appointed as Richmond's deputy and Kildare was permitt
to return to Ireland.[28] Alen declared himself a loyal servant of the crown, but
was not enough to protect him from a charge of *praemunire* in 1531 and a he1
fine as punishment for his collusion in the cardinal's legation. When Kilda
resumed the deputyship in 1532 he replaced Alen as lord chancellor. Two yea
later Alen was murdered by order of Kildare's son, Thomas Fitzgerald, Baro
Offaly: Geraldine revenge on the late cardinal was complete. Wolsey's Iris
policy had been late in maturing beyond anything other than efforts to contai
the violent feud between the leading families, efforts that were consistentl
frustrated. When Archbishop Alen attempted to introduce something tha
might be identified as joined-up government, it was rapidly snuffed out by
Wolsey's political demise. One conclusion that can be reached from reflecting
on this imposition of a tried and tested English solution to Irish problems is that
it confirmed Wolsey's confidence in what he had achieved in England, whether
in maintaining the rule of law or in continuing to reform the administrative
and legal structures of the English Church.

The Anglo-French peace of 1527 meant that Scotland provided Wolsey with
relatively few unsought distractions during his last two-and-a-half years in
power. Within a month of that peace, the sixteen-year-old King James declared
his majority by escaping from his step-father Angus and banning the entire
Douglas clan from government. Once again the earl fled to England and to
the active support of both Henry and his chancellor. Wolsey responded by
sending Thomas Magnus on another mission north of the border, in the hope
of persuading the young monarch to accept both the earl and the pro-English
policy he represented, but Magnus overplayed his hand by addressing James as
a callow youth rather than an anointed king. In the midst of the 'phoney' war
of 1528, the emperor-elect sought to foment insular tensions by proposing his
widowed sister, the former queen of Hungary, as a possible wife for James, but
that was a ruse which could fool no seasoned diplomat. English fears centred
on the possibility that James would commit himself to a French marriage, but
these were unfounded during Wolsey's lifetime and only borne out when he
married Madeleine de Valois in 1537 and Mary of Guise (Marie de Lorraine)
the following year. Meanwhile, Queen Margaret's third marriage proved to be
no more successful than her second, and there was even talk of her seeking
to divorce the unfaithful Henry Stewart – now Lord Methven – and remarry
Angus, presumably with a view to securing financial support from England. She

on the annulment, while Henry's impatience with his chancellor was reflected in open criticism of him and in the role he accorded to Norfolk, Suffolk and Rochford with regard to foreign policy, the realm that had long been Wolsey's preserve.

After two years of wrangling and prevarication, the legatine court finally sat at the London Blackfriars on 31 May to determine King Henry's 'Great Matter'. Henry and Katherine both lodged at neighbouring Bridewell, while Campeggi was housed at Bath Place, the London residence of the bishop of Bath and Wells. There was certainly tension between the two judges, Wolsey still hoping that this papally-sanctioned option was the route to achieving the king's objective, while Campeggi knew that he was there to prevent anything of the kind. One reflection of Wolsey's hope lay in his choice of William Benet, 'fixer' of various abbatial elections, as the latest English ambassador to the Curia. Cavendish's account of the trial includes a description of the layout of the courtroom and locates all the principal players, including Gardiner ('Dr Stephens'), who acted as chief scribe. Indeed, in the course of the trial Gardiner shrewdly transferred his allegiance from cardinal to king, succeeding William Knight as Henry's principal secretary. Henry was represented in the tribunal by younger men whose careers prospered as a consequence of taking on his case, including Richard Sampson and John Bell, who became bishops of Chichester and Worcester respectively. Katherine's counsel was more eminent: Cavendish names Bishops Fisher and Standish, but not Bishops Clerk and Tunstal, who were also vigorous in her cause. Much of the tribunal's business consisted of receiving and examining evidence from both sides in the case. Fisher spoke passionately in the queen's defence, thereby effectively setting his feet on the road to martyrdom, and Bishop West, one of her chaplains, was among those who testified on her behalf, but Katherine saw no hope of them winning and, in mid June, made her formal appeal for the case to be heard in Rome. According to Polydore Vergil, Katherine's problem with the court was that she had no faith in the impartiality of one of the judges and accused Wolsey of 'treachery, deceit, injustice and evil-doing in creating dissension', adding 'I deny, revolt from and shun such a judge, who is the bitterest enemy both of me and of law and justice.'[30] Presumably she had no problem with the impartiality of the other one, but Vergil happened to have no personal gripe against Campeggi. Cavendish counters Vergil by omitting much of the business and cutting straight to the high drama of 21 June, when Katherine made her passionate appeal to the king as his true wife of twenty years. After her dramatic departure from the court room, the cardinal's biographer turns to an exchange between Henry and Wolsey in which both commend the queen's virtues, the cardinal seeks to distance himself from the king's sustained attack on so innocent a woman, and Henry obligingly confirms that 'ye have been rather against me in attempting or setting forth thereof'.[31]

The next encounter between king and minister, as related by Cavendish, came some days later when Henry sent for Wolsey to meet him at Bridewell. It was not a comfortable experience, as a subsequent exchange between Wolsey and John Kite revealed. The bishop of Carlisle commented on the heat of the day. '"Yea," quoth my Lord Cardinal, "if ye had been as well chafed as I have been within this hour, ye would say it were very hot."'[32] Within a matter of hours, Henry instructed Wolsey and Campeggi to visit Katherine and persuade her to give up her opposition to Henry's course of action. As he prepared for this delicate mission Wolsey addressed Viscount Rochford in prophetic terms:

> Ye and other my lords of the council, which be near unto the king, are not a little to blame and misadvised to put any such fantasies into his head, whereby ye are the causes of great trouble to all the realm; and at length get you but small thanks either of God or of the world.[33]

Wolsey then met Campeggi at Bath Place and both cardinals proceeded to Bridewell, where Cavendish was in attendance for much of their audience with the queen. Instead of haranguing in the manner presented by Vergil, Wolsey's biographer relates Katherine's desperate plea to the two prelates:

> I am a poor woman, lacking both wit and understanding sufficiently to answer such approved wise men as ye be both, in so weighty a matter. I pray you to extend your good and indifferent minds in your authority unto me, for I am a simple woman, destitute and barren of counsel here in a foreign region: and as for your counsel I will not refuse but be glad to hear.[34]

The conversation then continued behind closed doors and the gentleman usher could discern no more, but there was clearly no decisive shift by any of the principals. Back in the courtroom the deadlock was finally broken on 31 July when Campeggi declared that the court was observing the dates of the Roman legal calendar and would therefore adjourn until October. According to Cavendish, it fell to the duke of Suffolk to respond on behalf of the king and to anticipate the Whig interpretation of history by declaring that 'It was never merry in England whilst we had cardinals among us.' 'Sir,' Cavendish has Wolsey respond:

of all men within this realm, ye have least cause to disprise or be offended with cardinals; for if I, simple cardinal, had not been, you should have had at this present no head upon your shoulders, wherein you should have a tongue to make any such report in despight of us, who intend you no manner of displeasure . . .[35]

Continuing his lecture, the cardinal-legate explains the challenges of serving the pope in a land far from Rome. What he omits to explain is the immeasurably greater challenge of serving simultaneously as papal legate and chancellor of a secular prince. That dual role had finally proved to be incompatible in practice, just as it had long appeared to be in theory. Now that it was obvious that no annulment could be decided in England and there was no prospect of Clement defying the imperial will, Wolsey's rivals sought to take immediate advantage of his misfortune and secure his dismissal from the chancellorship, but Henry frustrated them by doing nothing of the kind. By 6 August the decision had been taken to call a parliament to meet in early November, a decision which the plotters sought to use for their own purposes.[36]

The English end of the annulment campaign fell with remarkable rapidity into other hands, though they were not necessarily any safer hands than Wolsey's and met with only partial success, rending the unity of Christendom in a manner which has been no more than indifferently patched in the course of the intervening centuries. It seems to have been just two days after Campeggi's adjournment of the tribunal, on 2 August, that Stephen Gardiner and Edward Fox happened to lodge with the Cressy family of Waltham Holy Cross, on the London side of Essex, and there met Thomas Cranmer, who was a relative of the family. All three men were united by their Cambridge connections and by recent or current service to the king. Gardiner and Fox told Cranmer of the latest developments in London and he, a theologian rather than a canon lawyer, responded by suggesting a different approach to the dilemma, one designed to isolate Rome by securing the support of canonists throughout the continental universities. As the debate between Fisher and Wakefield had proved, this was not an entirely new departure; the difference would lie more in the weight of numbers than in the novelty of argument. It might have been a chance suggestion, but Gardiner and Fox had run out of alternative options. They easily persuaded Henry that this was the way forward and set an example the following February by canvassing expert opinion in Cambridge and garnering 200 signatures in the king's interest. A similar exercise was conducted in Oxford in April 1530 by Fox, Longland and Bell. In the autumn of 1529, though, priority went to winning over Parisian scholarly opinion, a task which fell to the king's bookish cousin Reginald Pole and the ambassador John Stokesley, a former vice-president of Magdalen who had risen to prominence through his association with Wolsey. Meanwhile, Ghinucci led the Italian arm of the campaign. Cranmer's initiative generated momentum and documentation, but no immediate solution to the problem of the royal marriage.

At the height of his power, Wolsey had been perfectly capable of pursuing apparently contradictory diplomatic threads simultaneously, keeping the French and the imperialists guessing about his real objective. He had also used the summer months, between the legal terms, to concentrate on foreign policy, venturing abroad or entertaining distinguished guests. By the summer of 1529, he had lost Henry's confidence and, with it, the ability to pursue even one serious diplomatic thread. He was also kept preoccupied by the Blackfriars tribunal, which denied him the opportunity to represent English interests at that season's north European diplomatic negotiations, the Franco-imperial summit at Cambrai, where the peace initiatives launched by Louise of Savoy and Margaret of Austria in 1528 came to fruition in the so-called Ladies' Peace (3 August). The English delegation at Cambrai included Tunstal and More, both of whom had ample experience of Anglo-imperial diplomacy, but their inclusion has nevertheless given rise to speculation that they were deliberately removed from London in order to deprive Katherine of two of her most elo-quent supporters. Such an anglocentric conspiracy theory makes no difference to the substance of international relations in that season, for that is what really mattered with regard to the outcome of the trial. At the beginning of May the pope decided that he had no option but to make peace with Charles, a decision confirmed at Landriano on 21 June, when another military defeat sealed the fate of French attempts to control Lombardy. The stark reality of Charles's complete dominance in Italy was recognized in the terms of the papal-imperial treaty of Barcelona, signed on 29 June, from which Clement gained a crumb of comfort in the imperial undertaking to defeat the Florentine republican government and create a Medicean principality. Thus the new treaty of Cambrai completed a more extensive peace process, one which effectively sidelined the English and gave the pope no choice but to advoke (recall) the annulment case to Rome. Wolsey appreciated the consequences of English isolation and urged Henry not to ratify the Cambrai treaty, but his opinion on such matters was now no more than one among many. However, the full measure of England's diplomatic isolation was realized after the cardinal's fall, first in Charles V's imperial coronation at Bologna in February 1530 and, six months later, when

Francis married the widow of King Manuel of Portugal, for she was none other than the emperor's eldest sister.

If Wolsey was the principal loser from the latest turn of Fortune's wheel, the man who gained most was his imperial counterpart, the grand chancellor Gattinara, for whom the treaties of Barcelona and Cambrai represented the apex of his diplomatic career. Charles expressed his gratitude in the traditional manner of a monarch towards his chancellor, by requesting a cardinal's hat for Gattinara. Clement not only obliged, but also overlooked the fact that Gattinara was a layman. He was admitted to the Senate of the Church on 13 August. For the sake of completeness, we may note that Clement created six more cardinals in what remained of Wolsey's lifetime: François de Tournon, archbishop of Bourges, Bernhard von Cles, prince-bishop of Trent, Louis de Gorrevod, bishop of Saint-Jean de Maurienne, García de Loaysa, bishop of Osma, and Íñigo de Mendoza, bishop of Burgos, on 9 March 1530, and Gabriel de Gramont, bishop of Tarbes, on 8 June. By this measure, too, England was frozen out by the continental powers. Not only had Mendoza and Grammont both been recent envoys to England on behalf of their respective princes, but Clement was under no pressure whatsoever to confer the hat on Henry's candidate, Girolamo Ghinucci. By the time Paul III did so in 1535, Ghinucci had been deprived of his see of Worcester by the Reformation Parliament. Cardinal Campeggi lost Salisbury by the same means. Thus concluded the practice that began with Giovanni Gigli's appointment to Worcester in 1497, by which Anglo-papal diplomacy had hinged on Italian prelates occupying English sees. It was a practice with which Wolsey worked throughout his career, especially when his legatine power allowed him to 'farm' the temporalities of those sees, and one that did not long survive him. The last half dozen cardinals to die before Wolsey were Domenico Jacovacci and Cristoforo Numai in 1528, Pirro Gonzaga and Silvio Passarini in 1529, Enrique de Cardona and Mercurino Arborio di Gattinara in 1530; Gattinara had been a non-curial cardinal for less than a year. Duprat, who died in 1535, was the last surviving member of Wolsey's generation of red-hatted chancellors.

Wolsey's personal contacts with his fellow cardinals were limited by the fact that he never travelled to Rome and, indeed, never ventured beyond a relatively small portion of north-west Europe. His last meeting with a fellow ecclesiastical prince was in the second half of September 1529 when he accompanied Campeggi to Grafton, where the latter took his formal leave of the king. For Cavendish, an account of the Grafton episode provided a useful opportunity to observe the relationships between Henry, Anne Boleyn, Wolsey and Norfolk. The king was amiable towards the cardinal; Anne was overtly hostile and sought to put physical and emotional distance between them. At dinner Wolsey confessed himself content to retire to his bishopric of Winchester, but that was not far enough from the court for Norfolk's liking and he declared that York would be better.[37] From Northamptonshire, Wolsey and Campeggi made their way to the More, near St Albans, and then went their separate ways. A relic of their relationship survives at Stonyhurst College in the form of an early fifteenth-century book of hours (MS 57) which an inscription on the flyleaf assures us was a gift from Campeggi to Wolsey.[38]

There followed an uneasy lull in the nation's affairs as the king postponed what now appeared to be inevitable, dropping the pilot who had guided him so imperiously through the twenty years of his reign. His hand was finally forced by the start of the Michaelmas law term and the revival of Wolsey's activities in the courts of chancery and star chamber. On 9 October the chancellor took his place in chancery but, at the same time, was indicted on a charge of *praemunire* in the court of king's bench by the attorney general, Sir Christopher Hales. This move should not be interpreted as a sign of royal hostility towards Wolsey's legatine power, for Henry had been a constant campaigner for and supporter of the legation and all that the cardinal attempted in that regard was perfectly compatible with good governance in the secular sphere. If the legation had really promoted papal power at the king's expense, then the popes would hardly have been so reluctant to concede it in the first place. Rather, the charge of *praemunire* was a clever choice because it provided a convenient excuse to remove Wolsey from secular office before parliament met at Blackfriars from 3 November and offered an opportunity for his enemies to unite behind an act of attainder. This procedure would have resulted in Wolsey's execution without trial, in comparison with which the accompanying forfeiture of his goods to the crown would have been somewhat incidental.

Again there was a pause, reflecting the king's lingering loyalty to his minister. Wolsey assumed that the dukes of Norfolk and Suffolk would come to demand the great seal from him the day after the charge was preferred, but they failed to make the journey from the court at Windsor. By the time they appeared at York Place on 11 October, he felt sufficiently emboldened to attempt a delaying tactic, demanding to see the commission under which they sought the great seal. This frustrated any further action, so that it was not until the following week – the sources are not consistent about the precise date – that the chancellor yielded up the great seal after nearly fourteen years in office. There followed some dispute over whether the chancellorship should continue to be held by a prelate, in this case Bishop Tunstal, or whether it was time to break with that tradition and appoint a layman, the duke of Suffolk, who had no legal qualifications. The lawyer Thomas More therefore emerged as a compromise candidate on 25 October and had just nine days in which to prepare for the opening of parliament.[39] In the meantime, Wolsey pleaded guilty to the *praemunire* charge, was secretly pardoned by the king on 1 November, and publicly accepted punishment in the form of deprivation from the office of lord chancellor, loss of the temporal property he possessed by virtue of his bishoprics and the abbacy of St Albans, together with house arrest at Esher, the Surrey manor he had recently acquired as bishop of Winchester. The proper penalty, from which Henry saved him, was life imprisonment. At this point Wolsey's career in secular government ceased. All subsequent contact between the king and his former minister was by means of letters, intermediaries or significant gestures, such as when Henry permitted Wolsey's importunate son Thomas Wynter to be included among his chaplains.

While More was handed the poisoned chalice of the chancellorship, Norfolk was the most obvious material beneficiary from the cardinal's fall. In addition to acknowledgement as the king's principal lieutenant, Norfolk acquired Wolsey's former responsibility for Henry Fitzroy, duke of Richmond, and bought the last year of the wardship of Edward Stanley, the young earl of Derby. Within weeks, Stanley was forced into marriage with Norfolk's daughter Katherine, but the bride died early in 1530 and a substitute had to be found in the person of the duke's sister Dorothy. Emboldened by this strategy, Norfolk developed it in 1533 when he secured the marriage of his daughter Mary to the fourteen-year-old Fitzroy. That union had not been consummated by the time of Fitzroy's death in 1536. In that same season, Norfolk's other royal ambition was thwarted by the execution of Anne Boleyn, and was not revived until 1540, when the king embarked on his relationship with another of the duke's nieces, Katherine Howard. In view of the fact that the later decades of Norfolk's long life were marked by opposition to Thomas Cromwell in the 1530s and to the Seymours in the 1540s, one can see his difficult relationship with Wolsey in the 1520s as part of a pattern and therefore surmise that it was something in the duke's character which provided the source of a recurring problem.

While the cardinal adapted to the privations of enforced retirement, public attention turned to the parliament – what turned out to be the Reformation

Parliament – which met from 3 November when, according to Edward Hall, the new chancellor employed conventional imagery by likening the people to sheep and the king to their shepherd and, maintaining the pastoral theme, identified his disgraced predecessor as a castrated ram:

> And as you see that amongst a great flock of sheep some be rotten and faulty, so the great wether, which is of late fallen, as you all know, so craftily, so scabbedly, yea, and so untruly juggled with the king, that all men must needs guess and think that he thought in himself, that he had no wit to perceive his crafty doing.[40]

If More was as much the king's agent in this parliament as he had been in that of 1523, then his speech was designed channel the heightened emotions about Wolsey, emphasize that he had already received his punishment, and try to shift attention elsewhere. In the event, the Commons certainly had other priorities and sent a number of essentially anti-clerical bills up to the Lords, where Bishop Fisher effectively accused their authors of heresy. When the bills were passed, three bishops – Fisher, Clerk and West – appealed to the pope against them and each received a brief term of imprisonment for his pains.

The only move made against Wolsey came in the form of a petition to the king, dated 1 December and signed by seventeen members of the political elite, most of whom can be recognized from the Eltham ordinances of less than four years earlier: Lord Chancellor More, the dukes of Norfolk and Suffolk, the marquises of Dorset and Exeter, the earls of Shrewsbury, Oxford and Northumberland, Lords Fitzwalter, Darcy, Rochford, Mountjoy and Sandys, together with William Fitzwilliam, Henry Guildford, Sir Anthony Fitzherbert and Sir John Fitzjames. Fitzherbert and Fitzjames were distinguished judges, the former best known for the legal writings, the latter as chief justice of king's bench in succession to Sir John Fyneux. Fitzjames also happened to be the nephew of Bishop Richard Fitzjames. Some of these men were certainly dedicated to Wolsey's total destruction and determined that he should never return to power; others, including More, were more measured in their opinions and appeared to have enjoyed constructive working relationships with the cardinal. Thus a diversity of opinions has arisen about the nature of the petition, ranging from Elton's assumption that it was designed to lead to Wolsey's attainder to Lehmberg's conclusion that it was intended to be no more than 'record Wolsey's misdeeds and to impress upon Henry the strength of the feeling against him'.[41]

The original petition has not survived. Hall's *Chronicle* lists some of the charges brought against the cardinal, but the most comprehensive version of the Lords' articles are those published in the seventeenth century and contain forty-four separate items.[42] If the articles really were some form of damage limitation exercise, then it is significant that the first of them overlapped with the charge of *praemunire*, for it accused Wolsey of injuring the king's prerogative by exercising legatine authority in England. In reality, Henry had been a consistent supporter of Wolsey gaining and retaining the legatine powers, and had done so because they represented the means by which the crown could gain greater control over the English Church. It was the English king's attempt to enjoy levels of power and patronage similar to those which Charles V exercised over the Church in Spain and the New World or, perhaps more pertinently, those negotiated by Francis I at Bologna in 1516. Opposition to the legation was most likely to arise from the bishops because of its threat to their jurisdictional and financial interests, but it did not follow that Wolsey wished to weaken the English Church as a whole. Rather, his attempts to strengthen it through sound governance were more evolutionary than revolutionary, and had not evolved very far by the time of his fall. Up to thirteen further articles relate to alleged abuses committed by Wolsey in his legatine capacity, some with an emphasis on financial gain. Many of the accusations are of a general nature, such as Wolsey's role in the election of monastic superiors and his 'slandering' of the English clergy in letters sent to Rome, and few identify specific wronged parties, though two bishops were said to have been prevented from visiting the university of Cambridge to prevent the spread of heresy, and Bishops Ruthall of Durham and Fox of Winchester were among half a dozen deceased clerics whose estates were appropriated by the legate.

No bishops signed the articles, but plenty of noblemen did so, and it was doubtless from among their number that charges arose relating to Wolsey's promotion of dissention in their ranks and to his arrogant demeanour in the council chamber. As Wolsey had taken exception to the livery of noblemen being worn by their retainers, in a similar fashion one of the articles accuses the cardinal of having his servants swear loyalty to himself alone, rather than to the king. The festering animosity of the king's alienated natural councillors, whose place had been usurped by the upstart from Ipswich, is surely reflected in the assertion that Wolsey endangered Henry's life by breathing on him when afflicted with the pox, for this appears in the midst of claims that the cardinal had overreached himself by entering into treaties with other states without the king's knowledge or warrant, that he saw all ambassadorial correspondence before Henry did so, and presumed to write to foreign princes using the phrase 'ego et rex meus', thereby not merely equating himself with the king's majesty but implying that the king was his servant. A parallel charge concerned the minting of coins on which the cardinal's hat appeared beneath the royal arms. From the lawyers came articles about Wolsey's abuse of power as lord chancellor, examining matters in his court of chancery after they had been dealt with under the common law, forbidding litigants who had been before him in star chamber from suing to the king for pardon, threatening judges, and rebuking Mr Justice Fitzherbert, one of the signatories to the articles. Three of the items concerned individual legal cases, among which was the wrongful imprisonment of the late Sir John Stanley. This accusation reflected more than a decade of complaints that the chancellor was motivated by vindictiveness against members of the nobility. Stanley had leased a certain farm from the abbot of St Werburgh, Chester. When Wolsey earmarked the land for George Legh of Adlington, Stanley was imprisoned in the Fleet until he relinquished his claim. As if to clinch the argument, the article identified Legh as the husband of Larke's daughter, 'which woman the said Lord Cardinal kept, and had with her two children'. This may or may not have been intended as a means to censure the worldliness of an ecclesiastical prince, because elsewhere in the list of articles Wolsey is said to have wronged his son, Thomas Wynter, by appropriating 2,700*l*. per annum from the boy's clerical income, leaving just 200*l*. to cover his living costs. Further financial irregularities were identified with reference to the illegal export of grain, fixing the price of corn, and interfering with the operation of the market at St Albans. By way of conclusion, in the forty-fourth article the signatories begged the king to make an example of the cardinal.

Whatever the precise purpose of the Lords' articles and however conveniently they summarized his manifold faults as perceived by the political elite, no further action was taken against the fallen minister. Removed from the trappings of power, all that remained was that elusive entity, the man called Thomas Wolsey.

6

Pastor Bonus, 1529–30

Thomas Wolsey's life story is a classic of the 'rise and fall' genre, and can be employed to illustrate both the upward social mobility of talented clerics and the humbling of anyone who exalts himself by means of extravagant outward display, no matter how great his talent. A chronologically balanced account of Wolsey's life must give relatively little attention to the 'fall', which occurred little more than a year before his death. An artistically balanced one, like that of George Cavendish, does otherwise and devotes half the text to an intimate portrait of the disgraced cardinal, a man who has gained wisdom through a long years of diplomatic and legal experience and has been humbled by his recent reversal of fortune. Penned so long after the events it recounts, though, not even Cavendish's life reveals a great deal about the man beneath the hat, for he is made to serve as much of a literary purpose as the real Wolsey schooled himself to serve a political one in his public career.

As related by Cavendish, the vision of humility is first seen on the day of the cardinal's departure from York Place. Observers expected him to be conveyed to the Tower, but the king spared him that fate and, instead, sent a ring and a message of continuing support by means of Henry Norris, who had served as groom of the stool and keeper of the privy purse since the time of the Eltham ordinances. The encounter between Wolsey and Norris took place in Putney, through which Wolsey was riding *en route* for Esher, and so moved was he by the warmth of Norris's message that he dismounted from his mule and knelt in the mud, rejoicing. Norris felt bound to do likewise, so knelt and embraced him, to the evident astonishment of the onlookers. 'And talking with Master Norris upon his knees in the mire, he would have pulled off his under cap of velvet, but he could not undo the knot under his chin; wherefore with violence he rent the laces and pulled it from his head, and so kneeled bare-headed.'[1] Before they parted, the cardinal gave Norris what was surely the most precious object he possessed, a piece of the True Cross which he habitually wore on a chain round his neck.

All that remains of Esher Place, Wolsey's place of enforced retirement, is Bishop Waynflete's entrance gateway, the character of which now owes more to the Gothick 'improvements' made by William Kent for Henry Pelham in the eighteenth century. This relic of the bishop of Winchester's palace now forms the centrepiece of as grand a vista as may be found in an English suburb, but in Wolsey's day it occupied a relatively isolated spot away from the main Portsmouth road, three miles along the river Mole from Hampton Court. In the autumn of 1529 it became quite literally a poor man's Hampton Court, when Wolsey and his household arrived there 'without beds, sheets, table-cloths, cups and dishes' and had to borrow such items from Bishop Kite and Sir Thomas Arundell, a former member of Wolsey's household. Thereafter it sufficed well enough, for the cardinal had no desire to be any further removed from the court and from the king who found his new advisers to be inadequate in comparison with Wolsey.

The fate of the fallen cardinal's servants and agents is highlighted by the case of Thomas Cromwell, with whom Cavendish happened to converse at Esher on the feast of All Saints. Unlike Stephen Gardiner, Cromwell had not been wily enough to seek alternative employment and feared that he was now too closely associated with Wolsey to acquire another patron: 'I am in disdain with most men for my master's sake; and surely without just cause. Howbeit, an ill name once gotten will not lightly be put away.' However, his dejection was soon replaced by resolution: 'And thus much I will say to you, that I intend, God willing, this afternoon, when my lord hath dined, to ride to London, and so to the court, where I will either make or mar, or I come again.'[2] That night Cavendish spied another sign of the king's continued favour towards Wolsey, when Sir John Russell rode to Esher and presented the cardinal with another ring. What Cavendish did not appreciate was that this was the means by which Henry secretly conveyed his pardon to Wolsey. Supplies of household goods arrived over the following days, suggesting that a greater revival of his fortunes might be imminent.[3] On 3 November the parliament opened, with Cromwell sitting as the member for Taunton.

The next notable visitor to Esher recalled by Cavendish was the duke of Norfolk, though only one detail of the duke's lengthy conversation with the cardinal is generally considered worthy of mention. Reflecting on his reduced circumstances, Wolsey indicated which of his many offices meant the most to him with the declaration 'for my authority and dignity legatine is gone, wherein consisted all my high honour', which certainly reflected his determination to secure and retain it. Norfolk replied brusquely: 'A straw ... for your legacy. I never esteemed your honour the more or higher for that.'[4]

At Christmas the emotional pressures of the previous months finally took their toll and Wolsey fell so ill that it was doubted he would survive. Henry sent his physician, Dr William Butts, to Esher. As related by Cavendish, Butts reported that Wolsey would surely die, unless Henry and Anne both sent him signs of their favour. Declaring that he would not lose the cardinal 'for twenty thousand pounds', the king chose another ring as his token of loyalty and encouraged the lady to make a corresponding gesture. 'She being not minded to disobey the king's earnest request, whatsoever she intended in her heart towards the cardinal; took incontinent her tablet of gold hanging at her girdle, and delivered it to Master Buttes, with very gentle and comfortable words and commendations to the cardinal.'[5] This is Anne's last appearance in the *Life* and effectively gives Wolsey some sort of moral victory over the woman previously presented as the source of his downfall.

By February it was clear that Wolsey had survived the diverse dangers of parliament and of life-threatening illness, and a more orderly arrangement of his affairs was required. For this Thomas Cromwell acted as an able intermediary. At Candlemas (2 February) the cardinal was permitted to move for the good of his health from Esher to a lodge in Richmond Park. On the 12th he received a general pardon and two days later the temporalities of his archbishopric were restored to him, providing him with estates, income, responsibilities and purpose. There was a firm intention among his noble enemies that any future he had should lie in the wilds of his distant northern province, and even the king was determined that Wolsey should not regain his London power base, York Place, which Henry and Anne had already appropriated for their own use. From it evolved the new, sprawling palace of Whitehall, as a character in Shakespeare and Fletcher's *King Henry VIII* points out:

> You must no more call it 'York Place' – that's past;
> For since the Cardinal fell, the title's lost.
> 'Tis now the King's and called Whitehall.[6]

This act created a precedent for royal appropriation of bishops' London palaces during the subsequent decades. By the end of the century the archbishops of York had acquired a property reasonably close to Wolsey's former residence. Located on a modern map, York Place was to the south west of Charing Cross

Station and the later York House to the east of the same. In 1622 Archbishop
Tobie Matthew exchanged the latter for a clutch of rural properties and James
I granted it to the duke of Buckingham. This palace was demolished in 1675,
leaving only the street names York Place and York Buildings. On 17 February
another agreement was signed between the cardinal and the crown, this time
regarding the temporal wealth of the see of Winchester with its numerous
estates in southern England, and that of the abbacy of St Albans. Although
Wolsey retained the titles and, at least nominally, the spiritual responsibilities
of both, their considerable wealth went to the crown, which allocated him a
lump sum and a pension by way of exchange.

What remained less certain and a cause of considerable unease to Wolsey was
the fate of his colleges at Ipswich and Oxford. The plunder began quickly, with
royal agents inventorying the wealth of the Ipswich college as early as November
1529 and removing a considerable quantity of plate.[7] Less easy to secure were
the lands from which their revenues were derived, for these had been carefully
protected under the terms by which they had previously been transferred
from their former monastic owners, terms confirmed by the king himself.
During the following months, the requisite legal loopholes were discovered, by
means of which the land could be declared forfeit to the crown. Both college
communities struggled on, but it was hardly surprising that some members
sought employment elsewhere. John Taverner, for example, seems to have left
Cardinal College, Oxford, after directing the Easter music in April 1530. By way
of comparison, Richard Pygott remained in post as master of the choristers in
Wolsey's reduced household through to the latter's death in November that year.
Like many another client of the cardinal, he seems to have found subsequent
employment with the king easy to obtain.

Wolsey observed his last Lent in suitably reflective mood, lodging with the
Carthusians at Sheen, contemplating the vainglory of this world and accepting
from the 'ancient fathers' a number of hair shirts. Only when the privy council
had granted him a sum of money from his own confiscated Winchester income
was he able to begin the journey towards his northern province, lodging for
the most part in monastic houses. Pausing at Hendon, Rye House, Royston and
Huntingdon, he came to Peterborough, where he spent Holy Week, washing
the feet of fifty-nine poor men on Maundy Thursday and celebrating Mass
on Easter Sunday. From Peterborough he proceeded to Stamford, Grantham,
Newark and Southwell, in the province of York, where he found the bishop's
palace in such a state of disrepair that he was obliged find temporary lodging

in a prebendary's house. Cavendish presents the cardinal's life in Southwell as that of a model bishop:

> He kept a noble house, and plenty of both meat and drink for all comers, both for rich and poor, and much alms given at his gates. . . . He made many agreements and concords between gentleman and gentleman, and between some gentlemen and their wives that had long been asunder, and in great trouble, and divers other agreements between other persons; making great assemblies for the same purpose, and feasting of them, not sparing for any costs, where he might make them peace and amity; which purchased him much love and friendship in the country.[8]

It was a pastoral interlude in more senses than one, but while the archbishop tended to the needs of his flock a number of senior clerics, including eight bishops, were arraigned in the court of king's bench and charged with *praemunire*, because they had made compositions with Wolsey and were therefore held to have acquiesced in his legatine authority. In the late summer he headed towards York, stopping with the Premonstratensians at Welbeck, the Cistercians at Rufford and the Benedictines at Blyth, and so reached Scrooby, where the Great North Road enters Yorkshire. In a particularly poignant passage, Cavendish relates how, at an abbey dedicated to St Oswald, the cardinal spent seven hours in a single day confirming children. More children appeared for confirmation the following morning, and when he journeyed from there to his archiepiscopal manor at Cawood he came across a further two hundred children waiting for him at Ferrybridge on the river Aire, 'where he alighted, and never removed his foot until he had confirmed them all'.[9] As events transpired, Wolsey spent little more than a month in Yorkshire, but such was his apparent transformation from worldly prelate to gentle pastor that Richard Morison could pronounce in his *Remedy for Sedition* of 1536: 'Who was less beloved in the North than my Lord Cardinal (God have his soul) before he was amongst them? Who better beloved after he had been there a while?'[10]

A chastened Wolsey emerging as a conscientious pastor – perhaps as a northern parallel to Bishop Gian Matteo Giberti in Verona – was something his enemies had certainly not anticipated. A revived Wolsey, throwing his energies into the repair of the castle at Cawood and meeting Dean Hygdon to arrange his enthronement in York Minster on 7 November, suggested that he might be cultivating a northern power base with a view to engineering his return to the government.[11] Meanwhile, Norfolk was taking a lead in ensuring the destruction of one of Wolsey's southern strongholds by ordering the dissolution of the Ipswich college and the demolition of his buildings, the valuable materials from which were to be shipped to London and incorporated into the new palace of Whitehall. However, what really exercised the duke and other courtiers determined to ensure Wolsey's final destruction was news of a papal brief prohibiting the king's marriage to Norfolk's niece. This contributed to their conviction that Wolsey, the master schemer, had been intriguing with both Charles and Francis, with a view to recovering his former authority and thus their removal from power. There is no definitive proof that Wolsey was doing anything of the kind, but the atmosphere grew increasingly fevered towards the end of October. Finally, the king took control of the situation by ordering Wolsey's arrest on a charge of treason. The men commissioned to execute this were Walter Walsh, who had become a gentleman of Henry's privy chamber after the Eltham ordinances of 1526, and Henry Algernon Percy, Anne Boleyn's frustrated suitor and earl of Northumberland since the death of his father in 1527. Walsh had effectively prospered from Wolsey's reforms, but the 'unthrifty' Percy resented the cardinal's interventions in his affairs, financial and otherwise. As they sped north on their commission, Wolsey was at Cawood on the feast of All Saints. Cavendish relates the occurrence of a 'malum omen' as the party concluded their meal. When Wolsey's Venetian doctor, Agostino Agostini – 'Doctor Augustine' – stood up from the table his 'boisterous' gown caught on the cardinal's one surviving ceremonial silver cross, which was standing nearby. The cross toppled over, catching Wolsey's chaplain, the future bishop of London Edmund Bonner, on the head and drawing blood. It boded ill, but also neatly reflected Agostini's role in betraying his master to Norfolk. Three days later, on 4 November, the cardinal was again at dinner when Walsh and Percy arrived at Cawood to arrest him. His fighting instincts revived, Wolsey asked to see the earl's commission and, when Percy refused to produce it, the cardinal declined to be arrested by him, surrendering instead to the more compliant Walsh.

It was on the Sunday that Wolsey, accompanied by Cavendish and four other servants, was taken from Cawood Castle, where three thousand dolorous persons gathered to watch the departure of their good lord. Their first night's stop was at Pontefract Abbey, their second with the Dominicans at Doncaster. From 8 to 24 November the party stayed at Sheffield Manor, one of the estates recently acquired in that region by George Talbot, earl of Shrewsbury. The earl and his wife greeted their distinguished guest and wished that his visit might have taken place in happier circumstances, and Wolsey took the opportunity to declare his innocence of treason to this loyal and highly respected servant of the crown. For two weeks there was suspense. Then the constable of the Tower,

Sir William Kingston, arrived to accompany the accused on the journey to London, but it was obvious by then that the cardinal was a very sick man and unequal to the rigours of the journey. Nevertheless, on Thursday 24 November Kingston and his charge rode from Sheffield to Hardwick Hall, and the following day on to Nottingham.[12] On Saturday 26th they rode the twenty-five miles from Nottingham to Leicester. Wolsey's physical condition was already 'lamentable' at Sheffield, but on the road to Leicester he was so weak that he nearly fell from mule a number of times. He knew he could not go on and, arriving at Leicester Abbey, met his host with the words 'Father Abbot, I am come hither to leave my bones among you.'[13] He took to his bed and did not rise again. Cavendish gives no details of what happened on the Sunday, but by the Monday morning the cardinal was surprised to be still alive, expressing a conviction that he ought to be dead by 'eight of the clock'. Later in the day he rallied sufficiently to give Kingston a report on his financial affairs. Early in the morning of Tuesday 29th he began to drink a chicken broth but then recalled that it was the eve of a feast day, and accepted no more. If Cavendish's memory was accurate after nearly three decades, Wolsey spoke at length before falling unconscious, reflecting on various aspects of his career in public service. Most famously, he confessed:

> Well, well, Master Kingston . . . I see the matter against me how it is framed; but if I had served God as diligently as I have done the king, he would not have given me over in my grey hairs. Howbeit this is the just rewards that I must receive for my worldly diligence and pains that I have had to do him service; only to satisfy his vain pleasure, not regarding my godly duty.[14]

Then, avoiding the foreign affairs which had tended to preoccupy him during the period of his greatness, he apparently turned his attention to matters that would have meant much more to Cavendish's audience in the reign of Mary Tudor, reflecting on the unfortunate discord between the king and 'good Queen Katherine', and urging Henry to have 'a vigilant eye to depress this new pernicious sect of Lutherans'. As life drained from him, he came to a good and pious end, his biographer pausing to reflect on the contrast with the cardinal in his prime, when he was the 'haughtiest' man alive. As he prophesied the previous day, he did indeed give up the ghost at eight of the clock that November morning. His body was prepared for burial and was found to be clad in a hair shirt, which came as a surprise to all but his closest servants. The mayor and other citizens were brought so that they could testify to his death and then the body was taken to the Lady Chapel, where it reposed until four o'clock the following morning, the feast of St Andrew, when the monks sang his funeral Mass. It was interred straightaway.[15]

Wolsey was not England's last great pre-Reformation prelate, for William Warham could claim that distinction, but Warham was buried in Canterbury Cathedral and that building was saved for the nation, whereas Wolsey's grave at Leicester was soon lost in the course of the monastic dissolution masterminded by his former servant Thomas Cromwell. Whatever Cromwell's reputation elsewhere in England, in Ipswich it is that of the man who intervened in the dissolution of Wolsey's college of priests in order to save the school. All the while, the man who arguably did most to ensure that the cardinal ultimately received a fitting tribute was John Hygdon, the dean of Cardinal College, Oxford. In January 1531, only a few weeks after Wolsey's death, his college was suppressed, but Hygdon remained in Oxford and ensured that he was able to resume his former office when it was refounded, as King Henry VIII's College, in July the following year. Hygdon died in 1533. A further refoundation ensued in 1546, but although it then went by the name of Christ Church and doubled up as the home of both a college and a cathedral community, somehow the force of Wolsey's personality, the scale of his vision and the intensity of his commitment meant that Cardinal College never ceased to be his real legacy to his university and his country.

England may have lost the statesman who enabled her to punch above her weight in the international arena, but the deaths of cardinals were regular events in Rome, where a new cardinal-priest of S. Cecilia was named as soon as 9 January 1531. This was Gabriel de Gramont, archbishop of Bordeaux and former French ambassador to England. Wolsey's posthumous impact on the English episcopate was limited to the vacancies at York and Winchester created by his death, though these were not filled until October 1531, when Edward Lee became archbishop of York and Stephen Gardiner bishop of Winchester. Thirteen of the English and Welsh bishops who held office throughout all or most of the period of Wolsey's prominence died during the tumultuous 1530s: Blyth in 1530, Warham in 1532, Skeffington and West in 1534, Booth, Fisher, Ghinucci and Standish in 1535, Nix, Rawlins and Sherborn in 1536, Kite and Ateca in 1537. Bishops Clerk, Longland and Veysey lived until 1541, 1547 and 1554 respectively. They soon perceived the distinctions between Wolsey's legatine efforts to reform the English Church and the strategies of Henry and Cromwell, which necessitated breaking with Rome and declaring the king to be supreme head of the Church in his realm. The aged Warham's identification with his predecessor Thomas Becket intensified as he prepared himself for martyrdom in the cause of ecclesiastical privilege and against another charge of *praemunire*. In the event, his death proved to be from natural causes, but Warham's neighbour at Rochester, John Fisher, was the target of assassination attempts and finally lost his life because of his resolute opposition to the royal supremacy.

At the Sign of the Red Hat, 1530–2009

As Wolsey himself appreciated all too well, red-robed cardinals seem to possess greater dramatic potential than virtually any other figures in history; with the possible exception of Alexander VI, not even popes have attracted similar attention.[1] By way of illustration, Cardinal Richelieu has enjoyed a particularly colourful afterlife, appearing in works as diverse as Alexandre Dumas's *The Three Musketeers* and its numerous cinematic adaptations, Aldous Huxley's *The Devils of Loudun* (filmed as *The Devils*) and on television in *Monty Python's Flying Circus*. Among the English cardinals, Wolsey is the one who lends himself most readily to such cultural games, which he originated through his devotion to the symbolism of the hat. The man behind the symbolism remains an enigma. Unlike Richelieu, he left no political testament, so his public career and his place in English history have been moulded to suit evolving political or religious priorities. Sybil Jack's examination of Wolsey historiography for the *Oxford Dictionary of National Biography* is so recent (2004) and so readily available (online, as well as in print) that it would be a superfluous exercise to confine our survey of the cardinal's 'afterlife' to purely academic matters and, accordingly, what follows weaves together primary sources, scholarship, fiction, images, theatre, film and television into one chronological whole.[2]

From the Venetian ambassador Sebastiano Giustinian we have gleaned something of the respect with which contemporary statesmen and diplomats regarded the cardinal in his omnipotence, and we have heard at rather greater length from those contemporaries – Skelton, Barlow and Roy, and Tyndale – who satirized the overmighty and overbearing minister and who were increasingly motivated by evangelical zeal to condemn the worldliness of an ecclesiastical prince and papal legate. Indeed, Greg Walker has described Wolsey as the first victim of English Protestant propaganda, adding that Catholic controversialists were reluctant to come to his defence.[3] Among those contemporaries who remained loyal to Rome, Thomas More appreciated his predecessor's achievements as lord chancellor but lamented his perceived defects of character: 'Vainglorious was he very far above all measure, and that was great pity; for it did harm and made him abuse many great gifts that God had given him.' Towards the end of More's life, 1534 saw the publication at Basel of Polydore Vergil's *Anglica Historia*, but only a version of the text that stopped at the death of Henry VII. Coverage of the years 1509 to 1538, including Vergil's literary revenge on the 'arrogant and ambitious' Wolsey, did not appear until the third edition, in 1555. It is to Vergil that most of the negative impressions perpetuated about Wolsey can ultimately be traced, and to his humanistic facility with words that his power to influence readers may be attributed.

Between Vergil's first and third editions, there appeared in 1548 the post-humous publication of the relevant portion of Edward Hall's *Union of the Two Noble and Illustre Famelies of Lancastre and Yorke*, which covers English history from the reign of Henry IV to that of Henry VIII. Although his taste for display and performance makes him an invaluable witness for episodes such as the Field of the Cloth of Gold, Hall's political priorities were those of the city of London, where the reformed religion became increasingly entrenched.[4] Consequently, his criticism of Wolsey was coloured by urban and religious considerations:

> This Cardinal . . . was of a great stomach, for he compted himself equal with princes and by crafty suggestion got into his hands innumerable treasure. He forced little on simony, and was not pitiful, and stood affectionate in his own opinion. In open presence he would lie and say untruth, and was double both in speech and meaning; he would promise much and perform little. He was vicious of his body and gave the clergy evil example. He hated sore the city of London and feared it.[5]

The Protestant bias of this work led to its official condemnation during Mary's reign (1553–8), though it did not follow that the queen was any more favour-ably disposed towards the memory of the cardinal who had at least attempted to engineer her parents' 'divorce'. It was, however, a most congenial climate in which to publish a life of the martyred More. Nicholas Harpsfield's *Life of More* appeared in 1557 and was based on the reminiscences of More's son-in-law William Roper, which were also published in due course. Although Roper's juvenile Lutheran inclinations had earned him no more than a mild rebuke from Wolsey, for the purposes of the hagiographical memoir the long-dead cardinal acted as a convenient foil for the saintly More, not least in coverage of the parliament of 1523.[6]

While Roper's public career profited from the brief Catholic resurgence, George Cavendish continued to live quietly in his native Suffolk, where he appears to have composed his famous biography, *Thomas Wolsey, Late Cardinall, his Lyffe and Deathe*, between 1554 and 1558. By that stage a consistent body of anti-Wolsey literature had built up, a corpus which Cavendish countered to such great effect that he single-handedly confounded the image of Wolsey as a convenient all-purpose villain. His close personal contact with the cardinal gave him an authoritative edge over Vergil and Hall, and his detailed recollections were carefully arranged in order to create a moving portrayal of the great statesman humbled and spiritually matured by his disgrace. That careful composition is perhaps never more obvious than in Cavendish's introduction of Anne Boleyn as the source of Wolsey's misfortune:

> Thus passed the cardinal his life and time, from day to day, and year to year, in such great wealth, joy, and triumph, and glory, having always on his side the king's especial favour; until Fortune, of whose favour no man is longer assured than she is disposed, began to wax something wroth with his prosperous estate, and thought she would devise a mean to abate his high port; wherefore she procured Venus, the insatiate goddess, to be her instrument.[7]

The detailed observations are balanced with more general comments reflecting Wolsey's public achievements. Looking back over four reigns, Cavendish concludes: 'I never saw this realm in better order, quietness and obedience than it was in the time of his authority and rule.'[8] If he wrote with conviction, it was in the wake of the fitful imposition of reformed religion during the latter years of Henry VIII's reign and the rise of the convinced Protestants under Edward VI, developments with which Cavendish was clearly not in sympathy. It was also with knowledge gleaned from the work of his father Thomas and brother William as financial officials in the service of Henry VII and Henry VIII, although in William's case that involved assisting Thomas Cromwell in the dissolution of monasteries in the 1530s. In 1547, nearly half a century after Wolsey spent Christmas with the marquis of Dorset at Bradgate Hall, that house was the venue for William Cavendish's third marriage, to Elizabeth Hardwick. William proved to be merely the second of Bess of Hardwick's four husbands, but it was a marriage that caused the Cavendish name to be associated with Derbyshire, rather than with the family's native Suffolk, and it was William's descendants, not George's, who achieved social and political eminence as dukes of Newcastle and Devonshire.

If the Derbyshire Cavendishes were in any sense custodians of the *Life* and, by extension, of the Wolsey flame, it does not appear to have loomed large in their considerations. Indeed, the text seems to have slipped from their hands.

By the late seventeenth century the original manuscript of the *Life* (BL Egerton 2,402) belonged to the Derbyshire gentleman Clement Rossington of Dronfield, which is not far from the Cavendish estates at Bolsover and Chatsworth. The Egerton manuscript also includes George Cavendish's *Metrical Visions*, poems on the reverses of fortune experienced by a number of his contemporaries, not least Wolsey ('Cardinalis Eboracensis'), though a few lines are sufficient to assure the reader that Cavendish's strength lay more in prose composition:

> Farewell Hampton Court, whose founder I was
> Farewell Westminster Place, now a palace royal
> Farewell the More, let Tyttenhanger pass.
> Farewell in Oxford, my college Cardinal
> Farewell in Ipswich, my school grammatical
> Yet once farewell I say, I shall you never see
> Your sumptuous building, what now availeth me.[9]

Cavendish's *Life* was not printed until 1641, leaving popular appreciation of Wolsey in the hands of his detractors, not least those of the martyrologist John Foxe. From the perspective of the hotter sort of English Protestants, history did not go back very far; it consisted of the heroism of those who dared to embrace the reformed religion, especially to the point of martyrdom, and had but one chronicler, Foxe, whose *Acts and Monuments* was first published in 1563. In that account Wolsey appears as an agent of the Antichrist in Rome and, far from being lenient towards reformers, as a persecutor of true believers such as Robert Barnes.

Thomas Churchyard was quite literally a fighter for the Protestant cause, his picaresque adventures taking him to many lands in the course of a long military career, but he was also a prolific poet and, at some point in the first half of Elizabeth's reign, composed a *Tragedy of Cardinal Wolsey* in seventy undemanding stanzas. The repentant cardinal relates the story of his rise and fall:

> Within one year three bishoprics I had
> And in small space a Cardinal I was made:
> With long red robes rich Wolsey then was clad
> I walked in sun when others sate in shade:
> I went abroad, with such a train and trade
> With crosses borne before me where I past
> That man was thought to be some god at last.[10]

Not to be outdone, a Christ Church man, Thomas Storer, published a similar poem in 1599: *The Life and Death of Thomas Wolsey, Cardinall* is another autobiographical reflection told by the cardinal's ghost. This time it is given a suitably learned twist, with its three parts subtitled 'Wolseius aspirans', 'Wolseius triumphans' and 'Wolseius moriens'.[11]

No such learning is evident in a piece entitled *Ballad on the Death of the Cardinal*, which Roger Bowers rates as 'little better than doggerel' and dates to the first half of the sixteenth century:

> By a forest as I came past
> I heard a voice ruefully complain
> Now may I mourn for my trespass
> For all my jewels are from me gone
> And every voice complained thus
> *Miserere mei deus, miserere mei deus*
> Some time in England lord that I was
> Chief of the spirituality and dread over all
> For my great pride now may I say alas
> My subtle deceit hath brought me to this fall
> Wherefore my song it may be thus
> *Miserere mei deus, miserere mei deus*
> I ruled and remitted all at mine own will
> Both mine estate full little did I know
> I oppressed the people and that to no skill
> Therefore my head lyeth now full low
> Wherefore my song it may be thus
> *Miserere mei deus, miserere mei deus*

More remarkable is the fact that the notation for this three-part song has survived and is a suitably mournful composition.[12] In the light of this, it is slightly curious that the only other piece of music which appears to have been inspired by the cardinal during the century after his death is an exceedingly jolly piece by William Byrd: *Wolsey's wilde*.

Elizabeth I's excommunication by Pius V in 1570 intensified the confessional conflict, forcing some English Catholics into recusancy and some into exile at Douai, Rome and elsewhere. If Wolsey was vilified by Protestant writers, that was reason enough for him to be championed by Catholic ones. Thus the Jesuit Edmund Campion permitted himself a digression on the subject of the cardinal's character in his *History of Ireland* (1571), a digression incorporated by Raphael Holinshed in his *Chronicles of England, Scotland and Ireland* later in the decade:

The cardinal (as Edmund Campion in his history of Ireland describeth him) was a man undoubtedly born to honor: 'I think' (saith he), 'some prince's bastard, no butcher's son; exceeding wise, fair spoken, high minded; full of revenge; vicious of his body; lofty to his enemies, were they never so big; to those that accepted and sought his friendship, wonderful courteous; a ripe schoolman; thrall to affections; brought abed with flattery; insatiable to get, and more princely in bestowing, as appeareth by his two colleges at Ipswich and Oxenford, the one overthrown with his fall, the other unfinished, and yet as it lieth for an house of students, considering all the appurtenances, incomparable through Christendom . . .'[13]

Holinshed was familiar with Cavendish's *Life*, as was the historian John Stow, who incorporated substantial quantities of it in his *Annales of England* (1592). It was from Stow, rather than the original text, that Shakespeare and Fletcher derived their knowledge of the Cavendish tradition about Wolsey.

In 1601 the meticulous Elizabeth Talbot, countess of Shrewsbury – formerly Elizabeth Cavendish – commissioned a detailed inventory of the decorations and furnishings at Hardwick Hall and Chatsworth House. Among the items listed was a portrait of Wolsey, its presence there possibly accounted for by the countess's earlier Cavendish marriage. This particular work cannot now be identified, nor can one even assume that it belonged to the 'family' of profile portraits which includes those in the National Portrait Gallery in London and in Oxford at Magdalen and Christ Church.[14] The frequently reproduced, arch-topped NPG portrait is anonymous, but the two Oxford paintings were made in 1610 by the Dutch-born artist Sampson Strong, who specialized in painting long-dead founders of Oxford colleges. This group provides the earliest depictions of Wolsey as a man of more than ample proportions and came to influence many subsequent paintings, prints and performances on stage and screen, but there is no contemporary evidence, written or pictorial, for him being uncommonly fat. Nor is there any evidence for him following the example of Clement VII and a number of curial cardinals of the period in growing a beard, yet the illustrations in a manuscript of Cavendish's *Life* depict him as a lean, frail old man with a long patriarchal beard such as became associated with the reformed religion.[15] The full-face drawing of Wolsey in the Bibliothèque d'Arras gives the impression of being a likeness from the life but is, in fact, a later sketch made from an original which Hilary Wayment has dated to 1508 and the occasion of the future cardinal's mission to Scotland. In her study of Wolsey's stained-glass commissions, Wayment has also identified his pre-1515 visage in the somewhat unexpected guise of a messenger in a window at St Mary's, Fairford, and his more mature but nevertheless lean self as the type of a cardinal in the glazing scheme for the chapel at Hampton Court, where he kneels in prayer opposite Henry, Katherine and Mary, supported by his name saint, Thomas of Canterbury, together with Sts Peter and Paul.[16]

Wolsey's first appearance as a character on the London stage seems to have been in *When you See me, you Know me* (c. 1604) by Samuel Rowley, but this was soon eclipsed by *The Famous History of the Life of King Henry VIII* (hereafter *King Henry VIII*) by William Shakespeare and John Fletcher, which was first performed at the Globe Theatre on 29 June 1613. In terms of dramatic action, Shakespeare and Fletcher's Wolsey is chiefly involved in a 'private difference' with the duke of Buckingham, which builds up aristocratic opposition to the base-born 'butcher's cur', in hosting a masque at which Henry dances with the seductive Anne Bullen, in the great set piece that is the Blackfriars trial, and in a rapid fall from power, much to the satisfaction of the earl of Surrey and other nobles. In terms of Wolsey's character, he might as well be on trial, with the playwrights' sources – including Hall and Campion (both via Holinshed) – standing as witnesses for the prosecution and defence. This is most apparent in the speeches given to Katherine and her servant when news reaches them of the cardinal's death:

KATHERINE   He was a man
      Of an unbounded stomach, ever ranking
      Himself with princes; one that by suggestion
      Tied all the kingdom. Simony was fair play.
      His own opinion was his law. I'th' presence
      He would say untruths, and be ever double
      Both in his words and meaning. He was never
      But where he meant to ruin, pitiful.
      His promises were as he then was, mighty;
      But his performance, as he is now, nothing.
      Of his own body he was ill, and gave
      The clergy ill example.[17]

GRIFFITH   . . . This Cardinal
      Though of humble stock, undoubtedly
      Was fashioned to much honour. From the cradle
      He was a scholar, and a ripe and good one
      Exceeding wise, fair-spoken and persuading;
      Lofty and sour to them that loved him not
      But to those men that sought him, sweet as summer.
      And though he were unsatisfied in getting –
      Which was a sin – yet in bestowing, madam
      He was most princely: ever witness for him

> Those twins of learning that he raised in you
> Ipswich and Oxford – one of which fell with him
> Unwilling to outlive the good that did it;
> The other, though unfinished, yet so famous
> So excellent in art, and still so rising
> That Christendom shall ever speak his virtue.
> For then, and not till then, he felt himself
> And found the blessedness of being little.
> And, to add greater honours to his age
> Than man could give him, he died fearing God.[18]

In the eyes of his numerous detractors, the nearest approximation that seventeenth-century Englishmen witnessed to a native cardinal was Archbishop William Laud. Indeed, there was talk of a red hat for Laud if he and Charles I could restore England to the faith. More precise comparisons between Laud and Wolsey could be made with regard to their ecclesiastical reforms, their activities in Star chamber – where landowners were still being tried for enclosing more than a century after the cardinal's death – and their educational patronage. In that last capacity Laud was a significant benefactor of Oxford's Bodleian Library, actively supported the teaching of Arabic and Hebrew in the university, and favoured his own college, St John's, by building the thoroughly classical Canterbury Quad. Although Laud could not match Wolsey in the matter of founding a college – his attachment to St John's was too intense for that – he did realize one of the cardinal's ambitions when he was able to use his authority as chancellor to impose a new set of statutes on the university. In terms of political power, there was no meaningful comparison. Elsewhere in Caroline Oxford, Christ Church was such a bastion of royalism and Laudian high churchmanship under Deans Brian Duppa and Samuel Fell that it was chosen by the king as his residence in times of peace and war. Duppa and Fell were also responsible for the first building campaign to be undertaken at the college since Wolsey's time, which included the fan vaulting over the stairway to the hall, the style of which deliberately recalled work of the cardinal's era.

The most explicit connections between Laud and Wolsey were made in two pamphlets printed in 1641, both of which were fancifully attributed in the eighteenth century to John Milton. One is a straightforward *True Description, or Rather a Parallel betweene Cardinall Wolsey, Archbishop of York, and William Laud, Archbishop of Canterbury*, but the other, *Canterburies Dreame*, is a soliloquy spoken by Laud, to whom the ghost of Wolsey appears as a warning on the 'third night after my lord of Strafford had taken his fare-well to the world'.

This ghostly Wolsey was presumably inspired by the verse of either Churchyard or Storer.

Like Laudianism and like the completion of the Great Quadrangle at Christ Church under the famously unloved Dr John Fell, the English theatre revived with the post-Commonwealth restoration of the monarchy. In 1660 Sir William Davenant formed the Duke's Company, under the patronage of James, duke of York, and went on to revive many Shakespearean plays for London audiences. These included a production of *King Henry VIII* in 1663, in which the king was played by Thomas Betterton, who was acclaimed as the finest actor on the Restoration stage, the queen by Betterton's wife, and Wolsey by Henry Harris. A portrait of Harris by John Greenhill is of note as one of the earliest depictions of an actor in costume as a Shakespearean character and shows him elegantly dressed in fine red robes, albeit with distinctly Anglican bishops' sleeves.[19] Between 1681 and 1684 the lawyer John Banks had three of his Tudor history plays staged in London. Wolsey was a character in *Vertue Betray'd, or, Anna Bullen* (1682), but the play never succeeded in rivalling the popularity of the Shakespearean version. Banks's interest in English history coincided with the 'popish plots', which anticipated the death of Charles II and the succession of the overtly papist duke of York. In that increasingly fevered atmosphere, Banks's play about Elizabeth I and Mary Stuart was considered so controversial that performances were banned.

With the accession of James II in 1685 and, more particularly, his deposition three years later, religion and politics in the island kingdoms acquired a new relationship, one based on party, faction and loyalty to either Catholic or Protestant claimants to the crown. It was in that context that Richard Fiddes wrote the first full-scale biography of our subject, published in 1724 as *The Life of Cardinal Wolsey*. It has been described as 'more dispassionate'[20] than the assessments of earlier commentators, but any notion that it was somehow characteristic of the Age of Reason is dispelled when one considers its author's firm convictions as a high churchman and a high Tory. Though he was not himself a Christ Church man, Fiddes' appreciation of Wolsey, whose 'injured memory' he was determined to restore, was nevertheless rooted in the college and he was a friend of two successive deans, Francis Atterbury and George Smalridge. By the time Fiddes' biography appeared, Atterbury had not only left Christ Church to become bishop of Rochester, but had been an active participant in the Jacobite plot which bears his name, deprived of his bishopric, exiled, and had thrown in his lot with the Old Pretender. Like Cavendish to

Wolsey, Fiddes remained loyal to the disgraced bishop and acknowledged his assistance in the biography. Wolsey appealed to Fiddes because he represented a combination of devotion to the crown, upholding the rule of law in Church and State, and championing orthodox churchmanship against rebellious dissent. With its 260 pages of primary source material, the book provides an illustration of how non-jurors contributed to the development of historical studies. It managed to attract criticism from both low churchmen, who could see no good in any Catholic, and from a Jacobite who considered it, as a piece of scholarship, 'a very indifferent Thing'.[21]

The cardinal's next biographer was considerably less prominent and controversial, for Joseph Grove turned to the writing of history as something of a recreation after retiring from the legal profession. The Cavendishes supplied a connection between his choices of subject matter: *The History of the Life and Times of Cardinal Wolsey, Prime Minister to King Henry VIII* (1742–4) and *The Lives of all the Earls and Dukes of Devonshire* (1764).

The rehabilitation of historical villains was not an exclusively Tory occupation, as Horace Walpole's immensely popular *Historic Doubts on the Life and Reign of Richard III* demonstrated in 1768. Earlier in the century it had been the turn of Walpole's father, Sir Robert, the dominant political figure of his age, to be cast as the cardinal in the satirical *Authentick Memoirs of the Life and Infamous Actions of Cardinal Wolsey* (1731). Walpole *père* also appears to have been the real target when Samuel Johnson wrote of Wolsey's wide-ranging power and its dramatic loss as an example of *The Vanity of Human Wishes* (1749).

No churchman of the period could reasonably be cast as a latter-day Wolsey: the only vaguely British cardinal of the eighteenth century was the lifelong exile Henry Benedict Stuart, hailed by diehard Jacobites as King Henry IX. The century's lord chancellors offer better parallels and none more so than Edward Thurlow, who was of relatively humble East Anglian birth and openly acknowledged his illegitimate children. His brother Thomas also rose to eminence, following in Wolsey's footsteps as bishop of Lincoln and Durham. Thurlow made his name in legal practice and became lord chancellor in 1778 through the personal intervention of George III, in consequence of which he regarded himself – Wolsey-like – as the king's servant and not as a member of a political party or faction. After long and distinguished service, Thurlow's position was weakened by a royal crisis, that of the king's mental incapacity and the regency claim of the prince of Wales in 1788–9, but it was in order to avoid William Pitt's threatened resignation that George sacrificed Thurlow to his political rivals in 1792. James Gillray's version of the episode has the beleaguered Thurlow assailed by the king from one side and by Pitt and his close ally William Grenville from the other; it is, tellingly, entitled *The fall of the Wolsey of the woolsack*. It was therefore merely a variation on this theme when a more recent lord chancellor, Derry Irvine, identified himself as Wolsey to Tony Blair's Henry VIII. One consequence of this was a particularly striking *Guardian* cartoon by Richard Wilson, in which the Blair figure is clearly inspired by Holbein and that of Irvine, less obviously, by a portrait of Henry Irving in the part of Wolsey.[22]

King Henry VIII became a patriotic staple of the London stage, and never more so than in 1727, when Colley Cibber's production at Drury Lane celebrated the coronation of George II, and in 1761, when David Garrick did likewise at the same theatre for the coronation of George III. Cibber had previously played Wolsey in both *Vertue Betray'd* and *King Henry VIII*, and is most unlikely to have been sympathetic towards a prince of the Church. As a young man he served in a regiment hastily assembled by William Cavendish, first duke of Devonshire, to support William of Orange's invasion in 1688. Throughout his career as an actor and writer he never missed an opportunity to demonstrate his staunch Whig allegiance, not least in his play *The Non-juror* (1717) and in his feud with the Catholic poet Alexander Pope. Towards the end of the century Drury Lane was in the hands of a Catholic actor-manager, John Philip Kemble, who came from a theatrical dynasty precisely because Catholics were still disqualified from more socially respectable professions. When Kemble took over Drury Lane in 1788 he chose to revive *King Henry VIII* in memory of Garrick and the theatre's Shakespearean heyday. Kemble, 'the Euclid of the stage', was too thoughtful an actor for many tastes, but it was that thoughtfulness which established Wolsey as a prominent and serious part for generations of actors. Kemble's education among the exiles of the English College in Douai presumably contributed to his rejection of the theatrical tradition of presenting clerics as figures of fun. Meanwhile, his sister Sarah Siddons triumphed as Katherine of Aragon, evoking considerable sympathy for the wronged Catholic wife losing her husband to a brazen Protestant strumpet.

Kemble revived *King Henry VIII* at Covent Garden in 1803 and 1811. Thereafter, each of the great nineteenth-century actor-managers took the part of Wolsey in ever more spectacular productions of the play: William Charles Macready at Covent Garden in 1822, Charles Kean in a highly successful 100-night run at the Princess's Theatre in 1855, and Samuel Phelps at Sadler's

Wells in 1865. Audiences whose knowledge of history may well have derived from Scott's Waverley novels demanded ever higher levels of historical detail and authenticity, and were rewarded with sets and costumes based on documentary research. 'Archaeological' authenticity was concentrated in set piece tableaux, at the expense of the text, which was liable to suffer severe cuts. Elsewhere, the actress Charlotte Cushman, who had played Katherine to Macready's Wolsey, created a gender-bending precedent by taking the part of the cardinal in her native America in 1859.

The gap of thirty-three years between the Macready and Kean productions witnessed profound changes in official attitudes towards Catholicism in Britain, with Catholic Emancipation in 1829, the creation of three new English cardinals between 1830 and 1850, and the restoration of the Catholic hierarchy in England and Wales, also in 1850. In addition, that gap witnessed the appearance of a rival cardinal on the London stage, Edward Bulwer-Lytton's *Richelieu* (1839), with Macready in the title role and Phelps as Father Joseph, the 'grey eminence'. Perceptions of Catholicism became more variegated as the century progressed, a development from which not even Wolsey was immune. Indeed, far from being agents of papist superstition, the English cardinals from Nicholas Breakspear to Wolsey found their own historian in Robert Folkestone Williams, whose *Lives of the English Cardinals* was published in two volumes in 1868.

So powerful was the impact of Phelps' Wolsey that he was depicted in the role by the actor and painter Johnston Forbes-Robertson in a portrait for the Garrick Club. When other painters took Wolsey as their subject, it was clearly the Wolsey of Shakespeare rather than the Wolsey of history. Neither of the cardinals devised by William Bromley in *Katherine of Aragon and the cardinals* (1866, Manchester City Art Gallery) makes a convincing Wolsey. Both are dressed in the manner of nineteenth-century ecclesiastical princes and one of them might even have been inspired by the portly Nicholas Wiseman, the first cardinal archbishop of Westminster. No more rotund a Wolsey can be imagined than that of the Edinburgh painter John Pettie in his *Disgrace of Cardinal Wolsey* (1869, Sheffield Galleries and Museums Trust), which has been described as 'a psychologically charged study of political humiliation'.[23] Sir John Gilbert was an illustrator of Shakespeare and an enthusiastic history painter whose twin interests combined in a couple of Wolsey paintings. The first, *Cardinal Wolsey, chancellor of England, on his progress to Westminster Hall* (1887, London, Guildhall Art Gallery) is clearly inspired by Cavendish's account of the daily term-time progress from York Place, for the attendants carrying his hat and antique-style pillars are prominent in the scene. Yet this is an ahistorical Wolsey, so unmoved by the pleas of the female petitioners that he carries a pomander to ward off the odour of their poverty. Gilbert chose a quotation from Act III, scene ii of *King Henry VIII* with which to assure the viewer that such a monstrous character would get his come-uppance:

> I have touched the highest point of all my greatness
> And from that full meridian of my glory
> I haste now to my setting. I shall fall
> Like a bright exhalation in the evening
> And no man shall see me more.[24]

In the event, he was seen in Gilbert's second study, *Ego et rex meus* (1888, London, Guildhall Art Gallery), the succinct title of which derives ultimately from one of the Lords' articles against Wolsey in 1529 and featured thereafter in the tradition of Holinshed, Shakespeare and Fletcher. Among the charges levelled against the fallen minister, the stage duke of Norfolk declares:

> Then, that in all you writ to Rome, or else
> To foreign princes, '*ego et rex meus*'
> Was still inscribed, in which you brought the King
> To be your servant.[25]

Gilbert conveys the cardinal's presumed personal and political priorities by causing the king's dull-coloured costume to merge with the dark background, while Wolsey himself is swathed in the swirling and strikingly red robes of his office.

In biographical terms the nineteenth century opened with the *Life and Administration of Cardinal Wolsey* (1812) by the Scottish novelist John Galt, followed by F. C. Laird (writing as George Howard), *Wolsey: the Cardinal and his Times, Courtly, Political and Ecclesiastical* (1824), and by Samuel Weller Singer's edition of Cavendish's *Life* (1825).[26] Joseph Hunter asked *Who Wrote Cavendish's Life of Wolsey?* (1814) and concluded that it was not the progenitor of the ducal dynasty. As long as archives remained largely unexplored and uncatalogued, historical novelists took their cue from Walter Scott and acted as highly influential interpreters of the past. Wolsey received fictional treatment from Richard Cobbold in *Freston Tower* (1850), a work which celebrates one of Suffolk's greatest sons as well as one of its architectural gems. Among the numerous collections of primary sources published in the course of the century, two had a particular impact on the study of Wolsey. First, the venetophile

Rawdon Brown edited the dispatches of Sebastiano Giustinian and published them as *Four Years at the Court of Henry VIII* (1854), a project which led to Brown's employment by the British government, calendaring other material in the Venetian archives relating to English history.[27] More significantly, from 1856 J. S. Brewer was similarly employed editing the *Letters and Papers, Foreign and Domestic, of the Reign of Henry VIII,* the volumes of which began to appear in 1862. In the light of his labours, Brewer concluded of Wolsey that 'No statesman of such eminence ever died less lamented.'[28] Wolsey nevertheless remained the classic model of the fallen statesman and was called upon to play that part at the fall of the Liberal administration in 1866: a satire called *The Gladstone Lament; or, Wolsey Personified* parodies the encounter between Wolsey and Cromwell in Act III, scene ii of *King Henry VIII.*[29]

In 1888 Wolsey gained a biographer worthy of his eminence, one who appreciated him as 'the greatest political genius whom England has ever produced'.[30] Mandell Creighton was at that point a canon of Worcester, the first Dixie professor of ecclesiastical history at Cambridge, and the founding editor of the *English Historical Review*. He had previously taught history at Oxford and combined scholarship and ministry by taking the Merton College living at Embleton, on the Northumberland coast. Creighton's episcopal career, at Peterborough and London, occupied the last decade of his life. He was probably younger than Wolsey at the time of his death and was buried in St Paul's Cathedral, home to Wolsey's sarcophagus. Creighton's scholarly reputation is founded on his five-volume *History of the Papacy* (1882–94), which provided not only the academic context for the writing of *Cardinal Wolsey*, a more concise work, but also the historical context, meaning that he could appreciate Wolsey's secular and ecclesiastical activities as part of the history of international relations and that of the Rome-centred Church. Then again, Creighton was not disposed to separate Church and State in any clinical fashion, as can be seen both in his study of papal history and in his opinions about the worldwide mission of Anglicanism. The figure of Wolsey offered a splendid illustration not only of how the study of Church and State might be conflated, but also of how the leadership of a man like Wolsey could be beneficial to both. It was an exalted vision, expressed with the assured touch of an able teacher:

> Politics to him was not a pursuit, it was a passion. He loved it as an artist loves his art, for he found in it a complete satisfaction for his nature. All that was best, and all that was worst, in Wolsey sprang from this exceptional attitude towards statecraft, which he practised with enthusiasm, not in the spirit of cold calculation. The world is accustomed

to statesmen who clothe the results of calculation in the language of enthusiasm; Wolsey's language was practical and direct, his passionate aspirations were restrained within his own bosom.[31]

Lord Acton's disappointment at Creighton's reluctance to censure the moral failings of Renaissance popes makes the reader alert to the same tendency in Creighton's study of Wolsey. Indeed, the cardinal's next biographer, A. F. Pollard, highlighted the fact that Creighton made no reference to Wolsey's two illegitimate children. Mentioning them simply did not serve Creighton's purpose, the nature of which can be gleaned from the fact that seven out of his eleven chapters are devoted to Wolsey's contribution to international relations, with the remaining four set aside for domestic policy, the royal divorce, Wolsey's fall, and an overview of his career.

Henry Irving's fascination with historical subjects made *King Henry VIII* a natural choice for the Lyceum, and his romantic interest in Catholicism meant that he could depict princes of the Church without being tempted to turn them into grotesque villains. In appearance he was perfect for the part of Richelieu, which he first played in 1873, but Phelps' success as Wolsey caused him to 'funk' that of the English cardinal for many years, and it was not until 5 January 1892, in the wake of Creighton's *Cardinal Wolsey*, that Irving's suitably spectacular, 'archaeological' and Holbeinesque production opened to enthusiastic reviews. Clement Scott, the doyen of theatre critics and himself a Catholic convert, revelled in the vision that was Irving's Wolsey and appreciated the subtle interpretation of character:

> Never before in our memory has Mr Irving made so wonderful a picture. He is swathed from head to foot in what is miscalled the cardinal's scarlet. It is not scarlet at all, but an indescribable geranium-pink, with a dash of vermilion in it. The biretta on his head is of the same blush-rose colour, and it hides every inch of hair, bringing into relief the pale, refined and highly intellectual face. We see at once, at the first glance, how Mr Irving intends to read Wolsey. He is to be far more like Richelieu than the humble trader's son of Ipswich. This is no man of ignoble birth who has risen by his brains to power. He is not coarse in feature, he is not gross, there is nothing of the vulgarian about him. There is majesty in his lineaments, a little foxiness in his face, but the power is that of the lynx, and not the British bull-dog. . . . Henry Irving's Cardinal Wolsey is a cultured and crafty ascetic, not a man of dogged determination and of iron will.[32]

The biretta, like the rest of Irving's costume, was a glaring anachronism and helped to prompt the *New York Times*' correspondent to describe Irving's Wolsey as a cross between Cardinal Manning and Louis XI. In that respect the production could not have been more timely, for the wraith-like Manning died just nine days after the opening night and performances continued while London witnessed an unprecedented outpouring of public grief for a Catholic prelate. That popular affection was inspired by Manning's championing of the poor in the face of exploitation by their employers, a nineteenth-century version of Wolsey's legal championing of the underdog against the rapacious nobility. The parallel might be continued in another sphere of mutual interest, for both cardinals were hugely ambitious but ultimately frustrated in their educational patronage.

Only after Mandell Creighton's death in 1901 did other historians venture to take Wolsey as their subject, E. L. Taunton's *Thomas Wolsey, Legate and Reformer* appearing the following year. Irving had been dead for more than four years when, in 1910, his successor as London's foremost actor-manager, Herbert Beerbohm Tree, assumed the part of Wolsey in an even more lavish and spectacular production of *King Henry VIII*, in which a grand total of 172 people appeared on stage in the course of the performance. His investment in actors, costumes and sets paid off: 254 performances over eight months gave it the longest continuous run of any Shakespearean production.[33] Whereas Irving's Wolsey had been elegant and cerebral, Tree's somewhat bulkier frame and strength as a character actor combined to make his Wolsey grand and imperious, complete with more authentic headgear. From that point onwards, Shakespeare and Fletcher's *King Henry VIII* became more of a theatrical curiosity, but Wolsey's wider symbolic potential remained undiminished, whether as a male model advertising the 'unshrinkable' woollen garments which were produced near the site of his death in Leicester, or as the inspiring patriot presented by Ernest Law in his wartime study of *England's First Great War Minister* (1916).[34]

A decade later, Wolsey featured in one of a series of eight history paintings commissioned for St Stephen's Hall in the Palace of Westminster, but this time he was cast not as a patriotic hero but as the bloated agent of a tyrannical monarch. *Sir Thomas More, as speaker of the House of Commons, in spite of Cardinal Wolsey's imperious demands, refuses to grant King Henry VIII a subsidy without due debate by the House, 1523* leaves neither the subject matter nor the subjectivity in doubt, and ultimately derives from Roper's account of the parliament. The painter, Vivian Forbes, followed Gilbert in presenting the cardinal in profile, the better to emphasize his ample girth. In keeping with an even longer pictorial tradition, he is accompanied by his crucifers and pillar-bearers, together with the armed escort that betokens a tyrannical regime. In contrast to the vibrant redness of Wolsey's robes, More is depicted in sombre black, quietly determined not to be bullied. Among the lesser figures crowding the scene, Thomas Cromwell appears on the Commons' side of the picture.[35]

Although Mandell Creighton's *Cardinal Wolsey* is so magisterial that it could easily be performed, it was Pollard's *Wolsey* that evolved out of the Ford Lectures, delivered at Oxford in 1927–8. Ford lecturers are chosen for their ability to draw upon a lifetime's experience of scholarship. In Pollard's case that included his biography of Henry VIII (1902), his chair at University College London since 1903, and his roles in founding the Historical Association in 1906 and the Institute of Historical Research in 1921. Pollard rejected Creighton's grand vision and, writing in a more uncertain world, reacted against nineteenth-century convictions, but his approach to the subject was conditioned most profoundly by Brewer's *Letters and Papers of Henry VIII*, and that kept his focus on the priorities of English domestic history. In successive chapters Wolsey is considered as 'lord chancellor', 'prime minister' and 'papal legate', with foreign policy firmly subsumed into the greater whole. Under each heading, Pollard consistently appears for the prosecution, possibly in order to make a clear distinction between king and minister, condemning one in order to exonerate the other. As we have observed with reference to the meeting of convocation in 1523, Pollard's deference to Vergil helped to perpetuate the negative views of a particularly hostile witness. Pollard's Wolsey is therefore a memorable figure ultimately derived from the satires and character assassinations of the cardinal's contemporaries:

> Getting and spending, he made waste his powers, and laid bare the poverty of his soul. His kingdom was all outside him, and he had little within on which to rely. His courage did not consist in the fortitude of his mind: no great man was ever more pitiably dependent upon externals; and when he looked upon the travail of his soul he found no satisfaction because there was no sacrifice. His dignity consisted in his dignities, his honour in his honours, and his welfare in his wealth.[36]

Pollard's insular priorities make his appreciation of Wolsey's foreign policy especially vulnerable to attack, for he wrongly assumed that the cardinal consistently aligned England with the papacy's changing French or imperial allegiances and was so ambitious for the tiara that he broke with Charles V and allied with Francis because the emperor-elect made no effort to secure his victory in the conclave of 1522–3.

Pollard's liberalism was at odds with the prevailing conservatism of Christ

Church, where Wolsey's name and attributes have been consistently venerated. Subsequent to the seventeenth-century building works mentioned above, the college obtained the foundation stone of Cardinal College, Ipswich, which can now be seen in the chapter house. From 1855 to 1892, Henry George Liddell was not only the longest-serving dean of Christ Church; in terms of building projects, he was also the most enterprising of the nineteenth-century deans. In 1870 Liddell had a statue of Wolsey placed in the outer niche of Tom Tower and in 1876–9 commissioned G. F. Bodley to create the belfry tower at the south-east corner of the Great Quadrangle, adorned with both the royal and cardinalitial arms. Its function as a gateway and its three gothic niches make it reminiscent of the fifteenth-century gateway at St Cross, Winchester, where only the *priant* figure of Cardinal Henry Beaufort has survived the ravages of time and ecclesiastical reform. In the Christ Church version Wolsey, acknowledging no higher authority, occupies the central niche, attended by angels. The cardinal's example, both before and since the erection of the statue, may well have inspired generations of statesmen, for Christ Church has produced far more British prime ministers, thirteen, than has any other Oxbridge college, not to mention men and women who have achieved eminence in many other fields. Wolsey's reputation for hospitality is arguably less likely to have inspired the Cardinals drinking society, which hosts termly events known as 'cardinals cocktails'. Wolsey's status as the college's original founder has had other miscellaneous cultural implications: the 1938 film *A Yank at Oxford* is set in Cardinal College; Colin Dexter cast Christ Church as Wolsey College in his Inspector Morse novels; in 1989 Andrew Carwood, then a Christ Church lay clerk, founded the early music ensemble The Cardinall's Musick.

   In his concise history of Christ Church, Hugh Trevor-Roper makes the intriguing statement that the college 'casually acquired' Wolsey's hat in 1898, since when it has been displayed in the library.[37] It is a felt hat of the broad-brimmed *galero* type, such as can be seen hanging above the tombs of cardinals, and has presumably lost whatever *fiocchi* (tassles) it once had. Its documented history reveals that it was found at the back of a wardrobe in Horace Walpole's house, Strawberry Hill, the contents of which were auctioned in 1842, and that it was worn by Charles Kean in his production of *King Henry VIII* in 1855. The material has been dated to the sixteenth century, but it cannot be proved to have adorned Wolsey's head. This last point was conveniently ignored by the literary critic Stephen Greenblatt, who assumed that hat and head had once been in contact and used the artefact as part of an argument about textual transmission through time.[38] His treatment of the hat and its assumed connection with Wolsey sparked Anne Barton's withering denunciation of 'Greenblatt's tendency to handle historical circumstances approximately', the evidence twisted to suit the pre-conceived argument.[39] It is a straightforward statement of fact, devoid of 'new historicist' spin, to say that Christ Church now celebrates its hat in media as diverse as stone, stained glass, wood, china and, at the commercial end of the range, on ties and wrapping paper for gifts. Elsewhere in Oxford there is an object which may or may not stand a better chance of providing a direct connection between Wolsey and the viewer: the polyhedral sundial in the Museum of the History of Science. Its base is decorated with the archbishop of York's heraldic crossed keys and by a rather fetching *galero*, and it is thought to have been made for Wolsey by Nicholas Kratzer *c*. 1525.

In an age when much attention was devoted to symbols and mottos, Wolsey matched the highly symbolic hat with a coat of arms which is thought to have been of his own devising and was formally granted by Garter and Clarenceux heralds in 1527. His complex design reflected multiple allegiances: to the county of Suffolk, the papacy, the royal house of Lancaster and his patron saint, expressed respectively by elements from the arms of the fourteenth-century Ufford earls and their more recent de la Pole successors, by the lion of Leo X, the familiar red rose of Lancaster, and the choughs of Thomas Becket.[40] When the shield is surmounted by a metropolitical cross it indicates Wolsey's status as archbishop of York. The *galero* is used in the heraldry of clerics from priests to cardinals, with ranks being identified by the number of *fiocchi* and only cardinals having the full complement of fifteen on each side. These various elements are prominently displayed on a terracotta plaque in the Clock Court at Hampton Court, supported by *putti*, bordered by classical columns and placed above Wolsey's motto *DOMINUS MIHI ADJUTOR* ('The Lord is my helper'). The founder's arms were adopted by Christ Church, where variations can be found throughout the college, with or without the cross or impaled with those of York.

In that same college history, Trevor-Roper quotes John Aubrey's seventeenth-century lament that Wolsey lay buried in Leicester '(to the shame of Christ Church men) yet without any monument', adding that no memorial existed there until 1934.[41] This last point refers to the 'tomb' made of concrete and brick, inscribed with the appeal made by Shakespeare and Fletcher's cardinal to the abbot of Leicester – 'Give him a little earth for charity' – and decorated with Wolsey's coat of arms, which stands in the Lady Chapel of the partially reconstructed walls of the Augustinian abbey. It is respectable enough for a municipal monument, but a far cry from the grandiose design of Benedetto da Rovezzano. Elsewhere in Leicester's Abbey Park stands a twentieth-century statue of the cardinal, originally commissioned *c.* 1920 by Wolsey Ltd to adorn its premises in the city. In scale it was presumably better suited to its first location than it is to its present one. The company donated it to Leicester City Council in 1979, since when it has been vandalized and has received a replacement head and right hand. The accompanying inscription does not exactly do justice to so great a statesman:

> CARDINAL WOLSEY
> CHANCELLOR TO HENRY VIII
> DIED AT LEICESTER ABBEY 1530
> BURIED IN ABBEY GROUNDS
> THE STATUE WAS DONATED TO THE CITY BY WOLSEY
> THE INTERNATIONAL KNITWEAR FIRM

The firm traced its origins back to the mid eighteenth century, but only acquired the Wolsey name between the First and Second World Wars. 'Wolsey' and 'Cardinal' became highly respected brand names for knitwear, stockings and, most famously, socks. Though the brand name survives, Wolsey Ltd no longer exists as an independent company; nor does its factory overlooking Abbey Park, for that industrial landmark was demolished in 2008.

It is entirely appropriate that Thomas Wolsey should have received greater and more diverse recognition in the city of his birth than in that of his death, though a parallel exists in the fact that Ipswich's Augustinian priory is now the site of the Wolsey Art Gallery, a charming Arts and Crafts building, and of the Wolsey Memorial Garden, both tucked behind the post-Dissolution Christchurch Mansion.[42] In terms of material remains relating to the cardinal, Ipswich retains both his birthplace and the brick gateway of his college. The attitude of his fellow citizens appears to be one of pride, respect and affection, and modern commemorations of the city's most famous son range in size from the New Wolsey Theatre to commercially produced key rings decorated with a design derived from Gilbert's *Ego et rex meus*.[43]

Twentieth-century stage productions of Shakespeare and Fletcher's *King Henry VIII* were too numerous to be listed here. In view of the fact that Donald Wolfit directed but did not star in the play, perhaps the most direct link with the world of the actor-managers was provided by John Gielgud, who played Wolsey at the Old Vic in 1958. His lean appearance meant that he did not conform to popular notions of the cardinal, but at least he was roughly the same age as the historical original. Since its foundation in 1960, the Royal Shakespeare Company has staged three productions of *King Henry VIII* at Stratford, with Brewster Mason as Wolsey in 1969, John Thaw finding himself somewhat overwhelmed by Richard Griffiths' Henry in 1983, and Ian Hogg as the most recent cardinal, in 1996. An alternative stage Wolsey became available in 1960 with Robert Bolt's acclaimed study of Thomas More, *A Man for all Seasons*. The nature of the subject – More's refusal to take the oath of supremacy – means that Wolsey is no more than a cameo part early in the proceedings, described by Bolt as 'a decayed body in scarlet, with ambition matched by an excelling intellect'.[44] In the original production he was played by Willoughby Goddard, described by Caryl Brahms as 'the fleshliest cardinal in the business'.

In 1911 Tree's Wolsey was the first to appear in film, when five scenes from *King Henry VIII* were recorded at Ealing. According to the terms of the contract, all prints of the twenty-five-minute recording were destroyed a few weeks later.[45] Consequently, the earliest surviving screen Wolseys are those of Adolf Klein in the German film *Anna Boleyn* (1920) and Arthur Forrest in *When Knighthood was in Flower* (1922). Charles Laughton was not a natural for dashing, heroic parts and might have made a memorable Wolsey, but his reputation rests in no small measure on *The Private Life of Henry VIII* (1933), in which he played the older king, paired with every wife except Katherine of Aragon and therefore in no need of a cardinal. Henry's sister Mary is the heroine of *The Sword and the Rose* (1953), in which D. A. Clarke-Smith appears as Wolsey. When *A Man for all Seasons* was adapted for the cinema in 1966, Orson Welles became arguably the definitive Wolsey, a jowelly, worldly-wise vision in scarlet, and a statesman of incomparable ability. It was a hard act for Anthony Quayle to follow in *Anne of the Thousand Days* (1969), but so successfully did he manage it that he was nominated for an Academy Award. Terry Scott was in no danger of receiving such a nomination for his Wolsey when the vogue for Tudor films resulted in the spoof *Carry on Henry* (1970), though his portrayal perhaps inadvertently recalled that theatrical tradition of presenting clerics as figures of fun.

Although Patrick Troughton had played Wolsey in *The White Falcon* (BBC, 1956), it was from 1970 onwards that Tudor costume dramas became regular treats of the small screen, with the little-known John Baskcomb cast as Wolsey to Keith Michell's Henry in *The Six Wives of Henry VIII* (BBC, 1970): he was not required beyond the first episode. When the phenomenal success of that production led to the feature film *Henry VIII and his Six Wives* (1972), John

Bryans took the part of the cardinal. An octogenarian Gielgud reprised the role in *A Man for all Seasons* (1988), as did Willoughby Goddard in *God's Outlaw* (also 1988), a William Tyndale 'biopic' made for the Bible Society. Timothy West (BBC, 1979) and David Suchet (Granada, 2003) have also been television Wolseys, playing opposite John Stride and Ray Winstone respectively. Most recently, *The Tudors* (BBC, 2007) plumbed new depths of historical fabrication, not least when Sam Neill's Wolsey died by his own hand, the production team effectively covering themselves by having Henry hiss 'No one must know of this.'

While popular appreciation of sixteenth-century English history snowballed in the second half of the twentieth century, Pollard's *Wolsey* remained the standard biography for many years, essentially untroubled by either Hilaire Belloc's 1930 character sketch, which that prolific author squeezed in between lives of Richelieu (also 1930) and Cranmer (1931), or by Charles Ferguson's labour of love, *Naked to Mine Enemies: the Life of Cardinal Wolsey* (1958). Along the way Garrett Mattingly abandoned academic caution and indulged in a vision of Wolsey that derived ultimately from the sixteenth-century satirists, revelling in the 'unwieldy hulk of corrupted flesh bearing perilously the supple, powerful, brain, a demoniac incandescence of ambition and pride driving and lighting from within the bloated, rotting, body'.[46] This was surely the Wolsey that Bolt and Welles brought to stage and screen. From the heart of the academy, Geoffrey Elton studied the 1530s so intensively that he spent nearly half a century zealously proclaiming that decade as a period of revolution in English government, with Thomas Cromwell as the minister at the hub of a modernizing and secularizing process.[47] In order to do this Elton was obliged to denigrate Wolsey as a 'medieval' figure whose tenure as lord chancellor was characterized not merely by continuity, but by sterility, rather than change. Elton's disinclination towards biography as a suitable genre for serious history left the field open for others, and the two Tudor ministers shared the billing in Neville Williams' *The Cardinal and the Secretary* (1975).

If teachers and their students and, more particularly, supervisors of doctoral theses and their supervisees are arranged in academic genealogies, then Elton was the academic grandson of Pollard, the intervening generation being supplied by the Elizabethan historian J. E. Neale, Elton's supervisor. As Patrick Collinson has noted, Pollard in 1903 and Elton in 1967 both chose to be professors of constitutional history when they acquired their personal chairs: an example of the so-called 'grandfather law' in practice.[48] Elton spent his career reacting against Neale's approach to Tudor history. In turn, he retained the respect of his own numerous students even when they chose to react against his obsession with Cromwell and the perceived revolution in government. Through their studies of cognate subjects, the first post-Elton generation of scholars has provided a variety of angles on Wolsey's career, with major contributions including J. J. Scarisbrick's biography of Henry VIII (1968), J. A. Guy's study of the court of star chamber (1977), and the biographies of Francis I (1982) by R. J. Knecht and of Anne Boleyn (1986) by Eric Ives. Scarisbrick presents Wolsey as the consummate statesman and as something of an Erasmian idealist, motivated above all by the cause of universal peace. This, Scarisbrick argues, accounts for Thomas More's ability to work with him so closely for much of the 1520s.[49] John Guy has concluded that, far from expressing sterility, Wolsey's legal reforms worked very effectively, speeding up the judicial process and demonstrably securing justice for the underdog.

In 1982 Wolsey became half of another double biography when Jasper Ridley, a seasoned biographer who had previously worked in the nineteenth century, matched him with his successor as lord chancellor in *The Statesman and the Fanatic: Thomas Wolsey and Thomas More*. Individual passages in this work bring its subjects to life, range widely and make good use of the primary sources, but the title of the book conveys a reluctance to acclimatize to the nature of religious belief in the sixteenth-century, while the Wolsey chapters are characterized by cynical anticlericalism. Much less easy to dismiss is Peter Gwyn, *The King's Cardinal: the Rise and Fall of Thomas Wolsey* (1990), which the author describes as a refutation of Pollard.[50] This is an utterly phenomenal work by any reckoning: eleven years of research fills more than 600 densely packed pages. Wolsey himself often disappears under the mass of thematically arranged material, thereby confirming Elton's point about the limitations of Tudor biography, but there are significant threads running through the work, not least Gwyn's insistence that Henry was no mere figurehead of a monarch, but one who actively initiated policies which Wolsey was then obliged to implement. Gwyn's asides on the nature of statesmanship, in which Margaret Thatcher looms uncomfortably large for some tastes, are now as dated as the contemporary allusions made by Law or Pollard. No less valuable, but more accessible, is the volume of essays, *Cardinal Wolsey: Church, State and Art* (1991), edited by S. J. Gunn and P. G. Lindley, which brings a refreshingly interdisciplinary approach to its subject.

As we have seen, each successive study of this well-worn subject offers subtle variations on its theme, but perhaps there is also a sense in which such studies can be likened to the types of pontiffs who are said to emerge from successive conclaves, fat popes alternating with thin popes, diplomats with pastors. If the present offering is interpreted in that light, then its modest scale is something of a reaction against Gwyn's highly ambitious scholarship and it will have achieved its purpose if it merely keeps interest in Wolsey ticking over. If, on the other hand, one is determined to find a further reason for studying the cardinal half a millennium after he rose to prominence in a small kingdom towards the edge of Christendom, then it must surely be found by presenting his career as an antidote to insularity, for his statesmanship, ecclesiastical responsibilities and cultural patronage were all exercised on a broad canvas. Thomas Wolsey's experience can therefore act as a useful – indeed, an eminently useful – guide to life in Renaissance Europe.

Notes

Notes to the Introduction

1   D. S. Chambers, 'Edward Armstrong (1846–1928), teacher of the Italian Renaissance at Oxford', in J. E. Law and L. Østermark-Johansen (eds), *Victorian and Edwardian Responses to the Italian Renaissance*, Aldershot and Burlington, 2005, pp. 211–32.
2   J. R. Hale, *Machiavelli and Renaissance Italy*, London, 1961.
3   This list does not include lord keepers of the great seal, who exercised some of the functions of the chancellorship, without enjoying its honours. It also omits the twelfth-century Robert de Gant, chancellor of King Stephen during a period of civil conflict when rival administrations contended for control of the kingdom.

Notes to Chapter 1: Apprenticeship, c. 1471–1515

1   On Wolsey's family background see T. W. Cameron, 'The early life of Thomas Wolsey', *English Historical Review* 3 (1888), 458–77; V. B. Redstone, 'Wulcy of Suffolk', *Suffolk Institute of Archaeology and Natural History*, 16 (1918), 71–89. 'Wulcy' was the cardinal's spelling of the name, perhaps suggesting a softer pronunciation than that adopted by posterity, though contemporaries would have been familiar with linsey-woolsey fabrics, the coarseness of which could be brought to mind when thinking of the base-born cardinal.
2   All information on Ipswich School and its antecedents is derived from J. Blatchly, *A Famous Antient Seed-plot of Learning: a History of Ipswich School*, Ipswich, 2003 sent to me by the author in electronic form.
3   G. Cavendish, *The Life of Cardinal Wolsey*, London, 1890, p. 38. All quotations in the present work are taken from this edition. The scholarly edition is *The Life and Death of Cardinal Wolsey*, ed. R. S. Sylvester, Early English Text Society, 1959.
4   M. Creighton, *Cardinal Wolsey*, London, 1888, p. 18; S. Jack, 'Thomas Wolsey', *Oxford Dictionary of National Biography* (hereafter *ODNB*), 60, p. 17, Oxford, 2004; A. F. Pollard, *Wolsey*, London, 1929, p. 12; J. Ridley, *The Statesman and the Fanatic: Thomas Wolsey and Thomas More*, London, 1982, p. 1; P. Gwyn, *The King's Cardinal: the Rise and Fall of Thomas Wolsey*, London, 1992, p. 1. The *ODNB* should be consulted for biographical and bibliographical information on most of the persons of English, Scottish and Welsh

birth mentioned in this text, together with those of non-insular birth who nevertheless developed significant connections with the island kingdoms.

5 *Calendar of State Papers and Manuscripts Relating to English Affairs, Existing in the Archives and Collections of Venice, and in other Libraries of Northern Italy* [hereafter *Cal. S. P. Ven.*], ed. R. Brown, London, 1867, 2 (1509–19), 1287. In the case of Italian personal names, I have adopted the spelling used in the *Dizionario Biografico degli Italiani*.

6 Cavendish, *Life*, p. 13.

7 *Cal. S. P. Ven.*, 2, 1287.

8 In cases where variant spellings of surnames exist, such as Winter and Wynter, Tunstal and Tunstall, those given in the *ODNB* are used here for ease of reference.

9 For Wolsey's Oxford, see J. I. Catto and T. A. R. Evans (eds), *The History of the University of Oxford*, 2: *Late Medieval Oxford*, Oxford, 1992, and J. McConica (ed.), *The History of the University of Oxford*, 3: *The Collegiate University*, Oxford, 1986.

10 Cavendish, *Life*, p. 14.

11 D. Mancini, *The Usurpation of Richard III*, ed. C. A. J. Armstrong, Gloucester, 1984.

12 Bradgate Park is less than five miles from the site of Wolsey's death at Leicester Abbey.

13 Not Lymington in Hampshire, as has occasionally been asserted.

14 Cavendish, *Life*, p. 15.

15 Cavendish, *Life*, p. 16.

16 Cavendish, *Life*, p. 17.

17 As with Archduke Philip, anglicizing the name of a prince known in his various realms as Charles, Carlos or Karl may be considered acceptable. For the sake of convenience, a handful of Christendom's most prominent rulers also appear in this text in anglicized form.

18 Cavendish, *Life*, pp. 17–21.

19 Pollard, *Wolsey*, p. 13.

20 For accounts of relations between these rulers, see F. J. Baumgartner, *Louis XII*, Stroud, 1994 and Basingstoke, 1996, and C. Shaw, *Julius II: the Warrior Pope*, Oxford, 1993.

21 On the Bridewell house see S. Thurley, 'The domestic building works of Cardinal Wolsey', in S. J. Gunn and P. G. Lindley (eds), *Cardinal Wolsey: Church, State and Art*, Cambridge, 1991, pp. 76–7, 83.

22 Gwyn, *The King's Cardinal*, p. 4.

23 B. J. Harris, *Edward Stafford, Third Duke of Buckingham, 1478–1521*, Stanford, 1986, pp. 162–3.

24 Cavendish, *Life*, p. 25.

25 See W. Ullmann, 'Julius II and the schismatic cardinals', in D. Baker (ed.), *Schism, Heresy and Religious Protest, Studies in Church History*, 9 1972, pp. 177–93.

26 *Letters and Papers, Foreign and Domestic, of the Reign of Henry VIII, 1509–1547* [hereafter *LP*], 1, ed. J. S. Brewer, London, 1862, p. 880.

27 Soderini and Wolsey were united in due course by having their tombs created by the same sculptor, Benedetto de' Grazzini da Rovezzano.

28 For the careers of all cardinals, patriarchs, archbishops and bishops, see initially K. Eubel, *Hierarchia Catholica Medii Aevi*, 2–3 Münster, 1913.

29 W. E. Wilkie, *The Cardinal Protectors of England: Rome and the Tudors before the Reformation*, Cambridge, 1974, pp. 17–28, 53–73.

30 Cardinal Galeotto Franciotti della Rovere had been protector of English interests from 1504 to 1508. For Della Rovere and Alidosi, see Wilkie, *The Cardinal Protectors*, pp. 34–40.

31 In 1517 Giulio consolidated his insular interests by becoming the first cardinal protector of Ireland.

32 S. Thurley, *Hampton Court: a Social and Architectural History*, New Haven and London, 2003, pp. 9–14.

33 *The Anglica Historia of Polydore Vergil, AD 1485–1537*, ed. D. Hay, Camden Society, 3rd ser., 74, 1950.

34 Pietro Vanni, a cousin of Ammonius, became Wolsey's Latin secretary.

35 Vergil, *Anglica Historia*, p. 225.

36 For all aspects of the reign, see R. J. Knecht, *Francis I*, Cambridge, 1982.

37 Creighton, *Cardinal Wolsey*, p. 38.

38 Cavendish, *Life*, p. 30.

39 Cavendish, *Life*, p. 31.

Notes to Chapter 2: Grand Chancellor, 1515–20

1 Thurley, *Hampton Court*, p. 26.

2 Thurley, *Hampton Court*, p. 20.

3 H. Wayment, 'Wolsey and stained glass', in S. J. Gunn and P. G. Lindley (eds), *Cardinal Wolsey: Church, State and Art*, Cambridge, 1991, pp. 116–30; T. Campbell, 'Cardinal Wolsey's tapestry collection', *Antiquaries Journal*, 76 (1996), pp. 77–83.

4 *Cal. S. P. Ven.*, 2, 1287.

5 For York Place, see Thurley, 'Domestic building works', pp. 77–81, 83–7.

6 Cavendish, *Life*, pp. 38–9.

7 For example, Gwyn, *The King's Cardinal*, p. 32.

8 Quoted by Gwyn, *The King's Cardinal*, pp. 49–50.

9 Quoted by Gwyn, *The King's Cardinal*, p. 49.

10 *LP*, 3, app. 21.

11 Cavendish, *Life*, p. 40.

12 For all aspects of Wolsey's role in star chamber, see J. A. Guy, *The Cardinal's Court: the Impact of Thomas Wolsey in Star Chamber*, Hassocks, 1977.

13 J. Skelton, 'Why come ye not to court', lines 326–45, ed. G. Walker, John Skelton, pp. 93–4. Wherever possible, I have followed Walker's edition of Skelton's poems, but in some cases the modernised spellings are my own. For comment on the poem and its political context, see G. Walker, *John Skelton and the Politics of the 1520s*, Cambridge, 1988, pp. 100–18.

14 *Cal. S. P. Ven.*, 2, 1287.

15 Guy, *The Cardinal's Court*, p. 31.

16 *BL Add.* 1938, f. 44: reproduced in this volume.

17 Guy, *The Cardinal's Court*, pp. 76–8.

18 *LP*, 4, 4796.

19 Wolsey's management of the council is described in detail by Guy, *The Cardinal's Court*, pp. 23–50.

20 Scarisbrick, *Henry VIII*, p. 45.

21 Gwyn, *The King's Cardinal, passim.*

22 Cavendish, *Life*, p. 40.

23 Fought on 13–14 September 1515. Knecht, *Francis I*, is a particularly good guide to relations between the various states.

24 Creighton, *Cardinal Wolsey*, p. 44.

25 For further details of the Petrucci conspiracy, see K. J. P. Lowe, *Church and Politics in Renaissance Italy: the Life and Career of Cardinal Francesco Soderini (1453–1524)*, Cambridge, 1993, pp. 104–13.

26 For example, Wolsey's suffragans at Bath and Wells were Thomas Wolf, a Franciscan, and William Gilbert, abbot of the Augustinian canons regular at Bruton.

27 K. M. Setton, *The Papacy and the Levant (1204–1571)*, 3: *the Sixteenth Century to the Reign of Julius III*, Philadelphia, 1984, p. 180.

28 *LP*, 2, 4034.

29 Scarisbrick, *Henry VIII*, p. 71.

30 *Cal. S. P. Ven.*, 2, 1085. On the celebrations surrounding the Universal Peace, see S. Anglo, *Spectacle, Pageantry, and Early Tudor Policy*, Oxford, 1969, pp. 124–36.

31 For details of the Anglo-French treaty, see Gwyn, *The King's Cardinal*, pp. 92–6.

32 *LP*, 2, 4540.

33 Lorenzo and the teenage Madeleine both died in 1519, leaving a baby daughter, Caterina, the future queen of France.

34 It is now the Palazzo Torlonia on via della Conciliazione.

35 Penny died at Leicester Abbey, where he had formerly been abbot, in 1520. In that respect he provided a precedent for Wolsey, who died there in 1530.

36 *LP*, 3, 1122.

37 Gwyn, *The King's Cardinal*, p. 268.

38 *Cal. S. P. Ven.*, 2, 1287.

39 *Cal. S. P. Ven.*, 2, 671.

40 Eubel, *Hierarchia Catholica*, 3, p. 283, Pacentin., n.4 misidentifies the archbishop as Bainbridge.

41 See Thurley, 'Domestic building works', in Gunn and Lindley, *Cardinal Wolsey*, p. 95, for a conjectural first floor plan of this structure.

42 Studies of this great festival include: J. G. Russell, *The Field of Cloth of Gold: men and manners in 1520*, London, 1969; Anglo, *Spectacle*, pp. 137–69; 'Jacobus Sylvius (Jacques

Dubois), *Francisci Francorum regis et Henrici Anglorum colloquium*', ed. S. Bamforth and J. Dupèbe, *Renaissance studies*, 5 (1991).

Notes to Chapter 3: Papal pretentions, 1520–3

1   For the college and its masters, see C. Crawley, *Trinity Hall: the History of a Cambridge College, 1350–1975*, Cambridge, 1976.
2   D. MacCulloch, *Thomas Cranmer: a Life*, New Haven and London, 1996, p. 24.
3   Gwyn, *The King's Cardinal*, p. 481.
4   On More's employment in the king's service see J. Guy, *The Public Career of Sir Thomas More*, Brighton, 1980.
5   Harris, *Edward Stafford*, p. 205.
6   Knecht, *Francis I*, p. 105.
7   See above, p. 21.
8   Crieghton, *Cardinal Wolsey*, p. 75.
9   *LP*, 3, 1762.
10 For Walker's analysis of the poem and its context, see *John Skelton*, pp. 53–100.
11 In 1549–50 over sixty ballots were required to reach a result.
12 F. J. Baumgartner, *Behind Locked Doors: a History of the Papal Elections*, New York and Basingstoke, 2003, pp. 95–7.
13 *Cal. S. P. Ven.*, 2, 1287.
14 Knecht, *Francis I*, p. 113.
15 E. Hall, *The Union of the Two Noble and Illustre Famelies of Lancastre and Yorke* [hereafter *Chronicle*], ed. H. Ellis, London, 1809, p. 634.
16 The festivities and their context are analysed by Anglo, *Spectacle*, pp. 170–206.
17 Thurley, *Hampton Court*, p. 24.
18 Skelton, *Why come ye not to court?*, lines 401–15.
19 Skelton, *Why come ye not to court*, lines 153–6.
20 In 1523 Inge was succeeded at Meath by Richard Wilson, bishop of Negroponte *in partibus*, who had been Wolsey's suffragan in York since 1516.
21 Vergil, *Anglica Historia*, p. 305.
22 Thurley, 'Domestic building works', p. 78, 91–3. It was demolished in 1650.
23 Thurley, 'Domestic building works', p. 87.
24 Cavendish, *Life*, pp. 53–4.
25 Hall, *Chronicle*, p. 642.
26 *LP*, 3, 2483.
27 Gwyn, *The King's Cardinal*, p. 356.
28 W. Roper, *The Lyfe of Sir Thomas More, Knight*, ed. E. V. Hitchcock, Early English Text Society, orig. ser. 197, 1935, pp. 16–20.
29 Gwyn, *The King's Cardinal*, pp. 369–77.

30　Vergil, *Anglica Historia*, p. 305.

31　Pollard, *Wolsey*, p. 187; Gwyn, *The King's Cardinal*, pp. 285–9.

32　Lowe, *Church and Politics*, pp. 132–9.

33　For this ill-fated expedition, see S. J. Gunn, 'The duke of Suffolk's march on Paris in 1523', *English Historical Review*, 101 (1986), pp. 596–634.

34　Gwyn, *The King's Cardinal*, p. 378.

35　D. S. Chambers, 'Papal conclaves and prophetic mystery in the Sistine chapel', *Journal of the Warburg and Courtauld Institutes*, 41 (1978), pp. 322–6.

36　Baumgartner, *Behind Locked Doors*, pp. 98–100.

37　*LP*, 3, 3389.

Notes to Chapter 4: Heretics and Rebels, 1524–7

1　Cavendish, *Life*, pp. 32–3.

2　Cavendish, *Life*, p. 34.

3　R. Bowers, 'The cultivation and promotion of music in the household and orbit of Thomas Wolsey', in S. J. Gunn and P. G. Lindley, *Cardinal Wolsey: Church, State and Art*, p. 180.

4　Bowers, 'Cultivation', pp. 191–2.

5　Bowers, 'Cultivation' p. 184, 186–8.

6　See above, pp. 91–2.

7　Cavendish, *Life*, p. 36.

8　*ODNB*, 70, p. 19.

9　Cited by D. S. Chambers, 'The economic predicament of Renaissance cardinals', *Studies in Medieval and Renaissance History*, 3 (1966), p. 293.

10　Wayment, 'Wolsey and stained glass', pp. 120–6.

11　Thurley, *Hampton Court*, p. 30.

12　Quoted by Gwyn, *The King's Cardinal*, p. 342.

13　H. R. Trevor-Roper, *Christ Church Oxford*, Oxford, 3 edn, 1989, p. 1.

14　J. Newman, 'Cardinal Wolsey's collegiate foundations', in S. J. Gunn and P. G. Lindley, *Cardinal Wolsey: Church, State and Art*, p. 108.

15　On the opposite side of St Aldate's, at the junction with Brewer Street, are almshouses founded by Wolsey as part of the college's wider community.

16　For details, see J. H. Harvey and J. G. Milne, 'The building of Cardinal College, Oxford', *Oxoniensia*, 8–9 (1943–4), pp. 137–53.

17　Newman, 'Cardinal Wolsey's collegiate foundations', pp. 108–9.

18　*ODNB*, 70, p. 159.

19　By D. MacCulloch, *Thomas Cranmer: a Life*, New Haven and London, 1996, p. 24. The most direct link between Cranmer and Wolsey was provided by William Capon, who doubled up as master of Jesus and the cardinal's almoner.

20　Newman, 'Cardinal Wolsey's collegiate foundations', p. 108.

21 Foxe, *Acts and Monuments*, London, 1877, 5, pp. 416–17.

22 The theme of B. M. Hallman, *Italian Cardinals, Reform, and the Church as Property, 1492–1563*, Berkeley and Los Angeles, 1985.

23 Gwyn, *The King's Cardinal*, p. 317, n. 2.

24 Pollard, *Wolsey*, p. 200.

25 Gwyn, *The King's Cardinal*, pp. 316–28.

26 Gwyn, *The King's Cardinal*, p. 273.

27 K. Brown, 'Wolsey and ecclesiastical order: the case of the Franciscan Observants', in S. J. Gunn and P. G. Lindley, *Cardinal Wolsey: Church, State and Art*, pp. 219–38.

28 J. Woolfson, *Padua and the Tudors: English Students in Italy 1485–1603*, p. 286.

29 For Campeggi as cardinal protector, see Wilkie, *The Cardinal Protectors*, pp. 141–239.

30 Knecht, *Francis I*, provides an excellent account of French foreign policy in this period.

31 On this episode, see G. W. Bernard, *War, Taxation, and Rebellion in Early Tudor England: Henry VIII, Wolsey and the Amicable Grant of 1525*, Brighton, 1986.

32 Knecht, *Francis I*, p. 185.

33 Quoted by Gwyn, *The King's Cardinal*, p. 367.

34 Gwyn, *The King's Cardinal*, p. 367.

35 *ODNB*, 53, p. 928.

36 L. Guicciardini, *The Sack of Rome*, trans. and ed. J. H. McGregor, New York, 1993.

37 J. Hook, *The Sack of Rome 1527*, 2nd edn, Basingstoke, 2004, p. 156.

38 Only two cardinals had died since Clement's election: Guillén-Ramón de Vich y de Vallterra in July 1525 and Sigismondo Gonzaga in October that year.

Notes to Chapter 5: A Great Fall, 1527–9

1 His wife was the sister of Madeleine de la Tour d'Auvergne and therefore the sister-in-law of Lorenzo de' Medici, duke of Urbino: see above, pp. 61, 198.

2 Baumgartner, *Louis XII*, pp. 71–9.

3 Scarisbrick, *Henry VIII*, pp. 153–4.

4 Cavendish, *Life*, p. 68.

5 Cavendish, *Life*, p. 81.

6 Cavendish, *Life*, pp. 87–8.

7 Cavendish, *Life*, p. 93.

8 On the trial, see G. Walker, 'Saint or schemer?: the 1527 heresy trial of Thomas Bilney reconsidered', *Journal of Ecclesiastical History*, 40 (1989), pp. 219–38.

9 For Wolsey's patronage of Skelton, see Walker, *John Skelton*, pp. 188–217.

10 G. Walker, 'Cardinal Wolsey and the satirists: the case of *Godly Queen Hester* re-opened', in S. J. Gunn and P. G. Lindley (eds), *Cardinal Wolsey: Church, State and Art*, Cambridge, 1991, pp. 239–0.

11 W. Tyndale, *The Practice of Prelates*, ed. H. Walker, Parker Society, 43, 1849.

12   S. J. Gunn, 'Wolsey's foreign policy and the domestic crisis of 1527–1528', in S. J. Gunn and
     P. G. Lindley (eds), *Cardinal Wolsey: Church, State and Art*, Cambridge, 1991, pp. 174–7.

13   On the sweating sickness, see J. L. Flood, '"Safer on the battlefield than in the city": England,
     the "sweating sickness", and the continent', *Renaissance Studies*, 17, 2, pp. 147–76.

14   *LP*, 4, 2, 4468.

15   *LP*, 4, 2, 4649.

16   Again, information on the Ipswich foundation comes from J. Blatchly, *A Famous Antient
     Seed-plot*.

17   Alas, there is no uniform opinion about whether or not Wolsey was the original Humpty
     Dumpty.

18   P. G. Lindley, 'Playing check-mate with royal majesty? Wolsey's patronage of Italian
     Renaissance sculpture', in S. J. Gunn and P. G. Lindley (eds), *Cardinal Wolsey: Church, State
     and Art*, Cambridge, 1991, p. 279.

19   Lindley, 'Playing check-mate', pp. 265–6. Lindley explains that Wolsey came to the
     commissioning of his own tomb with experience as the 'patron' of an unrealized tomb for
     Henry VIII and Queen Katherine commissioned from Torrigiano: pp. 262–3.

20   A point well illustrated by T. Tuohy, *Herculean Ferrara: Ercole d'Este (1471–1505) and the
     Invention of a Ducal Capital*, Cambridge, 1996.

21   On Wolsey's collection of plate and patronage of goldsmiths such as Robert Amadas, see
     P. Glanville, 'Cardinal Wolsey and the goldsmiths', in S. J. Gunn and P. G. Lindley (eds),
     Cardinal Wolsey: Church, State and Art, Cambridge, 1991, pp. 131–48.

22   For Wolsey and Katherine, see Gwyn, *The King's Cardinal*, pp. 505–7.

23   Cavendich, *Life*, p. 54.

24   *LP*, 4, 4477.

25   D. Knowles, '"The matter of Wilton" in 1528', *Bulletin of the Institute of Historical Research*
     31 (1958), 92–6; Gwyn, *The King's Cardinal*, pp. 321–3.

26   See Gwyn, *The King's Cardinal*, p. 294 for the exchange of Suffolk for Norfolk, which was
     at the insistence of Bishop Nix of Norwich.

27   Papal provision to Dublin was not granted until 3 September 1529.

28   Sir William was not related to Thomas Skeffington, bishop of Bangor, who was originally
     called Pace and was related to the dean of St Paul's.

29   E. Ives, 'The fall of Wolsey', in S. J. Gunn and P. G. Lindley (eds.), *Cardinal Wolsey: Church,
     State and Art*, Cambridge, 1991, p. 291.

30   Vergil, *Anglica historia*, p. 331.

31   Cavendish, *Life*, p. 119.

32   Cavendish, *Life*, p. 124.

33   Cavendish, *Life*, p. 125.

34   Cavendish, *Life*, p. 127.

35   Cavendish, *Life*, pp. 129–30.

36   Ives, 'The fall of Wolsey', p. 294.

37   Cavendish, *Life*, p. 135.

38 M. Whitehead (ed.), *Held in Trust: 2008 Years of Sacred Culture*, Stonyhurst, 2008, pp. 42–3.

39 Guy, *Public Career*, p. 97.

40 Hall, *Chronicle*, p. 764. The entire speech is summarized by Guy, *Public Career*, pp. 113–14.

41 Ives, 'The fall of Wolsey', pp. 308–9; G. R. Elton, *Reform and Reformation*, London, 1977, pp. 112–13; S. E. Lehmberg, *The Reformation Parliament, 1529–1536*, Cambridge, 1970, pp. 102–3.

42 Ives, 'The fall of Wolsey', p. 296; LP, 4, 3 pp. 2712–14.

Notes to Chapter 6: Pastor Bonus, 1529–30

1 Cavendish, *Life*, p. 146.

2 Cavendish, *Life*, pp. 149–50.

3 Cavendish, *Life*, pp. 156–9.

4 Cavendish, *Life*, p. 164.

5 Cavendish, *Life*, p. 171.

6 *Hen. VIII*, IV, i, 95–7.

7 As before, all information in this chapter relating to the Ipswich college is derived from Blatchly, *A Famous Antient Seed-plot*.

8 Cavendish, *Life*, pp. 194–5.

9 Cavendish, *Life*, pp. 202–3.

10 Quoted by P. Gwyn, *The King's Cardinal*, p. 616.

11 Unlike Wolsey's Hertfordshire building projects, Cawood Castle does survive, albeit subject to various alterations since the cardinal's day. It is now owned by the Landmark Trust.

12 Cavendish, *Life*, p. 243 distinguishes this Hardwick Hall as Hardwick-upon-Line, Nottinghamshire, though the more famous Hardwick Hall in Derbyshire does happen to stand half way between Sheffield and Nottingham.

13 Cavendish, *Life*, p. 244.

14 Cavendish, *Life*, p. 250.

15 Cavendish, *Life*, pp. 150–6.

Notes to Chapter 7: At the Sign of the Red Hat, 1530–2009

1 For the posthumous reputation of the Borgia, see J. N. Hillgarth, 'The image of Alexander VI and Cesare Borgia in the sixteenth and seventeenth centuries', *Journal of the Warburg and Courtauld Institutes*, 59 (1996), pp. 119–29.

2 *ODNB*, 60, pp. 34–6.

3 Walker, 'Cardinal Wolsey and the satirists', p. 240.

4   J. Dillon (ed.), *Performance and Spectacle in Hall's Chronicle*, London, 2002, highlights one dimension of the work.

5   Hall, *Chronicle*, p. 774.

6   W. Roper, *The Lyfe of Sir Thomas More, Knight*, ed. E. V. Hitchcock, Early English Text Society, orig. ser., 197, 1935.

7   Cavendish, *Life*, p. 46.

8   Cavendish, *Life*, p. 13.

9   Adapted from G. Cavendish, *Metrical Visions*, ed. A. S. G. Edwards, Columbia, 1980, p. 36, lines 232–8.

10 T. Churchyard, *Tragedy of Wolsey*, London, 1890, p. 271; originally published as *How Thomas Wolsey did Arise unto Great Authority . . . and was Arrested of High Treason*, in J. Higgins, *The Mirror for Magistrates*, 1587.

11 T. Storer, *The Life and Death of Thomas Wolsey, Cardinall*, London, 1599.

12 Bowers, 'Cultivation', pp. 206–18, which includes the score and from which I have taken and adapted the words.

13 Adapted from R. Holinshed, *Chronicles of England, Scotland, and Ireland*, 3, London, 1808, p. 756.

14 For the Magdalen portrait, see D. Roberts and R. Shepherd (eds), *Hidden Magdalen*, Oxford, 2008, pp. 50–1.

15 Bodleian MS Douce 363, reproduced in N. Williams, *The Cardinal and the Secretary*, London, 1975.

16 H. Wayment, 'Wolsey and stained glass' in Gunn and Lindley, *Cardinal Wolsey*, pp. 127–30.

17 *Hen. VIII*, IV, ii, 33–44.

18 *Hen. VIII*, IV, ii, 48–68.

19 There are versions in the Ashmolean Museum, Magdalen College, Oxford, and the Garrick Club.

20 The dispassion is asserted by Sybil Jack, *ODNB*, 60, p. 35.

21 *ODNB*, 19, pp. 462–3.

22 The Irving portrait is reproduced in J. Richards, *Sir Henry Irving: a Victorian Actor and his World*, London and New York, 2005.

23 *ODNB*, 43, pp. 938–9.

24 *Hen. VIII*, III, ii, 223–7.

25 *Hen. VIII*, III, ii, 313–16.

26 S. W. Singer: *The Life of Cardinal Wolsey and Metrical Visions*, 2 vols., London, 1825.

27 On which, see R. A. Griffiths and J. E. Law (eds), *Rawdon Brown and the Anglo-Venetian Relationship*, Stroud, 2005.

28 *LP*, 4, Introduction, p. dcxxxiii.

29 *The Gladstone Lament; or, Wolsey Personified*, London, 1866.

30 Creighton, *Cardinal Wolsey*, p. 2.

31 Creighton, *Cardinal Wolsey*, p. 213.

32 Quoted by Richards, *Sir Henry Irving*, pp. 138–9.

33   G. McMullan (ed.), *King Henry VIII (All is True)*, London, 2000, pp. 33–7.

34   The subtitle is even more revealing of the First World War context in which it was written: *How Wolsey Made a New Army and Navy and Organized the English Expedition to Artois and Flanders in 1513*.

35   C. A. P. Willsdon, *Mural Painting in Britain 1840–1940: Image and Meaning*, Oxford, 2000, p. 137, 140–1. Wolsey also appears in *The trial of Katharine of Aragon*, a mural commissioned from Frank Salisbury for the House of Lords.

36   Pollard, *Wolsey*, p. 327.

37   H. Trevor-Roper, *Christ Church Oxford*, p. 2.

38   S. J. Greenblatt, *Learning to Curse: Essays in Early Modern Culture*, New York and London, 1990.

39   A. Barton, 'Perils of historicism', *New York Review of Books*, 38, 6, 28 March 1991.

40   M. T. Elvins, *Cardinals and Heraldry*, London, *c*. 1988, p. 90, 92.

41   Trevor-Roper, *Christ Church Oxford*, p. 2.

42   Not to be outdone in the matter of Wolsey's cultural impact, Hampton Court boasts the Cardinal Wolsey public house and the large Cardinal spider, which is found only in the area around the palace.

43   In 1996 the (old) Wolsey Theatre premiered *The Devil's Cardinal* by Judith Cook, in which Michael Tudor Barnes played Wolsey.

44   A five-act play of 1874, *Cardinal Wolsey and the Loves of the Poets*, by 'Walter S. Raleigh', had never really taken off.

45   McMullan, *King Henry VIII*, p. 42.

46   G. Mattingly, *Catherine of Aragon*, London, 1942, p. 174.

47   Examples include: *The Tudor Revolution in Government: Administrative Changes in the Reign of Henry VIII*, Cambridge, 1953; *Reform and Renewal: Thomas Cromwell and the Common Weal*, Cambridge, 1973; *Studies in Tudor and Stuart Politics and Government: Papers and Reviews, 1946–1972*, 2 vols, London, 1974.

48   *ODNB*, 18, p. 352.

49   Scarisbrick, *Henry VIII*, p. 49.

50   Gwyn, *The King's Cardinal*, p. xvi, n. 3.

Bibliography

—— Anglo, S., *Spectacle, Pageantry and Early Tudor Policy*, Oxford, 1969

Authentick Memoirs of Life and Infamous Actions of Cardinal Wolsey, London, 1731

Baker, J., *The Oxford History of the Laws of England*, 6 (1483–1558), Oxford, 2003

Barlowe, J. and Roy, W., *Rede me and be not Wrothe*, ed. D. H. Parker, Toronto, 1992

Barton, A., 'Perils of historicism', *New York Review of Books*, 38, 6, 28 March 1991

Baumgartner, F. J., *Louis XII*, Stroud, 1994 and Basingstoke, 1996

—— *Behind Locked Doors: a History of the Papal Elections*, New York and Basingstoke, 2003

Belloc, H., *Wolsey*, London, 1930

Bernard, G. W., *The Power of the Early Tudor Nobility: a Study of the Fourth and Fifth Earls of Shrewsbury*, Brighton, 1985

—— *War, Taxation, and Rebellion in Early Tudor England: Henry VIII, Wolsey and the Amicable Grant of 1525* Brighton 1986

—— 'The fall of Wolsey reconsidered', *Journal of British Studies*, 35 (1996), pp. 292–310

Bingham, C., *James V: King of Scots 1512–1542*, London, 1971

Blatchly, J., *A Famous Antient Seed-plot of Learning: a History of Ipswich School*, Ipswich, 2003

Bowers, R., 'The cultivation and promotion of music in the household and orbit of Thomas Wolsey', in S. J. Gunn and P. G. Lindley (eds), *Cardinal Wolsey: Church, State and Art*, Cambridge, 1991, pp. 178–218

Broderick, J. F., 'The Sacred College of Cardinals: size and geographical composition (1099–1986)', *Archivium Historiae Pontificiae*, 25 (1987), pp. 7–71

Brown, K., 'Wolsey and ecclesiastical order: the case of the Franciscan Observants', in S. J. Gunn and P. G. Lindley (eds), *Cardinal Wolsey: Church, State and Art*, Cambridge, 1991, pp. 219–38

Brown, R. (ed.), *Four Years at the Court of Henry VIII*, 2 vols, London, 1854

Byatt, L. M. C., 'The concept of hospitality in a cardinal's household in Renaissance Rome', *Renaissance Studies*, 2 (1988), pp. 312–20

Calendar of State Papers and Manuscripts Relating to English Affairs, Existing in the Archives and Collections of Venice, and in other Libraries of Northern Italy, 2 (1509–19), ed. R. Brown, London, 1867

Cameron, T. W., 'The early life of Thomas Wolsey', *English Historical Review*, 3 (1888), pp. 458–77

Campbell, T., 'Cardinal Wolsey's tapestry collection', *Antiquaries Journal*, 76 (1996), pp. 77–83

Canterburies Dreame: in which the Apparition of Cardinall Wolsey did Present Himselfe unto him on the . . . Third Night after my Lord of Strafford had Taken his Fare-well to the World, London, 1641

Catto, J. I. and Evans, T. A. R. (eds), *The History of the University of Oxford*, 2: *Late Medieval Oxford*, Oxford, 1992

Cavendish, G., *The Life of Cardinal Wolsey and Metrical Visions*, 2 vols, ed. S. W. Singer, London, 1825

—— *The Life of Cardinal Wolsey*, London, 1890

—— *The Life and Death of Cardinal Wolsey*, ed. R. S. Sylvester, Early English Text Society, 243, 1959

—— *Metrical visions*, ed. A. S. G. Edwards, Columbia, 1980

Chambers, D. S., *Cardinal Bainbridge in the Court of Rome, 1509–1514* Oxford 1965

—— 'Cardinal Wolsey and the papal tiara', *Bulletin of the Institute of Historical Research*, 38 (1965), pp. 20–30

—— 'The economic predicament of Renaissance cardinals', *Studies in Medieval and Renaissance History*, 3 (1966), pp. 289–313

—— 'Papal conclaves and prophetic mystery in the Sistine Chapel', *Journal of the Warburg and Courtauld Institutes*, 41 (1978), pp. 322–6

—— 'Edward Armstrong (1846–1928), teacher of the Italian Renaissance at Oxford', in J. E. Law and L. Østermark-Johansen (eds), *Victorian and Edwardian Responses to the Italian Renaissance*, Aldershot and Burlington, 2005, pp. 211–32

Churchyard, T., *The Tragedy of Cardinal Wolsey*, London, 1890; originally published as *How Thomas Wolsey did Arise unto Great Authority . . . and was Arrested of High Treason*, in J. Higgins, *The Mirour for Magistrates*, 1587

Cobbold, R., *Freston Tower; or, the Early Days of Cardinal Wolsey*, London, 1850

Colvin, H. M. (ed.), *The History of the King's Works*, 4 London 1982

Crawley, C., *Trinity Hall: the History of a Cambridge College, 1350–1975*, Cambridge, 1976

Creighton, M., *History of the Papacy during the Reformation*, 5 vols, London, 1882–7

—— *Cardinal Wolsey*, London, 1888

Cruickshank, C. G., *Army Royal: Henry VIII's Invasion of France, 1513*, Oxford, 1969

—— *The English Occupation of Tournai, 1513–1519*, Oxford, 1971

Davis, J. F., 'The trials of Thomas Bylney and the English Reformation', *Historical Journal*, 24 (1981), pp. 775–90

Davis, V., *William Waynflete, Bishop and Educationalist*, Woodbridge, 1993

Dillon, J. (ed.), *Performance and Spectacle in Hall's Chronicle*, London, 2002

Dizionario Biografico degli Italiani, vols 1–70, 1960–2008

'Jacobus Sylvius (Jacques Dubois), *Francisci Francorum regis et Henrici Anglorum colloquium*', ed. S. Bamforth and J. Dupèbe, *Renaissance Studies*, 5 (1991)

Dymond, D., 'The famine of 1527 in Essex', *Local Population Studies*, 26 (1981), pp. 29–40

Elton, G. R., *The Tudor Revolution in Government: Administrative Changes in the Reign of Henry VIII*, Cambridge, 1953

—— *Reform and Renewal: Thomas Cromwell and the Common Weal*, Cambridge, 1973

—— *Studies in Tudor and Stuart Politics and Government: Papers and Reviews, 1946–1972*, 2 vols, London, 1974

—— *Reform and Reformation*, London, 1977.

Elvins, M. T., *Cardinals and Heraldry*, London, *c.* 1988

Emden, A. B., *A Biographical Register of the University of Oxford to 1500*, 3 vols, Oxford, 1957–9

—— *A Biographical Register of the University of Cambridge to 1500*, Cambridge, 1963

—— *A Biographical Register of the University of Oxford, 1501–1540*, Oxford, 1974

Eubel, K., *Hierarchia Catholica Medii Aevi*, 2–3, Münster, 1913

Ferguson, C., *Naked to Mine Enemies: the Life of Cardinal Wolsey*, London, 1958

Fiddes, R., *The Life of Cardinal Wolsey*, London, 1724

Flood, J. L., '"Safer on the battlefield than in the city": England, the "sweating sickness", and the continent', *Renaissance Studies*, 17, 2, pp. 147–76

Foxe, J., *Acts and Monuments*, 8 vols, London, 1877

Galt, J., *The Life and Administration of Cardinal Wolsey*, London, 1812

Gardiner, L. R., 'Further news of Cardinal Wolsey's end, November–December 1530', *Bulletin of the Institute of Historical Research*, 57 (1984), pp. 99–107

Giry-Deloison, C., 'A diplomatic revolution? Anglo-French relations and the treaties of 1527', in D. Starkey (ed.), *Henry VIII: a European Court in England*, London, 1991

The Gladstone Lament; or Wolsey Personified, London, 1866

Glanville, P., 'Wolsey and the goldsmiths', in S. J. Gunn and P. G. Lindley (eds), *Cardinal Wolsey: Church, State and Art*, Cambridge, 1991, pp. 131–48

Goring, J. J., 'The riot at Bayham Abbey, June 1525', *Sussex Archaeological Collections*, 116 (1978), pp. 1–10

Gouwens, K. and Reiss, S. E. (eds), *The Pontificate of Clement VII: History, Politics, Culture*, Aldershot and Burlington, 2005

Greenblatt, S. J., *Learning to Curse: Essays in Early Modern Culture*, New York and London, 1990

Griffiths, R. A. and Law, J. E. (eds), *Rawdon Brown and the Anglo-Venetian Relationship*, Stroud, 2005

Grove, J., *The History of the Life and Times of Cardinal Wolsey Prime Minister to Henry VIII*, 4 vols, London, 1742–4

—— *The Lives of all the Earls and Dukes of Devonshire*, 1764

Grummitt, D., *The Calais Garrison: War and Military Service in England, 1436–1558*, Woodbridge, 2008

Guicciardini, L., *The Sack of Rome*, ed. J. H. McGregor, New York, 1993

Gunn, S. J., 'The duke of Suffolk's march on Paris in 1523', *English Historical Review*, 101 (1986), pp. 596–634

—— 'The French wars of Henry VIII', in J. Black (ed.), *The Origins of War in Early Modern Europe*, Edinburgh, 1987

—— *Charles Brandon, Duke of Suffolk, c.1484–1545*, Oxford, 1988

—— 'Wolsey's foreign policy and the domestic crisis of 1527–1528' in S. J. Gunn and P. G. Lindley (eds), *Cardinal Wolsey: Church, State and Art*, Cambridge, 1991, pp. 149–77

Gunn, S. J. and Lindley, P. G. (eds), *Cardinal Wolsey: Church, State and Art*, Cambridge, 1991

Guy, J., *The Cardinal's Court: the Impact of Thomas Wolsey in Star Chamber*, Hassocks, 1977

—— 'Wolsey and the Tudor polity', in S. J. Gunn and P. G. Lindley (eds), *Cardinal Wolsey: Church, State and Art*, Cambridge, 1991, pp. 54–75

—— *The Public Career of Sir Thomas More*, Brighton, 1980

—— 'Wolsey, the council and the council courts', *English Historical Review*, 91 (1976), pp. 481–505

—— 'Wolsey and the parliament of 1523', in C. Cross, D. Loades and J. J. Scarisbrick (eds), *Law and Government under the Tudors: Essays Presented to Sir Geoffrey Elton*, Cambridge, 1988, pp. 1–18

Gwyn, P. J., 'Wolsey's foreign policy: the conferences at Calais and Bruges reconsidered', *Historical Journal*, 23 (1980), pp. 755–2

—— *The King's Cardinal: the Rise and Fall of Thomas Wolsey*, London, 1990 and 1992

Hale, J. R., *Machiavelli and Renaissance Italy*, London, 1961

Hall, E., *The Union of the Two Noble and Illustre Famelies of Lancastre and Yorke*, ed. H. Ellis, London, 1809

Hallman, B. M., *Italian Cardinals, Reform and the Church as Property 1492–1563*, Berkeley and Los Angeles, 1985

—— 'The "disastrous" pontificate of Clement VII: disastrous for Giulio de' Medici?', in K. Gouwens and S. E. Reiss (eds), *The Pontificate of Clement VII: History, Politics, Culture*, Aldershot and Burlington, 2005, pp. 29–40

Harris, B. J., *Edward Stafford Third Duke of Buckingham, 1478–1521*, Stanford, 1986

Harvey, J. H., 'The building works and architects of Cardinal Wolsey', *Journal of the British Archaeological Association*, 3rd ser., 8 (1943), pp. 50–9

Harvey, J. H. and Milne, J. G., 'The building of Cardinal College, Oxford', *Oxoniensia*, 8–9 (1943–4), pp. 137–53

Harvey, M. M., *England, Rome and the Papacy, 1417–1464: the Study of a Relationship*, Manchester, 1993

Hay, D., 'The life of Polydore Vergil of Urbino', *Journal of the Warburg and Courtauld Institutes*, 12 (1949), pp. 132–51

Heal, F., *Of Prelates and Princes: a Study of the Economic and Social Position of the Tudor Episcopate*, Cambridge, 1980

Heath, P., 'The treason of Geoffrey Blythe, bishop of Coventry and Lichfield, 1503–31', *Bulletin of the Institute of Historical Research*, 42 (1969), pp. 101–9

Higgins, A., 'On the work of Florentine sculptors in the early part of the sixteenth century: with special reference to the tombs of Cardinal Wolsey and King Henry VIII', *Archaeological Journal*, 51 (1894), pp. 191–7

Hillgarth, J. N., 'The image of Alexander VI and Cesare Borgia in the sixteenth and seventeenth centuries', *Journal of the Warburg and Courtauld Institutes*, 59 (1996), pp. 119–29

Holinshed, R., *The Chronicles of England, Scotland and Ireland*, 6 vols, London, 1807–8

Hollingsworth, M., *The Cardinal's Hat: Money, Ambition and Housekeeping in a Renaissance Court*, London, 2004

Hook, J., *The Sack of Rome 1527*, 2nd edn, Basingstoke and New York, 2004

Howard, G., *Wolsey: the Cardinal and his Times, Courtly, Political and Ecclesiastical*, London, 1824

Hunter, J., *Who Wrote Cavendish's Life of Wolsey?*, London, 1814

Hynes, H., *The Privileges of Cardinals*, Washington, 1945

Ives, E. W., *Anne Boleyn*, Oxford, 1986

——— 'The fall of Wolsey', in S. J. Gunn and P. G. Lindley (eds), *Cardinal Wolsey: Church, State and Art*, Cambridge, 1991, pp. 286–315

——— *Henry VIII*, Oxford, 2007

Jones, M. K. and Underwood, M. G., *The King's Mother: Lady Margaret Beaufort Countess of Richmond and Derby*, Cambridge, 1992

Knecht, R. J., *Francis I*, Cambridge, 1982

Knowles, D., '"The matter of Wilton" in 1528', *Bulletin of the Institute of Historical Research*, 31 (1958), pp. 92–6

Law, E., *England's First Great War Minister: how Wolsey Made a New Army and Navy and Organized the English Expedition to Artois and Flanders in 1513*, London, 1916

Lehmberg, S. E., *The Reformation Parliament, 1529–1536*, Cambridge, 1970

Letters and Papers, Foreign and Domestic, of the Reign of Henry VIII, 1509–1547, 1–4, ed. J. S. Brewer, London, 1862–76

Lindley, P. G., 'Playing check-mate with royal majesty? Wolsey's patronage of Italian Renaissance sculpture', in S. J. Gunn and P. G. Lindley (eds), *Cardinal Wolsey: Church, State and Art*, Cambridge, 1991, pp. 261–85

Loades, D. M., *The Tudor Court*, London, 1986

——— *The Life and Career of William Paulet (c. 1475–1572): Lord Treasurer and First Marquis of Winchester*, Aldershot, 2008

Lowe, K. J. P., *Church and Politics in Renaissance Italy: the Life and Career of Cardinal Francesco Soderini (1453–1524)*, Cambridge, 1993

MacCulloch, D. (ed.), *The Reign of Henry VIII: Politics, Policy and Piety*, London, 1995

——— *Thomas Cranmer: a Life*, New Haven and London, 1996

Mancini, D., *The Usurpation of Richard III*, ed. C. A. J. Armstrong, Gloucester, 1984

Mattingly, G., *Catherine of Aragon*, London, 1942

——— *Renaissance Diplomacy*, London, 1955

Mayer, T. F., *Reginald Pole, Prince and Prophet*, Cambridge, 2000

McConica, J. (ed.), *The History of the University of Oxford*, 3: *The Collegiate University*, Oxford, 1986

McMullan, G. (ed.), *King Henry VIII (All is True)*, London, 2000

Metzger, F., 'The last phase of the medieval chancery', in A. Harding (ed.) *Law-making and Law-makers in British History*, London, 1980, pp. 79–89

Miller, H., *Henry VIII and the English Nobility*, Oxford, 1986

Murphy, V. and Surtz, E. (eds.), *The Divorce Tracts of Henry VIII*, Angers, 1988

Oxford Dictionary of National Biography, 60 vols, Oxford, 2004

Newman, J., 'Cardinal Wolsey's collegiate foundations', in S. J. Gunn and

P. G. Lindley (eds), *Cardinal Wolsey: Church, State and Art*, Cambridge, 1991, pp. 103–15

Parmiter, G. de C., *The King's Great Matter: a Study of Anglo-papal Relations 1527–1534*, London, 1967

von Pastor, L., *The History of the Popes, from the Close of the Middle Ages*, vols 6–10, ed. F. I. Antrobus and R. F. Kerr, London, 1923

Pollard, A. F., *Wolsey*, London, 1929

Raleigh, W. S., *Cardinal Wolsey and the Loves of the Poets*, London, 1874

Rawcliffe, C., *The Staffords, Earls of Stafford and Dukes of Buckingham 1394–1521* Cambridge 1978

Redstone, V. B., 'Wulcy of Suffolk', *Suffolk Institute of Archaeology and Natural History*, 16 (1918), pp. 71–89

Redworth, G., *In Defence of the Church Catholic: the Life of Stephen Gardiner*, Oxford, 1990

Richards, J., *Sir Henry Irving: a Victorian Actor and his World*, London and New York, 2005

Ridley, J., *The Statesman and the Fanatic: Thomas Wolsey and Thomas More*, London, 1982

Roberts, D. and Shepherd, R. (eds), *Hidden Magdalen*, Oxford, 2008

Roper, W., *The Lyfe of Sir Thomas More, Knight*, ed. E. V. Hitchcock, Early English Text Society, orig. ser. 197, 1935

Russell, J. G., *The Field of Cloth of Gold: Men and Manners in 1520* London 1969

—— 'The search for universal peace: the conferences at Calais and Bruges in 1521', *Bulletin of the Institute of Historical Research*, 44 (1971), pp. 162–93

Sampson, A., *Wolsey*, London, 1935

Scarisbrick, J. J., *Henry VIII*, London, 1968

—— 'Cardinal Wolsey and the common weal', in E. W. Ives, R. J. Knecht and J. J. Scarisbrick (eds), *Wealth and Power in Tudor England: Essays Presented to S. T. Bindoff*, London, 1978, pp. 45–67

Setton, K. M., *The Papacy and the Levant (1204–1571)*, 3: *The Sixteenth Century to the Reign of Julius III*, Philadelphia, 1984

Shaw, C., *Julius II: the Warrior Pope*, Oxford, 1993

John Skelton, selected poems, ed. G. Walker, London, 1997

Starkey, D., *The Reign of Henry VIII*, London, 1985

—— (ed.), *Henry VIII: a European Court in England*, London, 1991

Storer, T., *The Life and Death of T. Wolsey, Cardinall*, London, 1599

Stow, J., *The Annales of England*, London, 1592

Sylvester, R. S., 'Cavendish's *Life of Wolsey*: the Artistry of a Tudor Biographer', *Studies in Philology*, 57 (1960), pp. 44–71

Taunton, E. L., *Thomas Wolsey, Legate and Reformer*, London and New York, 1902

Thurley, S., 'The domestic building works of Cardinal Wolsey', in S. J. Gunn and P. G. Lindley (eds), *Cardinal Wolsey: Church, State and Art*, Cambridge, 1991, pp. 76–102

—— *The Lost Palace of Whitehall*, London, 1998

—— *Hampton Court: a Social and Architectural History*, New Haven and London, 2003

Trevor-Roper, H., *Christ Church Oxford*, 3rd edn, Oxford, 1989

A True Description, or Rather a Parallel betweene Cardinall Wolsey, Archbishop of York, and William Laud, Arch-bishop of Canterbury, London, 1641

Tuohy, T., *Herculean Ferrara: Ercole d'Este (1471–1505) and the Invention of a Ducal Capital*, Cambridge, 1996

Tyndale, W., *The Practice of Prelates*, ed. H. Walker, Parker Society, 43, 1849

Ullmann, W., 'Eugenius, Kemp and Chichele' in J. A. Watt, J. B. Morrall and F. X. Martin (eds), *Medieval Studies Presented to Aubrey Gwynn, S. J.*, Dublin, 1961

—— 'Julius II and the schismatic cardinals', in D. Baker (ed.), *Schism, Heresy and Religious Protest, Studies in Church 9 History* 1972, pp. 177–93

Underwood, M. G., 'The Lady Margaret Beaufort and her Cambridge connections', *Sixteenth Century Journal*, 13 (1982), pp. 67–82

The Anglica Historia of Polydore Vergil, AD 1485–1537, ed. D. Hay, Camden Society, 3rd ser., 74, 1950

Walker, G., *John Skelton and the Politics of the 1520*, Cambridge, 1988

—— 'The "expulsion of the minions" of 1519 reconsidered', *Historical Journal*, 32 (1989), pp. 1–16

—— 'Saint or schemer?: the 1527 heresy trial of Thomas Bilney reconsidered', *Journal of Ecclesiastical History*, 40 (1989), pp. 219–38

—— 'Cardinal Wolsey and the satirists: the case of Godly Queen Hester re-opened', in S. J. Gunn and P. G. Lindley (eds), *Cardinal Wolsey: Church, State and Art*, Cambridge, 1991, pp. 239–60

Warnicke, R. M., *The Rise and Fall of Anne Boleyn*, Cambridge, 1989

Wayment, H. G., 'Twenty-four vidimuses for Cardinal Wolsey', *Master Drawings*, 23–4 (1985–6), 4, pp. 503–17

—— 'Wolsey and stained glass', in S. J. Gunn and P. G. Lindley (eds), *Cardinal Wolsey: Church, State and Art*, Cambridge, 1991, pp. 116–30

Wernham, R. B., *Before the Armada: the Growth of English Foreign Policy, 1485–1588*, London, 1966

Whitehead, M. (ed.), *Held in Trust: 2008 Years of Sacred Culture*, Stonyhurst, 2008

Wilkie, W. E., *The Cardinal Protectors of England: Rome and the Tudors before the Reformation*, Cambridge, 1974

Willen, D., *John Russell, First Earl of Bedford*, London, 1981

Williams, N., *The Cardinal and the Secretary*, London, 1975

Williams, R. F., *Lives of the English Cardinals*, 2 vols, London, 1868

Willsdon, C. A. P., *Mural Painting in Britain 1840–1940: Image and Meaning*, Oxford, 2000

Wodka, J., *Zur Geschichte der Nationalen Protektorate der Kardinäle an der Römischen Kurie*, Rome, 1938

Wooden, W. W., 'The art of partisan biography: George Cavendish's *Life of Wolsey*', *Renaissance and Reformation*, new ser., 1 (1977), pp. 24–35

Woolfson, J., *Padua and the Tudors: English Students in Italy, 1485–1603*, Cambridge, 1998

Worsley, L. and Souden, D., *Hampton Court Palace: the Official Illustrated History*, London and New York, 2005

Index of names

Accolti, Benedetto (1497–1549), cardinal 124
Accolti, Pietro (1455–1532), cardinal 22
Acton, John Emerich Edward Dalberg (1834–1902), 1st Baron Acton, historian 185
Adrian VI [Adriaan Florenszoon Dedel, Adrian of Utrecht] (1459–1523), pope 54, 79–81, 86, 88–9, 95–8, 107, 156
Afonso of Portugal (1509–40), son of King Manuel I, cardinal 54, 97
Agostini, Agostino, Wolsey's physician 166
Albany, duke of: see Stewart
Albrecht of Brandenburg: see Hohenzollern
Albret, Amanieu d' (c. 1478–1520), cardinal 22
Albret, Henri d' (1503–55), king of Navarre 74
Alcock, John (1430–1500), bishop of Ely, lord chancellor, founder of Jesus College, Cambridge 64, 102–3
Alen, John (1476–1534), archbishop of Dublin 89, 103, 107, 109, 148–9
Alexander VI [Rodrigo Borgia] (1431–1503), pope 13, 22–3, 79, 127–8, 171
Alidosi, Francesco (c. 1455–1511), cardinal 26
Amadas, Robert, goldsmith 202
Amboise, George d' (1460–1515), cardinal 35–6
Ammonius, Andreas: see Della Rena
Angus, earl of: see Douglas
Anne of Brittany (1477–1514), duchess of Brittany, queen of France, consort of Charles VIII and 1st consort of Louis XII 32, 127
Anne (1461–1522), princess, dame de Beaujeu, duchess of Bourbon 95
Aragona, Luigi d' (1474–1519), cardinal 22
Arborio di Gattinara: see Gattinara
Armellini, Francesco (1470–1528), cardinal 134
Armstrong, Edward (1846–1928), historian 1
Arthur (1486–1502), prince of Wales 13, 15, 17, 53, 128–9
Arthur, Thomas (d. 1532/3), religious reformer 136–8
Arundell, Sir Thomas (c. 1502–52), gentleman of Wolsey's privy chamber 162
Atterbury, Francis (1663–1732), dean of Christ Church, Oxford, bishop of Rochester 179
Aubrey, John (1626–97), biographer 189
Audley, Edmund (c. 1429–1534), bishop of Salisbury 27–8, 63, 112
Avalos, Ferdinando Francesco d' (1490–1525), marquis of Pescara, soldier 114

Bainbridge, Christopher (1462/3–1514), archbishop of York, cardinal 22, 26–9, 33, 35, 46, 78, 80, 198
Bakócz, Tamás (1442–1521), cardinal 22
Bangor, bishop of: see Deane; Penny; Skeffington
Banks, John (1652/3–1706), playwright 179
Barbo, Pietro: see Paul II
Barlow, Jerome, Franciscan friar and author 172
Barnes, Michael Tudor (1945–) 205
Barnes, Robert (c. 1495–1540), religious reformer 71, 105–7, 137, 174
Barton, Anne (1933–) 188
Baskcomb, John, actor 191
Bateman, William (c. 1298–1355), bishop of Norwich, founder of Trinity Hall, Cambridge 70
Bath and Wells, bishop of: see Castellesi; Clerk; Knight; Stillington; Wolsey
Beaufort, Henry (c. 1375–1447), bishop of Winchester, cardinal, lord chancellor 35, 58, 188
Beaufort, Henry (1436–64), 2nd duke of Somerset 119
Beaufort, Lady Margaret (1443–1509), countess of Richmond and Derby, founder of Christ's and St John's Colleges, Cambridge 9, 16–7, 27–8, 47, 53
Beaujeu, Anne de: see Anne
Pierre de: see Bourbon
Becket, Thomas (c. 1120–70), archbishop of Canterbury, lord chancellor 40, 90, 100, 131, 169, 177, 189
Bedford, earl of: see Russell
Bell, John (d. 1556), bishop of Worcester, 151, 153
Belloc, Hilaire (1870–1953), author and Catholic apologist 192
Bere, Richard (1455–1525), abbot of Glastonbury 108
Benedetto da Rovezzano: see Grazzini
Benet, Thomas, vicar-general of the Salisbury diocese 145
Benet, William, auditor of Wolsey's legatine court 108, 151
Bergavenny, Baron: see Neville
Besett, John, schoolmaster in Ipswich 6
Bessarion (d. 1472), cardinal 58
Betterton, Mary (c. 1637–1712), actress 179
Betterton, Thomas (1635–1710), actor and theatre manager 179
Bilney, Thomas (c. 1495–1531), religious reformer 71, 105, 136–8

Birchinshaw, Maurice, tutor 49–50

Blair, Tony (1953–) 181

Blount, Elizabeth (c. 1500–39/41), royal mistress 49

Blount, William (c. 1478–1534), 4th Baron Mountjoy 32, 158

Blyth, Geoffrey (c. 1470–1530), bishop of Coventry and Lichfield, 27–8, 168

Blyth, John (c. 1450–99), bishop of Salisbury 7, 12

Bodley, George Frederick (1827–1907), architect 188

Boleyn, Anne (c. 1500–36), queen of England, 2nd consort of Henry VIII 84–5, 91–2, 129, 132–3, 135, 140–2, 145–7, 150, 156–7, 163, 166, 173, 193

Boleyn, Elizabeth: see Howard

Boleyn, George (c. 1504–36), Viscount Rochford, 84, 152, 158

Boleyn, Mary (c. 1499–1543), later Carey 84, 91–2, 141

Boleyn, Thomas (1576/7–1539), Viscount Rochford, earl of Wiltshire and Ormond, 84, 91, 133, 145, 147, 151

Bolt, Robert (1924–95), playwright 191–2

Bonner, Edmund (d. 1569), bishop of London 166

Bonnivet, seigneur de: see Gouffier

Bonville, Cicely (d. 1530), marchioness of Dorset 10, 73

Booth, Charles (d. 1535), bishop of Hereford 53, 67, 107, 111, 168

Borgia, Cesare (1475–1507), cardinal, soldier 13

Bourbon, Charles III de (1490–1527), duke of Bourbon, constable of France, imperial commander 95–6, 113–4, 119, 121, 123–4, 135

Bourbon, duchess of: see Anne

Bourbon, Suzanne de (d. 1521), duchess of Bourbon 95

Bourbon, Pierre de (1438–1503), seigneur de Beaujeu, duke of Bourbon 95

Bourbon de Vendôme, Louis II de (1493–1557), cardinal 54, 97

Bourchier, Thomas (c. 1411–86), archbishop of Canterbury, cardinal, lord chancellor 30, 35

Bowers, Roger 175

Brahms, Caryl (1901–82), writer 191

Brandenburg, margrave of: see Hohenzollern

Brandon, Charles (c. 1484–1545), duke of Suffolk 24–5, 33, 44, 90, 95–6, 113, 115, 119, 133, 140, 151–2, 156–8

Breakspear, Nicholas (d. 1159), cardinal, later Pope Adrian IV 182

Brewer, John Sherren (1809–79), historian 184, 187

Briçonnet, Guillaume (d. 1514), cardinal 23, 34

Briçonnet, Guillaume (c. 1472–1534), bishop of Meaux 116

Brinknell, Thomas (c. 1479–1539), schoolmaster and theologian 102

Brinon, Jean (c. 1484–1528) diplomat 117

Bromley, William, painter 182

Brown, Rawdon (1806–83), historian of Venice 183–4

Bryans, John (d. 1989), actor 191

Buckingham, duchess of: see Percy
    duke of: see Stafford; Villiers

Bulmer, Sir William, courtier 43–4, 72

Bulwer-Lytton, Edward (1803–73), 1st Baron Lytton, writer and politician 182

Burgundy, duchess of: see Marie
    duke of: see Charles

Burnell, Robert (d. 1292), bishop of Bath and Wells, lord chancellor 2

Burnett, Avery, composer 100

Butler, James (c. 1496–1546), 9th earl of Ormond 84–5, 91

Butler, Piers (c. 1467–1539), 8th earl of Ormond and 1st earl of Ossory 84, 111, 148

Butts, Sir William (c. 1485–1545), physician 163

Byrd, William (1539/43–1623), composer 175

Cajetan: see Vio

Campeggi, Lorenzo (1471/2–1539), bishop of Salisbury, cardinal, 54, 58, 63–5, 81, 112–3, 125, 134, 141, 145, 150–3, 155–6, 201

Campion, Edmund (1540–81)), Jesuit 175–7

Canterbury, archbishop of: see Becket; Bourchier; Chichele; Cranmer; Deane; Kemp; Lang; Langton; Laud; Morton; Parker; Pole; Stafford; Warham

Capon, William (c. 1480–1550), master of Jesus College, Cambridge 142, 200

Carafa, Gianvincenzo (1477–1541), cardinal 134

Cardona y Enríquez, Enrique de (1485–1530), cardinal 134, 155

Carey, Eleanor, nun of Wilton, 146

Carey, Henry (1526–96), 1st Baron Hunsdon 91

Carey, Katherine (c. 1523–69) 91

Carey, Mary: see Boleyn

Carey, William (c. 1496–1528), courtier 84, 91, 146

Carlisle, bishop of: see Penny; Kite

Carvajal, Bernardino López de (1455–1523), cardinal 23, 79–80, 97

Carwood, Andrew (1965–) 188

Castellesi, Adriano (c. 1461–1521), bishop of Hereford and of Bath and Wells, cardinal, 22, 26–7, 32, 54–5, 63, 79

Castelnau, François Guillaume de (1480–1541), cardinal 22, 97

Casali, Gregorio [Sir Gregory Casale] (c. 1496–1536), diplomat 123, 140

Castiglione, Baldassare (1478–1529), diplomat and author of The book of the courtier 57, 79, 120

Cavendish, Elizabeth: see Hardwick

Cavendish, George (1494–c. 1562), Wolsey's gentle usher and first biographer 6–7, 10–5, 18, 36, 42–3, 48, 92, 99–100, 131–2, 145, 151–2, 155, 161–3, 165–7, 172–4, 176, 179, 182–3

Cavendish, Thomas (d. 1524), administrator 173

Cavendish, Sir William (1508–57), administrator 173

Cavendish, William (1720–64), 1st duke of Devonshire 181

Chapuys, Eustace (1490/2–1556), diplomat 135

Charles I (1600–49), king of England, Scotland and Ireland 144, 178

Charles II (1630–85), king of England, Scotland and Ireland 179

Charles V [Charles of Ghent] (1500–58), Holy Roman Emperor, king of Aragon and Castile, Sardinia, Sicily and Naples, ruler of the Low Countries and Franche Comté, and of Castile's New world possessions 1, 15–6, 24, 32–3, 50–2, 54, 56–7, 61–3, 66–7, 69–70, 74–7, 79–83, 90, 95–6, 98, 113–7, 120–2, 125–6, 129–31, 133–4, 140, 145, 149–50, 154–5, 159, 166, 187

Charles VII (1402–61), king of France 65

Charles VIII (1470–98), king of France 16, 23, 35, 65, 127

Charles of Ghent: see Charles V

Charles the Bold (1433–67), duke of Burgundy 13–4

Charlotte (1516–24), princess, daughter of Francis I 56, 69

Chichele, Henry (c. 1362–1443), archbishop of Canterbury 35, 102

Chichester, bishop of: see Sampson; Sherborn

Chiericati, Francesco (c. 1480–1539), papal diplomat 58

Chièvres, seigneur de: see Croy

Church, Augustine, suffragan bishop in the Salisbury diocese 7

Churchyard, Thomas (c. 1523–1604), writer and soldier 174, 178

Cibber, Colley (1671–1757), actor and writer 181

Cibo, Giovanni Battista: see Innocent VIII

Cibo, Innocenzo (1491–1550), cardinal 34

Ciocchi del Monte, Antonio Maria (1487–1555), cardinal, later Pope Julius III 22, 97

Cisneros, Francisco Jiménez de (1436–1517), cardinal, 23, 50

Clansey, Dorothy, daughter of Thomas Wolsey 17, 109, 160

Clarence, duke of: see George

Clarke-Smith, D. A., actor 191

Claude de France (1499–1524), queen of France, 1st consort of Francis I 32, 56, 91, 123

Clement VII [Giulio de' Medici] (1478–1534), pope 27, 34, 51–3, 78–81, 87, 97–8, 107, 109, 113–4, 121–7, 130–1, 133–4, 139–41, 145, 147, 150, 153, 155, 176, 197, 201

Clement, John (d. 1572), humanist scholar 101–2

Clerk, John (c. 1481/2–1541), bishop of Bath and Wells, master of the rolls 46, 78, 80–1, 89, 98, 105, 108, 112–3, 118, 120, 122, 130–1, 151, 158, 168

Cles, Bernhard von (1484–1539), cardinal 155

Cobbold, Richard (1797–1877), novelist 183

Colet, John (1467–1519), dean of St Paul's, founder of St Paul's School 9–10, 31, 36, 46, 49, 60, 63–4, 102, 143

Collinson, Patrick (1929–) 192

Cologne, archbishop of: see Weid

Colonna, Oddone: see Martin V

Colonna, Pompeo (1479–1532), cardinal 80, 82, 98, 125, 133

Colonna, Prospero (1452–1523), soldier 82

Columbus [Cristoforo Colombo] (1451–1506) 23

Condulmer, Gabriele: see Eugenius IV

Constable, John (d. 1528), dean of Lincoln 146

Contarini, Gasparo (1483–1542), Venetian statesman, cardinal 140

Cook, Judith (1933–2004), playwright 205

Corner, Francesco (1478–1543), cardinal 134

Corner, Marco (1482–1524), cardinal 22, 79, 134

Cornysh, William (d. 1523), composer 100

Courtenay, Henry (1498/9–1538), marquis of Exeter 119, 158

Coventry and Lichfield, bishop of: see Blyth; Smith

Coverdale, Miles (1488–1569), bishop of Exeter, biblical translator 105, 137

Cranmer, Thomas (1489–1556), archbishop of Canterbury, 71, 103, 122, 135–6, 140, 153–4, 192, 200

Creighton, Mandell (1843–1901), bishop of Peterborough and London, historian 6, 34, 52, 184–7

Cromwell, Thomas (c. 1485–1540), earl of Essex, royal minister 103, 142, 148, 157, 162–3, 168, 184, 186, 192

Croy, Guillaume de (1458–1521), seigneur de Chièvres 52, 60

Cushman, Charlotte (1816–76), actress 182

Dacre, Thomas (1467–1525), 2nd Baron Dacre 85–6

Darcy, Thomas (c. 1467–1537), Baron Darcy 158

Daubeney, Giles (1451/2–1508), 1st Baron Daubeney 13, 30, 37

Daundy, Joan (d. 1509), Thomas Wolsey's mother 6–7

Daundy, Mr, 142

Davenant, Sir William (1606–68), poet, playwright and theatre manager 179

Deane, Henry (c. 1440–1503), bishop of Bangor, bishop of Salisbury, archbishop of Canterbury, lord chancellor 12–3

Dedel, Adriaan Florenszoon, cardinal: see Adrian VI

Del Carretto, Carlo Domenico (c. 1451/3–1514), cardinal 22, 34

Della Rena, Andrea [Andreas Ammonius] (1476–1517) man of letters 31–2, 197

Della Rovere, Francesco: see Sixtus IV

Della Rovere, Giuliano: see Julius II

Derby, countess of: see Beaufort
    earl of: see Stanley

Devonshire, duke of: see Cavendish

Devlin, Baron: see Nugent

Dexter, Colin (1930–) 188

Docwra, Sir Thomas (d. 1527), prior of the hospital of St John of Jerusalem in England 30, 33
Doria, Andrea (1466–1560), naval commander 150
Doria, Girolamo (1495–1558), cardinal 150
Dorset, marchioness of: see Bonville
    marquis of: see Grey
Douglas, Archibald (c. 1489–1557), 6th earl of Angus 25, 34, 85, 112, 127, 149–50
Dovizi, Bernardo (1470–1520), cardinal, man of letters 34, 57
Du Bellay, Jean (1492–1560), diplomat 142, 144
Dudley, Edmund (c. 1462–1510), administrator 17
Dudley, William (d. 1483), bishop of Durham 7
Dumas, Alexandre (1802–70), novelist 171
Duppa, Brian (1588–1662), dean of Christ Church, Oxford, bishop of Winchester 178
Duprat, Antoine (1464–1535), cardinal, chancellor of France 68, 75–7, 131, 134, 155
Durham, bishop of: see Dudley; Fox; Neville; Ruthall; Sherwood; Thurlow; Tunstal; Wolsey

Easton, Adam (c. 1330–97), cardinal 35
Edmund (1499–1500), duke of Somerset 110
Edward (1475–99), earl of Warwick 11
Edward III (1312–77), king of England, 11
Edward IV (1442–83), king of England, 7, 9–11, 25, 37, 47–8, 111, 118
Edward VI (1537–53), king of England and Ireland, 173
Egidio da Viterbo (1469–1532), cardinal, theologian 54, 57
Eldon, earl of: see Scott
Eleanor of Austria (1498–1558), queen of Portugal, 3rd consort of Manuel I, and queen of France, 2nd consort of Francis I 61, 155
Elizabeth I (1533–1603), queen of England and Ireland, 174–5, 179
Elizabeth of York (1466–1503), queen of England, consort of Henry VII 10, 143
Elton, Sir Geoffrey Rudolph (1921–94), historian 158, 192–3
Ely, bishop of: see Alcock; Grey; Stanley; West
Empson, Sir Richard (c. 1450–1510), administrator 17–8
Enckenviort, Willem van (1464–1534), cardinal 97
Erasmus, Desiderius (1466–1536), humanist scholar 10, 31, 46, 63–4, 71, 102, 106, 125, 125
Essex, earl of: see Cromwell
Este, Alfonso d' (1505–34), duke of Ferrara 22, 140
Este, Ippolito d' (1479–1520), cardinal 22, 100
Eugenius IV [Gabriele Condulmer] (c. 1383–1447), pope 35
Exeter, bishop of: see Coverdale; Fox; Oldham; Veysey
Exeter, duke of: see Holland

Farnese, Alessandro (1468–1549), cardinal, later Pope Paul III 22, 57, 79–80, 97, 155
Felaw, Richard, educational benefactor in Ipswich 6

Fell, John (1625–86), dean of Christ Church, Oxford, bishop of Oxford 179
Fell, Samuel (1584–1649), dean of Christ Church, Oxford 178
Ferdinand II (1452–1516), king of Aragon, Sardinia, Sicily, Navarre and Naples 16, 19–21, 35, 50–2, 74
Ferguson, Charles, biographer of Wolsey 192
Ferrara, duchess of: see Renée
    duke of: see Este
Fiddes, Richard (1671–1725) biographer of Wolsey 180
Fieschi, Niccolò (1456–1524), cardinal 22, 79, 97
Filiberta of Savoy (1498–1524), 61
Fish, Simon (d. 1531), religious controversialist 106, 138, 148
Fisher, John (c. 1469–1535), bishop of Rochester, cardinal 27–8, 31, 64, 67, 72, 82, 94, 104, 106, 130, 135–6, 151, 153, 158, 168–9
Fitzgerald, Gerald (1487–1534), 9th earl of Kildare 84–5, 111, 148–9
Fitzgerald, James 111
Fitzgerald, Maurice, of Lackagh 84
Fitzgerald, Thomas (1513–37), Baron Offaly, 10th earl of Kildare 149
Fitzherbert, Sir Anthony (c. 1470–1538), judge 158, 160
Fitzjames, Sir John (c. 1470–c. 1538), chief justice of king's bench 158
Fitzjames, Richard (d. 1522), bishop of Rochester and London 27–8, 39, 46, 86, 89, 158
Fitzroy, Henry (1519–36), duke of Richmond and Somerset 49–50, 110–1, 124, 143, 148–9, 157
Fitzwalter, Viscount: see Radcliffe
Fitzwilliam, Sir William, (c. 1460–1534), sheriff of London 120
Fitzwilliam, Sir William (c. 1490–1542), earl of Southampton 117, 120, 158
Flandre, Louis de, seigneur de Praet, diplomat 115
Flemming, Robert (1416–83), dean of Lincoln 29
Fletcher, John (1579–1625), playwright 163, 176–7, 183, 186, 189–90
Florence, duke of: see Medici
Foix, Gaston de (1489–1512), duke of Nemours 20
Foix, Germaine de (1488–1538), queen of Aragon, 2nd wife of Ferdinand II 21, 50
Foix, Odet de (c. 1481–1528), seigneur de Lautrec, marshal of France 77, 139–40, 144
Foix, Pierre de (d. 1490), cardinal 35
Forrest, Arthur, actor 191
Forbes, Vivian, painter 186
Forbes-Robertson, Sir Johnston (1853–1937), actor and painter 182
Fox, Edward (1496–1538), bishop of Hereford 141, 153
Fox, Richard (1447/8–1528), bishop of Exeter, Bath and Wells, Durham and Winchester, founder of Corpus Christi College, Oxford 14–20, 24, 26–7,

33, 40, 45–6, 48–50, 60, 64, 83, 90, 92, 94, 101–2, 113, 120, 128–9, 142–4, 147, 159

Foxe, John (1516/17–587), martyrologist 71, 105, 174

Franciotti della Rovere, Galeotto (1471–1507), cardinal 197

Francis I (1494–1547), king of France 1, 32–4, 51–3, 56–7, 62–3, 65–9, 74, 76–7, 95–7, 112–6, 120–3, 131–2, 134, 140, 155, 159, 166, 187, 193

François, count of Angoulême: see Francis I

François (1518–36), dauphin, son of Francis I, king of France 60, 68, 120, 145

Friedrich III [Frederick the Wise] (1463–1525), duke of Saxony, imperial elector 62, 70

Fyneux, Sir John (d. 1525), chief justice of king's bench 41, 73, 107, 158

Gaddi, Niccolò (1490–1552), cardinal 124

Galt, John (1779–1839), novelist 183

Gara della Rovere, Sisto (1473–1517), cardinal 22, 53

Gardiner, Stephen (1495/8–1555), bishop of Winchester, lord chancellor 47, 71, 131, 135, 141, 150–1, 153, 162, 168

Garrick, David (1717–79), actor and theatre manager 181

Gattinara, Mercurino Arborio di (1465–1530), imperial chancellor, cardinal 75, 117, 155

George (1449–76), duke of Clarence 10–1, 49

George II (1683–1760), king of Great Britain and Ireland 181

George III (1738–1820), king of Great Britain and Ireland 180–1

Ghinucci, Girolamo (1480–1541), bishop of Worcester, cardinal 77, 79, 81, 87, 122, 133, 140, 142, 144, 154–5, 168

Ghislieri, Antonio: see Pius V

Giberti, Gian Matteo (1495–1543), bishop of Verona 125, 165

Gielgud, Sir John (1904–2000), actor 190–1

Gigli, Giovanni (1434–98), bishop of Worcester 26, 155

Gigli, Silvestro (1463–1521), bishop of Worcester 25–7, 29, 31, 33–4, 51, 55, 58, 70, 77, 87, 89

Gilbert, Sir John (1817–97), painter 182–3, 186, 190

Gilbert, William, suffragan bishop in the diocese of Bath and Wells 198

Gillray, James (1756–1815), caricaturist 180

Giovan Gioacchino da Passano [Jean-Joachim de Passano, Jean-Joachim de Vaux], diplomat 117, 121

Giovanni da Maiano, sculptor 82

Giulio Romano [Giulio Pippi] (1492–1546), painter 125

Giustinian, Paolo (1476–1528), Camaldolese hermit and ecclesiastical reformer 63

Giustinian, Sebastiano (1459–1543), diplomat 6–7, 38, 43, 46, 59, 66, 171, 183

Gladstone, William Ewart (1809–98), politician 184

Glastonbury, abbot of: see Bere; Whiting

Gloucester, duke of: see Richard III

Goddard, Willoughby (1926–2008), actor 191

Goldwin, William, grammar master in Ipswich 143

Goldwell, James (d. 1499), bishop of Norwich 6, 25

Gonzaga, Ercole (1505–63), cardinal 124

Gonzaga, Pirro (1505–29), cardinal 134, 155

Gonzaga, Sigismondo (1469–1525), cardinal 22, 124, 201

Gorrevod, Louis de (c. 1473–1535), cardinal 155

Gouffier, Adrien (c. 1479–1523), cardinal de Boissy 97

Gouffier, Guillaume (d. 1525), seigneur de Bonnivet, admiral of France 76

Gramont, Gabriel de (1486–1534), cardinal 155, 168

Grassi, Achille (1465–1523), cardinal 22

Grazzini, Benedetto de' [Benedetto da Rovezzano], (c. 1474–1554), sculptor 143, 189, 196

Greiffenclau von Vollrads, Richard (d. 1531), archbishop of Trier, imperial elector 62

Greenblatt, Stephen (1943–) 188

Greenhill, John (1644–76), painter 179

Gregory XV (1554–1623), pope 81

Grenville, William Wyndham (1759–1834), Baron Grenville, politician 181

Grey, Elizabeth (d. 1548), countess of Kildare 85

Grey, Thomas (c. 1455–1501), 1st marquis of Dorset 10–1, 14, 73, 85, 173

Grey, Thomas (1477–1530), 2nd marquis of Dorset 11, 21, 43, 119, 158

Grey, William (c. 1414–78), bishop of Ely, 29

Griffiths, Richard (1947–) 191

Griffo, Pietro (1469–1516), sub-collector of Peter's pence 31

Grimaldi, Girolamo (d. 1543), cardinal 134

Grimani, Domenico (1461–1523), cardinal 22, 79, 97, 124

Grimani, Marino (1488–1546), cardinal 124

Gritti, Andrea (1455–1538), doge of Venice, 124–5

Grocyn, William (1449?–1519), theologian 9, 46

Grosso della Rovere, Leonardo (1463–1520), cardinal, 22

Grove, Joseph (d. 1764), biographer of Wolsey 180

Guarino da Verona (1374–1460), teacher and educationalist 29

Guibé, Robert (c. 1460–1513), cardinal 22, 34

Guicciardini, Francesco (1483–1540), historian and diplomat 123

Guicciardini, Luigi (1478–1551), politician and historian 123

Guildford, Sir Henry (1489–1532), courtier 120, 158

Guise, Jean de (1498–1550), cardinal of Lorraine, 97

Guise, Marie de: see Mary

Gunn, Steven J. 193

Gunner, Christopher, royal servant 132

Guy, John (1949–) 193
Gwyn, Peter 6, 18, 48, 71, 93, 96, 108–9, 193–4

Hale, Sir John Rigby (1923–99), historian 1
Hales, Sir Christopher (d. 1541), attorney general, judge 156
Hall, Edward (1497–1547), chronicler 82, 92, 94, 110, 158, 172–3, 177
Hannibal, Thomas (d. c. 1530), master of the rolls 46, 81, 86, 88–9, 112, 131
Hardwick, Elizabeth [Bess of Hardwick] (c. 1527–1608), Lady Cavendish, countess of Shrewsbury 173, 176
Hardwicke, earl of: see Yorke
Harpsfield, Nicholas (1519–75), religious controversialist 172
Harris, Henry (1633/4–1704), actor and engraver 179
Hastings, George (1486/7–1544), second Baron Hastings, 1st earl of Huntingdon 43
Heneage, George (1482/3–1549), dean of Lincoln 146
Heneage, Sir Thomas (before 1482–1553), courtier 100, 103, 146
Henri (1519–59), duke of Orléans, later Henry II, king of France 120, 123, 131–2, 145
Henry IV (1366–1413), king of England, 172
Henry VI (1421–71), king of England, 8–9, 58, 102
Henry VII (1457–1509), king of England, 7, 10–2, 14–7, 20, 25–6, 43, 48, 58, 82, 110–1, 119, 128, 172–3
Henry VIII (1491–1547), king of England 7, 9, 11, 15, 17–21, 24–5, 27, 32, 34, 37, 39–40, 44, 47–8, 50–2, 55–6, 58–60, 62–3, 66–8, 69–70, 72–7, 79, 82, 84–6, 88, 91–3, 96, 98, 100–1, 111–4, 116–20, 126–32, 134–5, 139–54, 156–9, 163, 166–8, 172–3, 177, 179, 181, 183, 186, 191–3, 202
Henry II, king of France: see Henri
Henry (1483–1538), count of Nassau 74
Hereford, bishops of: see Booth; Castellesi; Fox; Mayhew
Hessler, Georg (d. 1482), cardinal 35
Hogg, Ian (1937–) 191
Hohenzollern, Albrecht von [Albrecht of Brandenburg] (1490–1545), cardinal, archbishop of Mainz, imperial elector 55, 62, 79, 97
Hohenzollern, Joachim I Nestor (1484–1535), margrave of Brandenburg, imperial elector 61–2
Holbein, Hans [the younger] (1497/8–1543), painter 181
Holinshed, Raphael (c. 1525–c. 1580), historian 175–7, 183
Holland, Henry (1430–75), 2nd duke of Exeter, 10
Holt, John, suffragan bishop in the diocese of London, 142
Hook, Judith (1941–84), historian 124
Hopkins, Nicholas, Carthusian friar 49, 72
Howard, Agnes: see Tilney

Howard, Dorothy, 157
Howard, Sir Edward (1476/7–1513), naval commander 19
Howard, Elizabeth (d. 1538), wife of Thomas Boleyn 84
'Howard, George': see Laird
Howard, Katherine, 157
Howard, Katherine (1518/24–1542), queen of England, 5th consort of Henry VIII 157
Howard, Mary (c. 1519–c. 1555), duchess of Richmond, 157
Howard, Thomas (1443–1524), earl of Surrey, 2nd duke of Norfolk, 11, 17, 19–20, 24–5, 33, 41, 47, 73, 90, 119–20
Howard, Thomas (1473–1554), earl of Surrey, 3rd duke of Norfolk, 47, 73, 83–4, 86, 90–1, 115, 119, 133, 140, 142, 145, 148, 151, 156–8, 162–3, 165, 167, 183
Hunne, Richard (d. 1514), merchant tailor 39–40, 63
Hunsdon, Baron: see Carey
Hunter, Joseph (1783–1861), antiquary 183
Huntingdon, earl of: see Hastings
Huxley, Aldous (1894–1963), novelist 171
Hygdon, Brian (d. 1539), dean of York 112, 165
Hygdon, John (d. 1532), dean of Christ Church, Oxford 103, 110, 168

Inge, Hugh (d. 1528), archbishop of Dublin 85, 111, 148, 199
Innocent VIII [Giovanni Battista Cibo] (1432–92), pope 22, 34, 58
Irvine, 'Derry' (1940–), Baron Irvine of Lairg, lord chancellor 181
Irving, Sir Henry (1838–1905), actor and theatre manager 181, 185–6
Isabella I (1451–1504), queen of Castile 14, 35, 50–1
Isabella of Austria (1501–26), queen of Denmark, consort of Kristian II 61
Isabella of Portugal (1503–39), empress, consort of Charles V 121
Islip, John (1464–1532), abbot of Westminster 41, 108
Ives, Eric (1931–) 150, 193

Jack, Sybil M. 6, 171
Jacovacci, Domenico (1444–1527), cardinal 155
James II and VII (1633–1701), king of England, Scotland and Ireland 179
James IV (1475–1513), king of Scots, 13, 15, 24–5
James V (1512–42), king of Scots, 25, 57, 86, 112, 149–50
Jeanne de France (1464–1505), queen of France, 1st consort of Louis XII 32, 127
Johnson, Samuel (1709–84), author and lexicographer 180
Johnson, William, master mason 103
Jordan, Isabel, abbess of Wilton 145–6

Jorge de Ateca [George de Athequa] (d. 1537), bishop of Llandaff 53, 67, 168

Juan (1478–97), prince of Aragon and Castile 16, 50, 61

Juana (1479–1555), queen of Castile 14–5, 61

Julius II [Giuliano della Rovere] (1443–1513), pope 16, 18–20, 22–3, 26–7, 31, 53, 128

Katherine of Aragon [Catalina], (1485–1536), queen of England, 1st consort of Henry VIII 13, 17, 37, 48–9, 51, 53, 56, 67–8, 74, 82, 90, 101–2, 126–30, 133, 135, 140–1, 145, 151–2, 154, 167, 177, 179, 181–2, 191, 202

Katherine of York (1479–1527), countess of Devon 48–9, 119

Kean, Charles (1811–68), actor and theatre manager 181–2, 188

Kemble, John Philip (1757–1823), actor and theatre manager 181

Kemp, John (1380/1–1454), archbishop of York and Canterbury, cardinal, lord chancellor 13, 35, 58

Kendall, John (d. 1501), prior of the hospital of St John of Jerusalem in England 30

Kent, William (1686–1747), painter and architect 162

Kildare, countess of: see Grey
  earl of: see Fitzgerald

Kingston, Sir William, (c. 1476–1540), constable of the Tower 120, 166–7

Kite, John (d. 1437), archbishop of Armagh and bishop of Carlisle 85–7, 89, 152, 162, 168

Klein, Adolf, actor 191

Knecht, Robert Jean (1926–) 193

Knight, William (1475/6–1547), bishop of Bath and Wells 21, 32, 47, 53, 81, 95, 119, 133, 135, 148, 151

Knyvett, Charles 72–3

Kratzer, Nicholas (c. 1487–1550), astronomer and horologist 189

Kristian II (1481–1559), king of Denmark 57, 61

Ladislas I [Lajos, Louis] (1506–26), king of Bohemia and Hungary, imperial elector 57, 61–2, 122

Laird, F. C. [George Howard] 183

Lajos II, king of Hungary: see Ladislas

La Marck, Robert de (d. 1536), seigneur de Sedan 74

Lang, Cosmo Gordon (1864–1945), archbishop of York and of Canterbury 2

Lang, Matthäus (1469–1540), cardinal 23, 35, 57–8, 65, 79, 97

Langton, Thomas (c. 1430–1501), bishop of Winchester, archbishop-elect of Canterbury 12, 28

Lannoy, Charles de (1482–1527), viceroy of Naples 114, 123

Larke, Jane/Joan, Wolsey's mistress 17–8, 110, 160

Larke, Thomas, master of Trinity Hall, Cambridge 17, 71

Latimer, Hugh (c. 1485–1555), bishop of Worcester 71, 104

La Tour d'Auvergne, Madeleine de (d. 1519) 61, 198, 201

Laud, William (1573–1645), archbishop of Canterbury 178

Laughton, Charles (1899–1962), actor 191

Lautrec, seigneur de: see Foix, Odet de

Law, Ernest (1854–1934), antiquarian 193

Lebons, John, master mason 38, 103

Lee, Edward (1481/2–1544), archbishop of York 122, 140, 168

Lefèvre d'Étaples, Jacques (1450–1536), humanist scholar 117

Legh, George, 18, 160

Legh, Thomas, 18

Lehmberg, S. E., 158

Leicester, abbot of: see Penny

Leo III (d. 816), pope 51

Leo X [Giovanni de' Medici] (1475–1513), pope 5, 20, 22–3, 27, 29, 31, 34, 39, 41, 47, 51–62, 65, 74–6, 78–81, 87, 98, 107, 121, 134, 156, 189

Le Sauvage, Jean, administrator 52

Liddell, Henry George (1811–98), dean of Christ Church, Oxford 187–8

Lily, William (c. 1468–1522/3), grammarian and schoolmaster 49, 101–2, 143

Linacre, Thomas (c. 1460–1524), physician 31, 46, 50

Lincoln, bishop of: see Longland; Rotherham; Russell; Smith; Thurlow, Wolsey

Lindley, Philip G. 193

Llandaff, bishop of: see Jorge de Ateca; Salley

Loaysa y Mendoza, García de (1478–1546), cardinal 155

London, bishop of: see Bonner; Creighton; Fitzjames; Stokesley; Tunstal; Warham

Longland, John (1473–1547), bishop of Lincoln 45, 72, 103–4, 107–9, 118, 130, 135–6, 146, 153, 168

Loredan, Leonardo (1438–1521), doge of Venice, 57

Louis XI (1423–83), king of France 32, 35, 58, 65, 95, 127, 185

Louis XII (1462–1515), king of France 14, 16, 18–20, 23–4, 32–3, 35–6, 51–2, 65, 127

Louise of Savoy (1476–1531), mother of and regent for Francis I 74, 81, 95, 116–7, 131, 145, 154

Louise (1515–17), princess, daughter of Francis I 52, 56

Lovell, Sir Thomas (c. 1449–1524), administrator 14–5, 17, 47

Ludwig V (1478–1544), elector palatine of the Rhine 62

Lupset, Thomas (c. 1495–1530), man of letters 102, 109

Luther, Martin (1483–1546), religious reformer 55, 57, 62, 69–72, 104

Luxembourg, Philippe de (1445–1519), cardinal 22

Machiavelli, Niccolò (1469–1527), administrator and political theorist 1, 13
Macready, William Charles (1793–1873), actor and theatre manager 181–2
Madeleine (1520–37), queen of Scotland, consort of James V 112, 149
Magnus, Thomas (1463/4–1550), administrator and diplomat 110, 112, 149
Manning, Henry Edward (1808–92), archbishop of Westminster, cardinal 185
Manuel I (1469–1521), king of Portugal 54, 57, 61, 128, 155
Margaret of Austria (1480–1530), imperial regent in the Low Countries, 15–6, 61, 91, 141, 145, 154
Margaret Tudor (1489–1541), queen of Scotland, consort of James IV, countess of Angus, Lady Methven 13, 15, 25, 34, 43, 49, 60, 85–6, 112, 127, 149–50
Margaret of York (1446–1503), duchess of Burgundy 13
Marguerite (1492–1549), queen of Navarre, consort of Henri d'Albret 116, 131
Maria (1482–1517), queen of Portugal, 2nd consort of Manuel I 128
Maria (1521–77), princess of Portugal 124
Marie (1457–82), duchess of Burgundy 14, 61
Mark, Eberhard von der (1472–1538), cardinal 97
Marney, Sir Henry (1456/7–1523), 1st Baron Marney 46
Martin V [Oddone Colonna] (1368–1431), pope 35, 58, 98
Mary (1496–1533), queen of France, consort of Louis XII, duchess of Suffolk 15–6, 24, 33, 49, 68, 91, 191
Mary [Mary of Guise, Marie de Lorraine] (1515–60), queen of Scots, consort of James V 149
Mary (1542–87), queen of Scots 179
Mary I (1516–58), daughter of Henry VIII and Katherine of Aragon, queen of England and Ireland 48–9, 56, 60, 68–9, 73, 76, 92, 86, 101, 111–2, 123–4, 129–33, 167, 172, 177
Mary of Austria (1505–58), queen of Bohemia and Hungary, consort of Ladislas I/Lajos II 122, 149
Mason, Brewster (1922–87), actor 190
Mason, John, composer 100
Matthew, Tobie (c. 1544–1628), archbishop of York 164
Mattingly, Garrett (1900–62), historian 192
Maximilian I (1459–1519), holy Roman emperor 14–6, 19, 23–4, 32–3, 52–3, 56–8, 60, 65
Mayhew, Richard (1439/40–1516), bishop of Hereford 16, 27, 53
Medici, Alessandro de' (1510–37), duke of Florence 126

Medici, Caterina de' (1519–89), queen of France, consort of Henry II 124, 127, 198
Medici, Giovanni de', cardinal: see Leo X
Medici, Giovanni de' (1498–1526), dalle bande nere, soldier 121–3
Medici, Giuliano de' (1478–1516), duke of Nemours 61, 150
Medici, Giulio de', cardinal: see Clement VII
Medici, Ippolito de (1511–35), cardinal 150
Medici, Lorenzo de' (1449–92), il magnifico, head of Florentine dynasty 61
Medici, Lorenzo de' (1492–1519), duke of Urbino 61, 198, 201
Medici, Piero de' (1418–69), head of Florentine dynasty 1
Mendoza, Íñigo López de (1489–1535), cardinal 129–30, 155
Mendoza, Pedro González de (d. 1495), cardinal 35
Methven, Lady: see Margaret
    Lord: see Stewart
Michell, Keith (1928–) 191
Milton, John (1608–74), poet 178
More, Sir Thomas (1478–1535), lord chancellor 31, 39, 46–7, 72, 93, 102, 105, 107, 120, 136–8, 154, 157–8, 171–2, 186, 191, 193
Morison, Sir Richard (c. 1510–56), diplomat and man of letters 165
Morton, John (d. 1500), archbishop of Canterbury, cardinal, lord chancellor 8, 12–3, 20, 35, 37, 58, 87–8
Mountjoy, Lord: see Blount

Nanfan, Sir Richard (1445–1507), lieutenant of Calais 13–4
Nassau, count of: see Henry
Neale, Sir John Ernest (1890–1975), historian 192
Neill, Sam (1947–) 192
Nelson, Horatio (1758–1805) Viscount Nelson, naval commander 144
Nemours, duke of: see Foix; Medici
Neville, George (1432–76), archbishop of York, lord chancellor 8–9, 25, 38, 88
Neville, George (c. 1469–1535), 3rd Baron Bergavenny 43, 73
Neville, Ralph de (d. 1244), lord chancellor 2
Neville, Ralph (1498–1549), 4th earl of Westmorland 73, 112
Neville, Richard (1428–71), 16th earl of Warwick 9
Newcastle, duke of: see Cavendish
Nix, Richard (c. 1447–1535), bishop of Norwich 28–9, 107, 136, 168, 202
Norfolk, duke of: see Howard
Norris, Henry (before 1500–36), courtier 161
Northumberland, countess of: see Talbot
    earl of: see Percy
Norwich, bishop of: see Bateman; Goldwell; Nix
Nugent, Richard (d. 1538), 3rd Baron Devlin 111, 148
Numai, Cristoforo (d. 1528), cardinal 54, 155

Offaly, Baron: *see* Fitzgerald
Oldham, Hugh (*c.* 1450–1519), bishop of Exeter 27, 63, 102
Old Pretender: *see* Stuart
Orford, earl of: *see* Walpole
Orléans, duke of: *see* Henri
Ormond, earl of: *see* Butler
Orsini, Franciotto (1473–1534), cardinal 98
Ossory, earl of: *see* Butler
Oxford, earl of: *see* Vere

Pace, Richard (*c.* 1483–1536), dean of St Paul's, administrator, diplomat and man of letters 46–7, 52, 60, 62, 78, 80, 98, 113, 119–20, 129, 135, 202
Parker, Matthew (1504–75), archbishop of Canterbury 71, 103
Palmieri, Andrea Matteo (1493–1537), cardinal 134
Pappacoda, Sigismondo (1456–1536), cardinal 134
Paris, bishop of: *see* Poncher
Passerini, Silvio (1469–1529), cardinal 79, 155
Paul II [Pietro Barbo] (1417–71), pope 32
Paul III: *see* Farnese
Paulet, Sir Amias (*c.* 1457–1538), landowner and soldier 11, 44
Pelham, Henry (1694–1754) politician 162
Penny John (d. 1520), abbot of Leicester, bishop of Carlisle 28, 64, 198
Percy, Eleanor (d. 1530), duchess of Buckingham 73
Percy, Henry (*c.* 1449–89), 4th earl of Northumberland, 73
Percy, Henry Algernon (1478–1527), 5th earl of Northumberland 43–4, 91–2
Percy, Henry Algernon (*c.* 1502–37), 6th earl of Northumberland 91–2, 100, 145, 158, 166
Percy, Mary, countess of Northumberland: *see* Talbot
Perugino, Pietro Vanucci (*c.* 1440–1523), painter 97
Pescara, marquis of: *see* Avalos
Peterborough, bishop of: *see* Creighton
Pettie, John (1839–93), painter 182
Petrucci, Alfonso (d. 1517), cardinal, 22 54, 79, 97
Petrucci, Borghese, Sienese politicial figure 54
Petrucci, Raffaele (d. 1522), cardinal 54, 79
Phelps, Samuel (1804–78), actor and theatre manager 181–2, 185
Philibert II (1480–1504), duke of Savoy 16, 61
Philiberte of Savoy: *see* Filiberta
Philip [Felipe I] (1478–1506), archduke, ruler of the Low Countries, king of Castile, consort of Juana 14–5, 61
Philip [Philip II of Spain] (1527–98), king of England and Ireland, consort of Mary I 125
Phillips, Rowland, vicar of Croydon 94
Piccolomini, Enea Silvio: *see* Pius II
Pisani, Francesco (1494–1570), cardinal 124
Pitt, William (1759–1806), politician 180
Pius II [Enea Silvio Piccolomini] (1405–64), pope 58

Pius III [Francesco Todeschini-Piccolomini] (1439–1503), pope 23, 26, 128
Pius V [Antonio Ghislieri] (1504–72), pope 175
Platina: *see* Sacchi
Poland, king of: *see* Zygmunt
Pole, Edmund de la (*c.* 1472–1513), 8th earl of Suffolk, claimant to English throne 14, 24
Pole, Margaret (1473–1541), countess of Salisbury 48–9, 73
Pole, Reginald (1500–58), archbishop of Canterbury, cardinal 81, 110, 154
Pole, Richard de la (d. 1525), soldier, claimant to English throne 14, 24, 33, 61, 86, 113–5
Pole, Ursula (d. 1570), Lady Stafford 73
Pollard, Albert Frederick (1869–1948), historian 6–7, 15, 94, 108, 185, 187, 192–3
Poncher, Étienne (1446–1524), bishop of Paris 59
Ponzetti, Ferdinando (1444–1527), cardinal 134
Pope, Alexander (1688–1744), poet 181
Poynings, Sir Edward (1459–1521), administrator and diplomat 12
Praet, Louis de: *see* Flandre
Prie, René de (1451–1519), cardinal 23
Pucci, Lorenzo (1458–1531), cardinal 34, 79
Pygott, Richard (d. 1549), composer 99–100, 164
Pynson, Richard (*c.* 1449–1529/30), printer 20

Quayle, Sir Anthony (1913–89), actor 191
Querini, Pietro, Camaldolese hermit and ecclesiastical reformer 63–4
Quiñones, Francisco de (1475–1540), cardinal 134

Radcliffe, Robert (1482/3–1542), Viscount Fitzwalter, earl of Sussex 158
Radcliffe, Roger, courtier 112
'Raleigh, Walter S.' 205
Ramryge, Thomas (d. 1521), abbot of St Albans 87
Rangone, Ercole (*c.* 1491–1527), cardinal 134
Ranulf (d. 1123), lord chancellor, 2
Raphael [Raffaello Sanzio] (1483–1520), painter 51
Rawlins, Richard (*c.* 1460–1536), bishop of St David's 89, 168
Redman, Henry (d. 1528), master mason 103
Remolins, Francisco de (1462–1518), cardinal 22
Renée de France (1510–75), duchess of Ferrara, daughter of Louis XII, king of France 32, 52, 61, 129, 132, 140
Richard III (1452–85), king of England, 7, 10–1, 14, 25–6, 28, 72
Richelieu, Armand-Jean du Plessis de (1585–1642), cardinal 171, 182, 185, 192
Richmond, countess of: *see* Beaufort duke of: *see* Fitzroy
Ridley, Jasper (1920–2004), biographer 6, 193
Ridolfi, Niccolò (1501–50), cardinal 79
Robert de Gant (d. *c.* 1158), chancellor to King Stephen 195
Rochester, bishop of: *see* Fitzjames; Fisher
Rochford, Viscount: *see* Boleyn

Roo, John, sergeant-at-law 106

Roper, John (d. 1524), attorney general 107

Roper, William (1495/8–1578), biographer 93, 107, 172

Rossington, Clement, Derbyshire gentleman 174

Rotherham, Thomas (1423–1500), archbishop of York, lord chancellor 28–9

Rowley, Samuel (d. 1624), actor and playwright 177

Roy, William (d. c. 1531), Franciscan friar and author 109, 137–8, 171

Ruiz de la Mota, Pedro 67

Russell, John (c. 1430–94), bishop of Lincoln, lord chancellor 7–8, 29

Russell, Sir John (c. 1485–1555), 1st earl of Bedford 123, 162

Ruthall, Thomas (d. 1523), bishop of Durham 17, 25, 27, 38, 46, 64–5, 67, 75, 88–9, 159

Sacchi, Bartolomeo [il Platina] (1421–81) historian of the popes 32

Sacheverell, Sir Richard 43

Sadoleto, Jacopo (1477–1547), cardinal, humanist scholar 57

Salisbury, bishops of: see Audley; Blyth; Campeggi; Deane; Woodville
countess of: see Pole

Salisbury, Francis Owen [Frank], (1874–1962), painter 205

Salley (Sawley), Miles (d. 1516), bishop of Llandaff 53

Salviati, Giovanni (1490–1553), cardinal 79

Sampson, Richard (d. 1554), bishop of Chichester and of Coventry and Lichfield 31, 47, 119–20, 151

Sandys, William (c. 1470–1540), 1st Baron Sandys 120, 158

Sanseverino, Antonio di, (c. 1477–1543), cardinal 134

Sanseverino, Francesco di (d. 1516), cardinal 23

Sansoni-Riario, Raffaele (1461–1521), cardinal 22, 54

Sansovino, Jacopo (1486–1570), architect and sculptor 125

Sauli, Bandinello (c. 1494–1518), cardinal 22, 54

Savonarola, Girolamo (1452–98), Dominican friar 125

Savoy, duke of: see Philibert

Saxony, duke of: see Friedrich

Scarisbrick, John Joseph (1929–) 48, 59, 193

Schiner, Matthäus (c. 1465–1522), cardinal 22, 52, 79, 81, 97

Scott, Clement (1841–1904), theatre critic 185

Scott, John (1751–1838), 1st earl of Eldon, lord chancellor 2

Scott, Terry (1927–94), actor 191

Scott, Sir Walter (1771–1832), poet and novelist 181, 183

Sedan, seigneur de: see La Marck

Selim I (c. 1465–1520), Ottoman sultan 55–6

Serra, Jaime (d. 1517), cardinal 22

Sforza, Bianca Maria (1472–1510), empress, 2nd consort of Maximilian I 61

Sforza, Francesco II (1495–1535), duke of Milan 82, 95, 121

Sforza, Massimiliano (1491–1530), duke of Milan 20, 23, 33–4

Shakespeare, William (1564–1616) 10, 163, 176–9, 181–3, 186, 189–90

Sheffield, Sir Robert (before 1462–1518), lawyer 44

Sherborn, Robert (c. 1454–1535), bishop of Chichester 27, 107, 168

Sherwood, John (d. 1493), bishop of Durham 25–6

Shrewsbury, countess of, see Hardwick; Talbot
earl of: see Talbot

Siddons, Sarah (1755–1831), actress 181

Singer, Samuel Weller 183

Sixtus IV [Francesco della Rovere] (1414–84), pope 22, 57, 143

Skeffington, Thomas (d. 1533), bishop of Bangor 27, 135, 168, 202

Skeffington, Sir William (d. 1535), lord deputy of Ireland 149, 202

Skelton, John (c. 1460–1529), poet 42, 83, 86, 94, 106, 137, 171, 201

Smalridge, George (1662–1719), dean of Christ Church, Oxford, bishop of Bristol 179

Smith, William (d. 1514), bishop of Coventry and Lichfield and of Lincoln, founder of Brasenose College, Oxford 16, 25, 27, 29, 32, 53

Soderini, Francesco (1453–1524), cardinal 22, 54, 79, 95, 97

Soderini, Piero (1452–1522), gonfalonier of the Florentine republic 20, 22, 54, 143, 196

Somerset, duke of: see Edmund; Fitzroy

Somerset, Charles (c. 1460–1526), 1st earl of Worcester 76, 119

Spinola, Agostino (c. 1482–1537), cardinal, 124

Squyer, John, schoolmaster in Ipswich 6, 9

St Albans, abbot of: see Ramryge; Wolsey

St Asaph, bishop of: see Standish

St David's, bishop of: see Rawlins; Vaughan

Stafford, Edward (1478–1521), 3rd duke of Buckingham 11, 37, 44–5, 49, 59, 67, 72–4, 84, 90–1, 95

Stafford, Eleanor, duchess of Buckingham: see Percy

Stafford, Henry (1455–83), 2nd duke of Buckingham 7, 11, 72

Stafford, Henry (c. 1479–1523), earl of Wiltshire 44, 90

Stafford, Henry Stafford (1501–63), 10th Baron Stafford 73, 90

Stafford, John (d. 1452), archbishop of Canterbury, lord chancellor 2

Stafford, Ursula, Lady Stafford: see Pole

Standish, Henry (c. 1475–1535), bishop of St Asaph 39–40, 63, 109, 111, 151, 168

Stanley, Edward (1509–72), 3rd earl of Derby 100, 157

Stanley, James (c. 1465–1515), bishop of Ely 17, 28, 33

Stanley, Sir John 160

Stanley, Thomas (before 1485–1521), 2nd earl of Derby 28, 44, 100

Stephen (c. 1092–1154), king of England 195

Stewart, Lady Jane 127

Stewart, John (c. 1482–1536), duke of Albany 25, 33–4, 60, 85–6, 112, 114, 127

Stewart, Henry (c. 1495–1553/4), 1st Lord Methven 127, 149

    see also Stuart

Stillington, Robert (d. 1491), bishop of Bath and Wells, lord chancellor 28

Stokesley, John (1475–1539), bishop of London 154

Storer, Thomas (c. 1571–1604), poet 178

Stow, John (1524/5–1605), historian 176

Strafford, earl of: see Wentworth

Stride, John (1936–) 192

Strong, Sampson, painter 176

Stuart, Henry Benedict [King Henry XI] (1725–1807), cardinal, Jacobite claimant to the thrones of England, Scotland and Ireland 180

Stuart, James Francis Edward [King James VIII and III, the Old Pretender] (1688–1766), Jacobite claimant to the thrones of England, Scotland and Ireland 179

Suchet, David (1946–) 191

Suffolk, duke of: see Brandon

    duchess of: see Mary

    earl of: see Pole

Süleyman (1494–1566), Ottoman sultan 74, 122

Surrey, earl of: see Howard

Sussex, earl of: see Radcliffe

Talbot, Elizabeth: see Hardwick

Talbot, George (1468–1538), 4th earl of Shrewsbury, 91, 119, 158, 166

Talbot, Mary (d. 1572), countess of Northumberland 91–2

Taunton, Ethelred Luke (1857–1907), historian 186

Taverner, John (c. 1490–1545), composer 104, 165

Taylor, John (d. 1534), master of the rolls 46, 117, 121, 131

Tetzel, Johann (1465–1519), Dominican friar 62

Thatcher, Margaret (1925–), Baroness Thatcher 193

Thaw, John (1942–2002), actor 190

Thurley, Simon (1963–) 101

Thurlow, Edward (1731–1808), 1st Baron Thurlow, lord chancellor 2, 180

Thurlow, Thomas (1737–91), bishop of Lincoln and Durham 180

Tilney, Agnes (before 1477–1545), duchess of Norfolk 49

Todeschini-Piccolomini, Francesco: see Pius III

Torregiano, Pietro (1472–1528), sculptor 143, 202

Tournon, François de (1489–1562), cardinal 155

Tree, Sir Herbert Beerbohm (1852–1917), actor and theatre manager 186, 191

Trevor-Roper, Hugh (1914–2003), Baron Dacre of Glanton, historian 102, 188–9

Trier, archbishop of: see Greiffenclau

Trivulzio, Agostino (c. 1485–1548), cardinal 79

Trivulzio, Scaramuccio (c. 1465–1524), cardinal 134

Troughton, Patrick (1920–87), actor 191

Tuchet, James (d. 1459), 5th Baron Audley 28

Tuke, Sir Brian (d. 1545), administrator 141

Tunstal Cuthbert (1474–1559), bishop of London and of Durham 45–6, 52, 69, 75, 86–7, 92–3, 115–6, 118, 130–1, 136–7, 141–2, 147, 151, 154, 157

Tyndale, William (c. 1494–1536), religious reformer, biblical translator 106, 109, 117, 136–9, 171, 191

Vanni, Pietro, Wolsey's Latin secretary 197

Vaughan, Edward (d. 1522/3), bishop of St David's 28, 88

Venice, doge of: see Gritti; Loredan

Vere, John de (1499–1526), 14th earl of Oxford 119–20

Vere, John de (1482–1540), 15th earl of Oxford 120, 158

Vergil, Polydore (Polidoro Virgili, c. 1470–1555) historian of England 32, 38, 46, 87, 94, 151–2, 172–3, 187

Verona, bishop of: see Giberti

Veysey, John (c. 1464–1554), bishop of Exeter 63, 111, 168

Vich y de Valterra, Guillén-Ramón de (d. 1525), cardinal 201

Vigerio della Rovere, Marco (1446–1516), cardinal 22, 53

Villiers, George (1592–1628), 1st duke of Buckingham 164

Vio, (Giacomo) Tommaso de [Cajetan] (1469–1534), Dominican theologian 54, 57

Virgili, Polidoro: see Vergil, Polidore

Vives, Juan Luís (1492–1540), humanist scholar 102

Wakefield, Robert (d. 1537/8), Hebraist 129, 133, 153

Walker, Greg (1959–) 138, 171

Walpole, Horatio [Horace] (1717–97), 4th earl of Orford, politician, writer and cultural patron 180, 188

Walpole, Sir Robert (1676–1745), 1st earl of Orford, politician 180

Walsh, Walter (d. 1538), courtier 166

Warbeck, Perkin (c. 1474–99), claimant to the English throne 11

Warham, William (c. 1450–1532), bishop of London, archbishop of Canterbury, lord chancellor 2, 15, 17–8, 27–9, 31, 35–6, 38–40,

Warham, William (*continued*)
  45–6, 51, 63–4, 67, 82, 89–90, 92, 101, 107, 129,
  142, 168–9
Warwick, earl of: *see* Edward; Neville
Wayment, Hilary 176
Waynflete, William (*c.* 1400–86), bishop of
  Winchester, lord chancellor, founder of Magdalen
  College, Oxford 8, 37, 50, 102, 104, 162
Welles, Orson (1915–85), actor 191–2
Wentworth, Thomas (1593–1641), 1st earl of
  Strafford, 178
West, Nicholas (d. 1533), bishop of Ely, 33, 41, 59,
  67, 72, 76, 104–5, 107, 130, 135–6, 151, 158, 168
West, Timothy, actor 191
Westminster, abbot of: *see* Islip
Westminster, archbishop of: *see* Manning; Wiseman
Westmorland, earl of: *see* Neville
Whiting, Richard (d. 1539), abbot of Glastonbury
  108
Weid, Hermann von (1477–1552), archbishop of
  Cologne, imperial elector 62
Wilfrid (d. 744/5), archbishop of York 2
Willaert, Adriaan (*c.* 1490–1562), composer 100
William III and II [William of Orange]
  (1650–1702), king of England, Scotland and
  Ireland 181
Williams, Neville (1924–77), biographer 192
Williams, Robert Folkestone (*c.* 1805–72), historian
  of the English cardinals 182
Willoughby, Cecily (d. 1528), abbess of Wilton
  145
Wilson, Richard, bishop of Meath 199
Wilson, Richard, cartoonist 181
Wilton, abbess of: *see* Jordan; Willoughby
Wiltshire, earl of: *see* Stafford
Winchester, bishop of: *see* Beaufort; Duppa; Fox;
  Gardiner; Langton; Waynflete; Wolsey; Wykeham
Wingfield, Sir Richard (*c.* 1469–1525), diplomat
  33, 115–6
Wingfield, Sir Robert (*c.* 1464–1539), diplomat 52
Winstone, Ray (1957–) 192

Wiseman, Nicholas (1802–65), archbishop of
  Westminster, cardinal, 182
Wolf, Thomas, suffragan bishop in the diocese of
  Bath and Wells 198
Wolfit, Sir Donald (1902–68), actor and theatre
  manager 190
Wolman, Richard (d. 1537), dean of Wells 119–20
Wolsey, Joan: *see* Daundy
Wolsey, Robert (d. 1496), father of Thomas 5–7
Wolsey, Thomas (*c.* 1471–1530), abbot of St
  Albans, bishop of Lincoln, Bath and Wells,
  Durham, Winchester, archbishop of York,
  cardinal, lord chancellor, founder of Cardinal
  College, Oxford and Cardinal College, Ipswich
  passim
Woodville, Elizabeth (*c.* 1437–92), queen of
  England, consort of Edward IV 10
Woodville, Lionel (*c.* 1454–84), bishop of Salisbury,
  7
Worcester, bishop of: *see* Bell; Ghinucci; Gigli;
  Latimer
  earl of: *see* Somerset
Wyatt, Sir Henry (*c.* 1460–1536), courtier 120, 123
Wyatt, Sir Thomas (*c.* 1503–42), poet and
  ambassador 123
Wykeham, William [William of Wykeham]
  (*c.* 1324–1404), bishop of Winchester, lord
  chancellor, founder of Winchester College and
  New College, Oxford 8, 102, 104, 123
Wynter, Thomas (*c.* 1510–post 1543), son of
  Thomas Wolsey 7, 17, 109, 143, 146, 157, 160

Yonge, John (1466/7–1516), master of the rolls 45
York, archbishop of: *see* Bainbridge; Kemp; Lang;
  Lee; Matthew; Neville; Rotherham; Wilfrid;
  Wolsey
  duke of: *see* James II
Yorke, Philip (1690–1764), 1st earl of Hardwicke,
  lord chancellor 2

Zygmunt I (1467–1548), king of Poland 57